Praise for *Build Your Autho. ⸺⸺*

"A rapid-fire, soup-to-nuts overview that will help authors see just how much they're able to choose from in building a platform."
> —Seth Godin, author of 17 bestselling titles,
> translated into more than 35 languages

"An author who knows and is known by their potential readership can be the difference between a book being signed or not, between succeeding or failing, between having sustained success or being soon forgotten. Author platforms are not given; they are hard earned. This book will show you how to build yours."
> —Craig Smith, Executive Commissioning
> Editor at John Wiley & Sons

"A fantastic book for any aspiring or established author. Publishers seek authors who know their audience, know how to reach them, and know how to grow them . . . *Build Your Author Platform: The New Rules* provides the perfect path to turning a great book into a great, *successful* book."
> —Kevin Harreld, Executive Editor of Cengage Learning

"As the waters in the publishing world get muddier and it gets tougher to rise above the noise, it's more critical than ever to build the right audience and platform to get noticed and get your work published. This book is your road map to making that happen."
> —Brook Farling, Senior Acquisitions Editor at
> Alpha Books and member of Penguin Group

"One of the first criteria a publisher utilizes when assessing a proposal is the evaluation of the author's platform for marketing and publicity. This practice has been consistent for much longer than my forty years in book publishing. However, the Internet and social media have created a whole new dimension to gaining an audience. By offering clear definitions and 'how to' procedures for authors in her well-written book, Carole Jelen has provided much-needed clarity to this fast-evolving, confusing topic."

—Kenzi Sugihara, Publisher at SelectBooks, Inc. and former VP/Publisher at Bantam/Doubleday/Dell and Random House

"Even experienced authors will find the advice and new rules in *Build Your Author Platform* are worth their weight in gold."

—Bob "Dr. Mac" LeVitus, author

"This is a great reference and how to guide for any author who is looking to navigate the perils and opportunities of today's social media outlets!"

—Christopher Will, Senior VP of Jones & Bartlett Learning

"This book will be required reading for my authors! Carole Jelen and Mike McCallister really nail it in *Build your Author Platform: The New Rules*. These 14 New Rules are what every author needs to know."

—Steven Elliot, Publisher at Morgan Kaufmann & Syngress Imprints, Elsevier

"This book will show you all of the tricks, tips, tools, and loopholes you'll need—empowering you to take control of and build your author platform. When pitching a new author, one of the first questions I'm always asked by my publisher and our sales force is, 'How's the author's platform?' In the new age of publishing, nothing is more important for success (aside from great writing, of course!)."

—Andrew Yackira, Associate Editor at Tarcher/Penguin Group USA

"With increasing amounts of books coming to market, authors must build up a wide audience platform ready to buy their books. A strong author platform is the most important factor in making or breaking initial and long term sales. Here in this book you will find the keys to the castle."

—Glenn Yeffeth, Publisher at Benbella Books, Inc.

BUILD YOUR
AUTHOR
PLATFORM

BUILD YOUR AUTHOR PLATFORM

THE NEW RULES

*A Literary Agent's Guide to
Growing Your Audience in 14 Steps*

Carole Jelen
and Michael McCallister

BenBella Books
Dallas, TX

BenBella Books, Inc.
10300 N. Central Expressway
Suite #530
Dallas, TX 75231
www.benbellabooks.com

Send feedback to feedback@benbellabooks.com

Printed in the United States of America
10 9 8 7 6 5 4 3 2 1

Library of Congress Cataloging-in-Publication Data
Jelen, Carole, date
    Build your author platform : the new rules: a literary agent's guide to growing your audience in 14 steps / Carole Jelen, Michael McCallister.
       pages   cm
    Includes bibliographical references and index.
    ISBN 978-1-939529-25-1 (pbk.) — ISBN 978-1-939529-29-9 1. Authorship—Marketing.
I. McCallister, Michael. II. Title.
    PN161.J45 2014
    808'.02—dc23

                                     2013045454

Editing by Paul Eisenberg
Copyediting by Stacia Seaman
Proofreading by Cape Cod Compositors, Inc. and Chris Gage
Indexing by Clive Pyne
Cover design by Sarah Dombrowsky
Text design and composition by Publishers' Design and Production Services, Inc.
Printed by Bang Printing

Distributed by Perseus Distribution
www.perseusdistribution.com
To place orders through Perseus Distribution:
Tel: (800) 343-4499
Fax: (800) 351-5073
E-mail: orderentry@perseusbooks.com

Significant discounts for bulk sales are available. Please contact Glenn Yeffeth at glenn@benbellabooks.com or (214) 750-3628.

*In the memory of and dedicated to
Dr. Rudolph Scott Langer,
a mentor, a sage, and a gentleman.*

Contents

New Rules by Chapter Number

"If you have built castles in the air, your work need not be lost; that is where they should be. Now put the foundations under them."

—Henry David Thoreau

1. **Author Website**

   New Rule: Online tools must work together. Learn how to set up your author site as your central location that all other online locations point to so that you can keep control of your platform.

2. **Your Blog**

   New Rule: Draw in and converse with your audience through comments. We show you how and where to set up your blog and suggest best practices, including how to enable and pursue comments.

3. **Twitter**

   New Rule: Build social authority and influence by having others share your ideas with their network. Learn how to jump into the huge pool of your audience that participates on Twitter, get set up easily, and gain a following.

4. **Google**

   New Rule: Search engines like Google define your findability via keywords, metadata, and more. We help you understand the power of Google and how to harness it, how Google is continuing to reward authors who create great written content, and why Google+ is far more than a social network.

5. **Facebook**

   New Rule: Authors must create motivation for interaction among members of their audience to rank higher and be found more often.

We show you how to use Facebook as a billboard (while still maintaining your privacy with your friends and family) and why "likes" on your author/book page are important.

6. LinkedIn

New Rule: Expand your network of supporters by joining the networks of many others. We show the power of using LinkedIn to grow community with peers, add to visibility, and add to your following through posting, joining LinkedIn groups, and using LinkedIn Tools.

7. Personal Appearances

New Rule: Success depends on how well you understand and speak from your audience's point of view. We show how to use tools that maximize audience by teaching, training, and speaking.

8. Articles

New Rule: Open up multiple avenues for others to talk about you and your work. We illustrate the value of creating an article bank and repurposing your written content for maximum exposure.

9. Audio

New Rule: Your audience needs interaction with you, and you'll learn how to use audio to connect personally with readers. We lay out the many avenues of audio available and why it's an especially effective medium for authors.

10. Video

New Rule: Video is a huge and growing draw on the web; authors must use multiple media. Discover how to maximize your author brand by creating video interviews, YouTube videos, channels, book trailers; repurposing your videos; and more.

11. Book Website

New Rule: Become an online bookseller with the Buy button. We show you how and why to build your book site and how it sells books.

12. Amazon

New Rule: Align with the "customer experience" at Amazon. Learn how to use Amazon, with all the tools in this author toolbox, to build your audience.

13. Reviews

    New Rule: In public view, authors must showcase reviews and praise from your audience. We show you how to go about getting solid book reviews.

14. Book Launch

    New Rule: Authors must search for their audience in multiple locations, using virtual and in-person appearances. We'll walk you through how to combine all of these into a fireworks show to launch your book with parties and virtual tours so that you can break into new audience networks.

Acknowledgments

PIECES OF A LIFE and of every creation come together in ways we never expected or anticipated. This book combined the puzzle pieces with many contributions to allow a complete vision. The number of people who helped, influenced, and supported us over the years to create this book is countless, and we send out our thanks to you all.

First, thanks to three thought leaders whose work greatly influenced our book and shaped our approach to our audience of authors. These three saw and articulated the paradigm shift that allowed first a glimpse, then a full grasp of the magnitude of change that the move to a digital world has encompassed:

- Nicholas Negroponte, author of the paradigm shift title that moved awareness from atoms to bits and bytes: *Being Digital*. He is also founder of the MIT Media Lab and the One Laptop per Child Association.
- Tim O'Reilly, publisher, speaker at conferences, including ones at Waterside, a renowned tech expert who popularized the term *Web 2.0*. He envisions the Internet developing into a sort of global brain, an intelligent network of people and machines to function as a nervous system for our planet.
- David Meerman Scott, online marketing strategist and author of *The New Rules of Marketing & PR*, who saw immediately the shift away from media controlling a message and toward a democracy of influencers with ideas, enabled by the tools of social media and all other online media.

Thank you Glenn Yeffeth, Publisher at BenBella, for supporting and believing in our vision to publish our book to enable authors. Thanks to all of the publishing experts at BenBella who supported us and contributed their time and expertise throughout the book-writing process. First and foremost, thank you to our editor, "Saint" Paul Eisenberg, for your patience, and for your development, ideas, contributions, and editorial skills par excellence. We could not have had a better editor. Thank you to Sarah Dombrowsky for creating our blue branding color and cover design and typography, to Publishers' Design and Production Services for the clean, compelling visual book design.

Many thanks to all at BenBella: to Debbie Harmsen and Vy Tran for editorial support, to Jessika Rieck for guiding our book through production, to Jenna Sampson for assistance with photo-wrangling, to Jennifer Canzoneri and Lindsay Marshall for their marketing expertise, and to Adrienne Lang, who understood and applied her knowledge of publishing to every aspect of our book process. Our thanks as well to Stacia Seaman for copyediting.

Deepest thank-yous to all who shared their time and talent in quotes, models, and formats, and to the many author client influencers for this book who shared their expertise so that others can benefit; to mention a few: George Plumley, Eric Butow, Jesse Feiler, Bud Smith, Dave Taylor, Jesse Stay, Ray Anthony, Bob LeVitus (Swifty's favorite), Ed Tittel, Barbara Boyd, Tee Morris, Evo Terra, Chuck Tomasi, Rebecca Bollwitt, Andy Rathbone, Jesse Feiler, John Havens, John Carucci, David Busch, and many more. Former lines have blurred; author clients have now become lifelong friends.

Thank you to the many publishers, editors, and publishers' marketing departments who contributed by sharing their advice over the many years, including ideas and success stories for authors to benefit. Thank you to those at Waterside who supported our efforts and visions in creating this book, with special thanks to Bill Gladstone, Margot Hutchinson, and Maureen Maloney; you are amazing in your experience and dedication to making authors successful. Thank you, Jack Canfield, for sharing your exceptional story and advice in the Foreword. More shoutout thanks to Richard Greninger (video), Karen Sterling (photography), Melissa Cavazos (transcription), and Doug Holliday (audio).

Most importantly, we could not have gotten through this long and arduous task and process of turning ideas into book form without support and encouragement from our friends, loved ones, colleagues, and supporters. Thank you all for your care and encouraging words and for never stopping your belief in us. Special thanks to Doug and Yvette, Jeanette McCallister, Karl Auker, Dory Willer, Gail Doering, Peter Gregory, Becky Gregory, Don Bangs, Glenn Reid, Zachary Romano, Michael Alves, and Michael McGrath to name a few. It's been a long road of travel in the publishing world, and sending out thanks to all friends and colleagues from Prentice Hall, Addison-Wesley, and Sybex for the many years (growing into a lifetime) of staying in touch.

Foreword

I'M NOT A BOOK PUBLICIST BY TRADE. In fact, I had to learn how to do that. Given that I was not a "natural born salesman," it's fascinating that the year that Mark Victor Hansen and I won the ABBY Award (the American Booksellers Book of the Year award), we also won the Southern California Book Publicists Award. As I always say to authors, "You've got to become a master of book promotion. You've worked too hard writing it to let it die a slow death due to lack of promotion."

July 1993 marked the publication of our first Chicken Soup for the Soul book. Great, it's published! Now what? We had to ask ourselves, "How do we do this book-promotion thing? How do we get our book out to all our possible buyers?"

This question had a life of its own, and to be successful, this question has to permeate all your efforts—as it did ours, throughout the creation, promotion, and distribution of more than 200 separate volumes in our Chicken Soup book series.

So where is the right place to start book promotion? At the very beginning, we gravitated to a book that answered the question in a multitude of ways: *1000 Ways to Promote Your Book* by John Kremer. Here was our start, a book chock full of promotion ideas. We were delighted to find these and decided to write out about 900 ideas on little yellow Post-it Notes. Then we stuck each one of those Post-its to a long wall in our office. You can imagine the look of 900 little yellow squares on the wall, defining our goal: Complete each suggestion until each one of these Post-its was taken off the wall. From that day on, we made it a daily game, to do everything on that wall to promote our book. Open all the doors. Talk to every possible distributor and buyer. Shake every hand. Consider how everything could contribute to the sales of our book.

We started in, doing unconventional things like calling up the buyers at the PX stores on military bases. We called and said, "We've got a great book we think your readers will be interested in! Would you be interested in purchasing it for your store?" For every "yes" we got, we sent out a free copy. One less Post-it on the wall, and it worked—we usually got orders! Next we called over 100 multilevel marketing companies, finding anyone interested, to say we created a book we believed would be motivational for their distributors. Yes, it's true that we got a lot of rejections, but it didn't matter. We contacted one company that bought 1,000 copies, and another that bought 1,700 copies. One more Post-it came off the wall!

We also gave lots of speeches and seminars anywhere we could— companies, direct sales organizations, chambers of commerce, hospitals, and universities. Every time we spoke, we would hold the book up high, saying, "You know, there's one thing that's stopping people from being successful more than anything else. And I'm going to demonstrate what that is by doing the following: I'm going to give away a copy of this *Chicken Soup for the Soul* book. Who would like it?" Then we just stood there until someone got up out of their chair, walked or ran up to the front of the room, and took it out of our hands. Then we'd say, "That's right! You've got to get off your butt and take action in order to succeed in life!" At that point, everyone else in the room wanted a copy of the book, too, and we would sell fifty percent of the audience a book.

Then came the many in-store promotional book signings that bookstores love to hold. I'll share a secret I learned by accident at one memorable signing. On that particular evening, we were all set up, sitting in front of the table at the bookstore, but nobody had arrived yet. Normally the crowd arrives at the specified time, we stand up, give a short fifteen-minute presentation, and then the audience lines up to pick up our book and get it autographed. On this evening, for some reason people were slow to arrive. Looking at the seats yet to be filled, I started thinking, *Hmm, what if I put a copy of my book on everyone's chair? While the audience waits for the talk to begin, they'll start reading . . . and then maybe they'll get hooked.* The surprise result? We sold five times more books that night than we ever had before. I realized once people held our book in their hands, and especially if they started to read it, they actually started to "own" it, and then they wanted to take it home.

As we expanded and followed more book-promotion paths, we began to get better at working with the bookstore staff members. For example, we learned about the importance of book signing "bag stuffers." About a week before the date of the book signing, we found we could provide the stores with a full ream of paper printed with our message on it: "On XX date and time, Jack Canfield and/or Mark Victor Hansen will be at our store for a book signing! Please be sure to mark your calendar and come early. You can meet the authors in person, shake their hands, receive their autographs on your books," and so on. These printed sheets were invaluable as invitations and reminders, and steadily increased the numbers of people who attended our book signings.

Starting out is always humbling, yet we all must start out somewhere on our path upward. That first step is the one that counts most. The first step takes the most courage and faith, especially when there is no evidence of success in sight. My own first book signing had an audience of three people: one was the owner of the store and one was the janitor. Of the three people, the janitor was the only one who bought our book that night.

Later on, as our book climbed up the bestseller lists, we attracted more people to our book signings. However, I remember one night when Mark and I were signing books at a Waldenbooks store at a large shopping mall in Los Angeles, and the foot traffic had slowed down in the store. Mark left the store and walked up to people out in the mall and said, "You can't believe what's happening down here at the Waldenbooks store. Jack Canfield and Mark Victor Hansen are signing their *Chicken Soup for the Soul* book. It's a rare opportunity to get a book signed by two famous authors! And they are perfect gifts for your friends and family members." Pretty soon a line of people would find their way into the bookstore where Mark and I would then sign their books. Sometimes, we would hear "Wait, weren't you the guy out in the hall!" and by that point, we had already hooked them with our humor into buying our book.

With our first Chicken Soup book, we truly dedicated ourselves non-stop to doing anything and everything to get our book into the hands of people everywhere. We completely believed in what we were doing. So we next started working on something we called the "Rule of Five." This is probably the most important message for authors to hear. The "Rule of Five" means that every single day, without any lapse, you do five action steps—in this case, five action steps to help promote or sell your book. On

Monday, for example, we would choose to contact five churches and say, "Do you have a bookstore? Would you carry our book in your bookstore? Can we speak to your minister?" And if we were able to get through to the minister, we would say, "How would you like to have a Sunday off where you don't have to prepare a sermon? We have prepared a sermon using stories from *Chicken Soup for the Soul* to illustrate biblical principles. We are offering to come in and do a great talk for your congregation on some future Sunday." By that point, we had a track record, so people already knew we were strong speakers, and we found people trusted us to deliver an inspirational message. All we asked in return was to be able sell our books somewhere afterward; it didn't matter where—in the back of the room, outside on a table, or in the bookstore. Almost everyone agreed with a big "yes." That's dedication! Even on Sunday when most people take a day off to relax, we were out there selling our books.

Sometimes we would draw a blank on five places to send books or five things to do next to promote our book. When we couldn't think of anything else, we would just choose five celebrities and send them each a free book. I remember coming across a book in a Vons supermarket called *The Celebrity Address Book*, which seemed like a major find for us! I've since learned that over 90% of these addresses were the celebrity's agent's addresses, but we didn't know any better then. We just used the addresses to send out five books to people like Harrison Ford, Sidney Poitier, Paula Abdul, or whoever was listed there. And this is the best part of this story: One day the earth moved. We got a call back from a woman, the producer of the television show *Touched by an Angel*. Here it was for us, the reward for our perseverance and our belief; this woman had decided that the quality of the stories in our book mirrored the exact quality that she wanted to project in *Touched by an Angel*. She bought copies for all of her writers and asked them to read our book to get the feel for the kind of stories she wanted to portray on the series. She bought a book for everyone on her staff and production crew. That was one of the most important sets of books we ever sold. She gave copies of our book to the sound people, the cameramen, the gaffers, the lighting people, and to the editors, in addition to the writers and the actors. She asked everyone that had any role in the show to read *Chicken Soup for the Soul*, stating, "I just want this feeling to come through on the set." The new term for the way our idea took off is *viral*, which is a pretty good term for how the word spread from there. Next, that story made news in the *Hollywood Reporter*. Then *Variety* picked up the story. Then the Associated Press wrote up the story, and onward from there until it became a national press story. The significance of *Chicken Soup for the Soul* and our story found readership in about a hundred newspapers. Well, needless to say, once our book became known and loved by so many, even more people went running out to buy our book. Our audience began to expand beyond our wildest dreams.

Then we looked to get excerpts of our book placed in magazines and felt that a story in the first book called "We're Raising Children Not Flowers" would be a good candidate for parent magazines. We decided to inquire at a local newspaper in L.A. called *L.A. Parent*. I wrote the editor and said, "Here's an article you might be interested in. It's about a parent and their six-year-old son, and it's a very moving story. Would you publish it in your magazine? And if you would, at the end could you put a little box that says 'Excerpted from *Chicken Soup for the Soul* . . . available from your local bookstore, etc.'?" I'll never forget the response we received from Jack Bierman, the editor, who responded in a really funny letter. He wrote, "I read your mail and I thought how dare you tell me to put something at the end of your article! And then I read the article. I'll put that in and more! And by the way, did you know that there are 75 of these parent magazines? There's the *L.A. Parent*, the *San Diego Parent*, the *San Francisco Parent*, the *Denver Parent*. . . . We're all part of a consortium, and you can submit this to all 75 at once." Suddenly our article not only got published in *L.A. Parent*, but also in about 50 more magazines, all across the country.

Our attention and focus were on constantly promoting our book, and because of this intense focus, we were able to realize that all the little weekly community newspapers, like the *Malibu Times*, are pretty much advertising vehicles for local businesses. These local weeklies have a hard time finding a lot of copy, so if you can provide them with interesting reading, they're usually very happy to print it! Of course we followed this lead and compiled the master list of all of these local weekly papers across the USA. We started sending all of these stories they were mostly happy to print, and the doors opened wider, this time leading to loads of print space for our book-promotion purposes.

Every single day we asked ourselves, "What promotion can we do today that is unique?" We'd call five radio producers and ask, "Can I send you a copy of our book?" From there, we found our way to speaking on long lists of radio shows; in fact, I've personally spoken on over 600 radio shows. It's amazing; sometimes I've even spoken on five shows in a single day. When your book is fresh and you are in the mode of promoting it, there is no action that is too small to take. They all add up over time.

One day we were scratching our heads over the question, "What the heck can we do to promote today?" We took a look at the headlines and saw that the O.J. Simpson trial was happening. Mark and I looked at each other and said, "What if we send books to the jury?" The jury is sequestered, so they can't read magazines. They can't read newspapers. They can't watch television. And our collective lightbulb went on: "All the jury can do is read books, so let's send them ours!" Instantly we sent the famous box of books over to the O.J. Simpson trial. Judge Ito was moved! He sent us back a nice letter saying, "Nobody ever thinks of the jury. I'm going to distribute these to them. Thank you very much." I still have that letter framed. About a week later, all these jurors walked back into court, with almost every member carrying a copy of *Chicken Soup for the Soul*. Then the press saw the personal angle opportunity: "Why are all these people in the court reading the same book?" Once again, our story became a press story, and it spread, virally, across more papers in the country.

Then one day I read in the *San Diego Union-Tribune* about a woman who had been raped. My wife and I were visiting my sister-in-law in San Diego at the time. The victim of the rape seemed like a very compassionate woman. She was kind of a new-age person who hadn't let the experience devastate her, so I reached out to her. I sent her our book with a note saying, "I was inspired by your story and I just wanted to send you a copy of our book." What happened next is phenomenal—at the sentencing hearing she asked the jury for leniency for the man who had raped her, and then she offered a copy of *Chicken Soup for the Soul* to the defendant and said, "This book helped me a lot. I hope it will help you, too." That story ended up on the front page of the *San Diego Union-Tribune* the next day.

Several years later we compiled a book of stories under the title *Chicken Soup for the Unsinkable Soul*. Very soon after, in October of 2000, one of our naval ships, the U.S.S. *Cole*, was attacked by terrorists and badly damaged while it was refueling in the Yemen port of Aden.

Seventeen American sailors were killed and 39 were injured. It was later towed from the Gulf all the way back to Norfolk, Virginia.

We had sent copies of *Chicken Soup for the Unsinkable Soul* to many of the wives of the sailors on that ship. As the sailors disembarked from the ship and were met by their wives, photographers and photojournalists were snapping hundreds of pictures. And there, front and center, appeared a woman hugging her sailor in one arm and holding in her hand a copy of *Chicken Soup for the Unsinkable Soul*. It ended up being the front-page color photograph on the next day's issue of *USA Today*. You can't even buy an ad on the front page of *USA Today*! That had to be worth hundreds of thousands of dollars to us.

So every day we continued with the question, always asking, "What are five things that we can do today?" One day we decided to take a drive to the *Los Angeles Times*. You know how hard it is to get reviewed by a major metropolitan newspaper? It's almost impossible. So we just went in and walked from desk to desk. We started with the obituary writer. Next, the Living section writer, who covers things like what's happening in Jennifer Aniston's life. We talked to everyone, including the sports writers. We said, "Here's our book. We thought you might be interested in it. You know, if you could find a way to write about it if you like it, great. If not, just enjoy the book." We did not stop until we had talked to almost every writer and had given them a book. Our efforts paid off: One month later, our perseverance became a front-page story in the View section. It was not a book review, but a story about these authors with all this chutzpah! With a distribution of about 1.3 million readers, we became the lead story, pictures and all!

We were constantly looking for ways to promote, no matter what. With everything we looked at we'd constantly ask, "How can we use this to promote the book?" One day I was driving to the airport, still holding that question. I looked around at my immediate surroundings and I thought, "I'm in a limousine. . . . How can we use a limousine to promote our book?" I remembered an author I'd met from Australia by the name of Bryce Courtney, who had written a book called *The Power of One*, which was made into a movie with Morgan Freeman. When Bryce was promoting a new book he would print a couple of thousand copies of the first chapter of his book, and he would hand them out free to people congregated at bus stations, railroad stations, and the like. That first chapter was a teaser, sort of like a chapter in a Harry Potter novel ending like this: "and there was a knock at the door." You are compelled to turn the page to see who's there! The idea occurred to me, "What about having limousine companies put copies of our book on the backseat of their limos, and then people riding in them would start to read the book, and at the end of the trip the limo driver would ask the client if they wanted to buy the book." We ended up with several companies doing that.

Another technique I learned from Bryce was to call in to the local talk shows and say things like, "As I say in my book *Chicken Soup for the Soul . . .*" or "You know, there is a story in my book *Chicken Soup for the Soul* that I think is relevant to this discussion." As our book began selling in bigger numbers, we started to become more well known, so we were recognized when we called in. The subject of the talk show didn't matter! They might be talking about the problem of the loggers and the tree huggers in Oregon protecting the white owls and we'd call in and hold a conversation about that. But guess what they would always say? "Oh, our next caller is Jack Canfield, the author of *Chicken Soup for the Soul*. What's new with you guys?" That's how we got even more free advertising.

Here's the main point for authors: Don't stop promoting! Our first Chicken Soup for the Soul book did not immediately hit it big. It took 14 months after it was published before it appeared on a bestseller list: The book published in July 1993 and didn't hit its first bestseller list until September of 1994. We were #15 on the *Washington Post* list. The next week it jumped up to 13. The next week it was #15 on the *New York Times* list, and then it kept moving up, up, and up until it became #1 on the *Times* list and stayed there for three years.

Several years later we set a Guinness World Record for having seven books on the *New York Times* bestseller list on the same day. We broke another Guinness record (it's actually been broken by someone else since then) for the largest book signing ever held. It was a multicity book signing, with all the contributors from *Chicken Soup for the Preteen Soul* signing at the same time at different locations. It was everywhere! It was in Denver, in Philadelphia, in Washington, in Los Angeles and San Francisco and several other cities. Thousands of people came to get their books signed.

Remember this: When your book first comes out, you may experience "the calm before the calm"—not the calm before the storm. Your book comes out and you're waiting for it to suddenly take off, and it doesn't. I tell authors that most publishers are printers. They're not good at promotion. That's not true of all publishers, but it's true of far too many. Therefore, you literally have to become a skilled book promoter. If you can afford a PR company, great! If not, read everything you can absorb in the pages of this book you are holding in your hand: *Build Your Author Platform: The New Rules: A Literary Agent's Guide to Growing Your Audience in 14 Steps.*

Today authors have advantages and additional promotion channels that we didn't have in our early days of promoting *Chicken Soup for the Soul.* As authors using the new rules of Internet promotion, you have access to all the tools covered in this book: social media, blogs, websites, audio, video, and more amazing tools that reach huge numbers of people that we would have jumped on and used in every possible way if they had been available to us.

There's a lot more you can do today that you couldn't back then, and using social media and these other channels is a big piece of it for you. So study what is in *Build Your Author Platform: The New Rules* and then apply it . . . day after day after day. If you do that, you will get to experience the unparalleled fulfillment of having entertained, uplifted, inspired, informed, and transformed the lives of hundreds of thousands of people. I promise you that it is worth all the effort.

—*Jack Canfield*
Motivational Speaker and Author,
Co-Creator of Chicken Soup for the Soul

Preface

Why This Book Was Written

This book is a product of years of collecting strategies, best practices, pre-digested routes, and major elements in getting up and running with a solid author platform. It will be a relief to be able to do my job more efficiently, to be able to simply hand authors this book and say, "All of your questions about the author platform are answered in this book. Just follow the 14 steps."

The beauty from an agent's and author's and publisher's perspective is that this is a complete system that covers all the bases. We've identified 14 steps that work together to supercharge author visibility and audience. Once a platform is built, it has a magnetic power of its own and can be expanded. We've found that author platforms impact sales in major positive ways, which affects the bottom line for everyone involved in creating books. The motivation for taking the time to create this book is that our authors demanded it, knowing that an effective author platform directly increases sales and publishing opportunities.

For decades, I have been listening to authors' concerns about platform and promotion. As they work hard on their books, consulting, and other day jobs, they wonder, where will they find the time to research, much less create a successful author platform? Finally, the time has come to answer every question, concern, problem, and complaint right here, under one roof.

Our Unique Experience and Value to Authors

You'll find a unique and valuable perspective here. We wrote this book from two unique perspectives and sets of experience that will benefit you in many ways: more than 30 years of my own publishing experience and background helping give voice to authors' ideas via books, coupled with an equal number of years of tracking and understanding technology, right as it's being created, by my coauthor, Mike McCallister. Mike is personally dedicated to simplifying and clarifying technology and making it accessible to all. There are many online short articles and blogs about how authors can use tech, but these pieces are often written by those who are still figuring it out, not having come from the depth of experience offered here. Misinformation online is frustrating at best, time wasting at worst, and can set authors in the wrong direction to the point of losing motivation to finish creating a cohesive author platform.

As a former editor at top publishing houses for a decade and current literary agent for two decades, I've worked closely with trendsetters, idea makers, and inventors of the technology we use today, alongside writers, many of whom have given voice to clarifying tech tools. Over many years, I've worked to create success for authors in every way possible, which has led to many millions in book sales. My publishing work has included all aspects of the book creation process, from nurturing ideas to editing, acquiring, and promoting the final book products. Far beyond agenting, I've created, responded to, and applied audience building and promotion strategies for authors who have proved successful at the element that gets book deals secured: building an author platform.

Mike McCallister, my coauthor and author client, is a technology wizard and pro writer who has lived and breathed the Internet since the World Wide Web was born. He can offer a perspective that few people have, showing you tips, tricks, and techniques hidden all over the web that you can in turn use for maximum outreach and maximum return of audience loyalty. We're sharing our decades of combined experience in publishing and technology to dispel confusion, zap misinformation, and help author clients to succeed with a minimum investment of both time and money.

Our Unique Agency at Waterside

We're a top literary agency in the USA, and as a team of agents, we've been involved with multimillions of book sales over the years. We're still doing something very right at the leading edge of publishing, even as we build bestsellers in today's chaotic publishing climate. I still place 100+ books a year from my own desk into contracts, including a large percent of revisions of books that sold so well that we updated them multiple times. The fundamental understanding of what publishers are looking for, and understanding what audiences need, are the driving forces that move us along on the cutting edge. You can see some of the successes our authors have had in the stories concluding the chapters of this book.

Our agency platform at Waterside has been built over three decades. Our own database of author clients numbers in the thousands, and with each author comes our connection to their network of author friends, colleagues, and associates. The Waterside website has solid traffic along with newsletter subscriptions. The appreciation notes and thanks we receive as Waterside agents often show up online through ebook publications. While showcasing our numerous contributions in the trade, they also help widen our audience outreach online. My own LinkedIn network, which I've cultivated over years, reaches over a million targeted and interested individuals through connections and groups; my Google+ circles include a variety of publishing-related groups and thousands of authors and their networks. Our book now has a growing Facebook fan page along with a budding blog and website enhanced by incoming links and Twitter. For years Waterside Conferences were well known in the publishing industry, bringing authors and publishers together to exchange ideas. Our website, massive author network, and longstanding relationships with publishers are fundamental measures of Waterside's well-established social presence and authority in the publishing industry. Top-selling titles and expansive series such as the For Dummies line began with Waterside clients. Our agency of author clients is more akin to a tribe-type membership who we listen to and dialogue with regularly. Our major success and top ranking in the publishing industry was built on longstanding relationships with authors and publishers, resulting in mega book sales over the years.

Our Author Clients and Publishing Partners

Our biggest inspiration has come from working with the amazing cutting-edge thinkers who have shared their techniques, ideas, and best practices with us. It's through this group of exceptional writers, thinkers, innovators, and pioneers in new publishing techniques (that we're proud to call clients) that we're able to articulate proven methods here to propel you to your goals.

We're greatly appreciative to all of the many authors who have shared their successes and insider knowledge over the years, and to the talented and dedicated publishers, editors, and marketing departments who have shared their time, insights, and long-standing and in-depth knowledge. We are privileged to work with you. It's a monumental task to acknowledge all of your contributions over the years that have made their way into this book of solutions for authors. A heartfelt thanks to all of you who have helped transform these ideas into book form!

—Carole Jelen

Introduction

It Takes an Audience

Authors need readers, and to build audience, this is not the time to remain anonymous! This book solves challenges in growing readership in an era of change. Now even the way the written word reaches your audience is new.

This book teaches you how to build your author platform, also known as your public persona, to serve as a magnet for building up your audience. We show you the essential elements to build your platform into one that attracts media, loyal audience followers, and buyers of your book. Like every strong relationship, your readers need to feel they can trust you, that they can talk to you, that you are the authentic "real deal," and that you have the expertise in the subject matter or entertainment they're interested in. This isn't about advertising or selling. It's about informing, entertaining, and knowing that sales will follow.

Strong author platforms that combine these very elements usually accompany best-selling book titles. Exemplary platforms include the author sites of best-selling authors Malcolm Gladwell (author of *Blink*, *Outliers*, and *The Tipping Point*; gladwell.com) or Steven Levitt and Stephen Dubner (freakonomics.com).

We know you're busy! You're following your mission and life's work, and you want to work on your manuscript without being distracted by yet another job: marketing your book. But we also know that technology has changed something fundamental in the way we communicate. By holding this book in your hand, you already understand that it's critical for you to learn to harness new enabling tools on the web and to build your public persona, too. The problem is carving out the time to explore how to do it and then taking the time to figure it out. That's why we organized this book into self-contained, one-step-at-a-time chunks. Once through the process, you'll see your own author platform materialize and bring in far more people than you can imagine.

We're living in an increasingly enlightened and exciting time when people come together and collaborate, when we can even talk directly to the president of our country, to a CEO of a large company, to a thought leader who influenced us, or to a celebrity who used to be out of reach. For authors, that means people want to talk to you, too, to make comments and ask you questions. It means taking your audience into account in writing your manuscript, listening to and responding to comments, and adding your own spin far beyond what a publisher could possibly advertise for you. With digital tools on the web, you're more empowered as an author to expand your influence and make connections all over our planet.

Advertising claims and push are slowly going by the wayside, being replaced with interactive dialogue. Now companies selling potato chips on television are asking their audience to vote online for their favorite flavor. News and entertainment shows like *American Idol* show hashtags on screen to bring audience into the show with Twitter comments on the screen. Live audience comments via Twitter can influence the outcome of a reality show (or shape the outcome of a presidential debate) and always add perspective.

All authors, experienced and new, nonfiction and fiction, best and brightest and novice, need to know and harness the new rules explained here to create a platform. Here we motivate you to promote and then give you the blueprint and step-by-step how-to. It's time to run with it!

This is the era of creating dialogue with an audience.

All too often authors run in the other direction from the very thought of promotion.

This Book Propels You Forward

You're reading this book because you've taken precious time to seek out specialists with decades of expertise in the publishing and tech industries to translate, pre-digest, and give you strategies, models, and steps that fit your criteria: simple, quick, and clear.

You're holding the 14-point author platform guide developed and used by successful authors, with interim steps, checklists, and a plan infused with the best of technology available to you. Here you're given a choice to go quick and easy by using these standard models or to go a step beyond and customize to fit your purpose and unique author brand.

You're holding the blueprint of your own author platform here, and in the summary at the back of this book are tearout sheets that form a complete platform publicity plan. We include some tutorial guides to keep everything under one roof for you and success stories and advice from our successful author clients. We've researched and made recommendations based on successful author platforms so that busy authors (you) can save money and a lot of time by avoiding the task of sifting through massive amounts of information. We've done that for you.

Authors who resist the shift from monologue to dialogue are falling behind; those who embrace this shift find that using the power of the crowd and the strength of the Internet engine propels them to their goals.

How you build your author platform, widen your audience efficiently, and increase book sales as a result are the questions answered for you in these pages. The method in this book involves multiple, discrete steps, but it's kept simple as a program, deliberately uncomplicated, devoid of jargon, and thorough in its coverage of basic elements.

Your secret advantage to carve a path to higher book sales resides in the visibility that these tools create for you. Added to the overarching strategies we present here, you will find proven methods to save time often lost through wasteful experimenting. With the 14-step mixture we have identified for you, you'll create a digital footprint that will carry you and your books far beyond the initial creation of your platform. When you build Web 2.0 interactivity tools into your plan, your author platform

A 2012 survey by Cisco revealed that 82% of organizations have a Facebook presence, 68% have presence on Twitter, 68% have presence on LinkedIn. But less than 20% of organizations surveyed have built any cohesive strategy for using these social networks to interact and engage with their audience.

> *There's no way around the fact that the joys of receiving the world's communications right in our pockets through a handheld device also means that you as an author must participate.*

will magnetize audience over time through word of mouth, search engine optimization (SEO), and more.

In these pages you'll find a cohesive, overarching author strategy to reach your audience to lead them to your book. Outside of this book, you can find great ideas in many places, but this book is largely a response to author complaints about collecting sand particles of individual ideas that just don't adhere and slip through their fingers. Authors need a well-defined platform strategy to implement with intelligence and efficiency. The end result of following the 14 steps? You'll still have time to write and run your business, and you'll still have your money staying securely in your wallet where it belongs.

The New Rules Apply to All Authors

> *New rules surround each wave of innovation, and those who align with these are able to progress toward their goals faster and easier.*

These principles and strategies are based on new tools and new rules that work for and apply to all authors, whether you write fiction, children's books, graphic novels, or whatever. We often talk in this book about defining and working in your "niche." You can define that term as any genre you write in or any audience you write for. Customize from the examples we show you here and creatively spin them to fit your audience.

More people than ever are choosing to be heard through content and the written word, so chaos and confusion is at an all-time high among book buyers. If an author is not findable on the web, we run the risk of lost sales. With mass production and self-publishing being so easy, we've seen a rise in some poor-quality content that actually sells because of confusion about whether it's a quality product or junk.

Why Are There 14 Steps?

There is no way around the fact that an author can no longer have a book appear in the bookstore, do a book signing, and expect the book to sell in large numbers—that is, unless you already have a strong platform and following.

Why 14 steps? Because people are now tuned in to many locations, including their laptops, phones, and tablets, not to mention radio, video, television, and auditoriums, so authors need to show up in as many of those locations as they can.

To get the word out about your book, it's necessary to write great content, appear in many media, and then distribute to as many of these places as possible. It's important to understand how content is best delivered,

> *The danger you face is this: If your own author platform is created badly, you may lose readers to an inferior product that was simply easier to find because its platform was superior to yours.*

with such visual elements as photos, diagrams, videos, and audio. Multidistribution includes making sure your materials are mobile-friendly so that they are easily accessed on any device.

It's a necessity for authors to post social content across multiple social media sites, a process that we simplify for you in this book. Volume isn't the answer: It's not just enough to post, post, post. Whether you're writing a post, video blogging, or tweeting, your posts need to be well timed and well crafted to begin a conversation, easy to digest, and really, really easy to share. If you set up your platform using the strategies in this book, you'll have an efficient communications framework to engage with your audience, no matter what site, device, or media they are using.

How This Book Is Organized

Each element of this 14-step author platform is organized into one step per chapter so that authors can stop between steps or read only the steps that they need.

This book is intended as an "elements of" title, a guidebook. Our goal is to save authors time as they quickly and easily build a successful platform. We don't intend for a single chapter to substitute for a whole book on a particular aspect of an author platform; we focus on what you need to know to create this step in your platform. You can go far beyond if you have the time and inclination, since there are whole books written on each step in this book. For every step, we include additional reading, in many cases books written by our author clients.

Each chapter includes these sections:

Why you need this: In this section, we motivate! This section encourages you to stretch your boundaries and gives you a rationale for including this step in your platform.

Strategy: After motivation, we give a section on author strategy for using that step and show how it works together with the whole 14-step platform. According to Cisco's study mentioned earlier, even though all businesses are using social networking in one way or another, less than 20% have any type of strategy about how they are using it; there is a lot of trial and error, frustration, and wasted time while overcoming the learning curve. The method in this book is pre-digested specially for authors, simply presented to show how to craft a strong platform as an author so that the framework is solid and can be built upon as time goes on.

How To: Step-by-step advice on the fastest route our authors have found and advice on getting each of the 14 steps accomplished. It's a high priority to show you how to save time, prioritize, and automate as much as possible while maintaining an authentic, consistent voice throughout your author platform. Using our own authors' experiences as a guide, we try to show you the quickest route to get where you need to go.

Best Practices: You say you don't have time to create a platform? These sections are taken from successful author practices that were already gleaned through trial and error to find what works best. We don't focus on "worst practices," although we will occasionally point some out if we have heard authors mention notable errors that they've seen over and over.

Simple Model: Where appropriate, we give a model format for a speech, an article, a short book launch event, etc. You can use the exact format we give you as your own model to save time, or you can customize further depending on your schedule and budget. We give you the essentials, and you can build from there in a way that's appropriate for your goals.

Final steps: Each chapter ends with a checklist covering the main chapter points. We also summarize all of these end-of-chapter steps as a worksheet at the back of the book to jump-start your author platform.

Success Stories: End-of-chapter success spotlights provide solid advice for authors looking to successfully build audience.

Read the Book Through...

If you are just starting out, it's easy to follow the 14 steps to get up and running with an efficient author platform that will serve you for many years to come. We advise reading through all the steps sequentially, even if, as most authors, you already have a presence in some of these areas. Use the standalone chapters in this book to supercharge, revamp, and consolidate any platform segments you already have created, and keep revisiting the book as a whole to catch things you may have missed in creating any portion of your platform.

...But First, Take the "Acid Test"

Try this self-assessment now. Google the name Dan Brown (thriller fiction) or David Meerman Scott (nonfiction), both authors with well-developed web presence. Immediately on the results page you'll see photos, books, considerable social network presences, URLs for websites and blogs, and more. Now type in your own name and see what appears. If your presence is not as easily identifiable, that should give you all the motivation you need! Follow the points in this book beginning with Step 1, creating your author website. After following all 14 steps in this book, type your own name again to see the profound transformation of your professional online author identity. These tools and techniques work for authors regardless of genre. Fiction authors need to connect to readers as much as nonfiction authors, and in these pages we suggest paths and examples for both nonfiction and fiction authors.

Then Build Your Author Platform

As you follow and build your author platform with the 14 steps in this book, when you or one of your readers searches your name, you'll find professional, impressive search results about you and your book that are clear and well-organized. Your fans will get an optimal first impression of you and will be set on an easy path toward finding out more about you and your book. By harnessing the power of the Internet and learning how the various online tools in your toolbox work together, you'll lead your audience to your unique message and author brand.

> *The sound of platform necessity coming was like a locomotive in the distance, and it has arrived.*

Good luck! There's no time like the present to begin. Build your platform right the first time, and as time goes on you'll see it grow with minimal effort. Devote the time you need to plan, customize, and execute your platform. Once created, it will take on a life of its own that works to increase your book sales for many years to come.

Visit our book site at BuildAuthorPlatform.com for links, new information, and more. Please contact us at jelenpub.com and michaelmccallister .com for Q&A on our blogs, and please participate in future editions of this book by sending in your success tips and stories via our website and the Contact Us form.

CHAPTER 1

Your Author Website: Home Central

"I enjoy the Web site a lot and I like being able to talk to my readers. I've always had a very close relationship with them."

—*Anne Rice, best-selling author*

AUTHORS WHO HAVE ANY SHRED of resistance to connecting with readers via platform-building, please consider these words of Rick Riordan, best-selling fiction author: "My goal is always to create life-long readers." And the words of Felix Dennis, best-selling nonfiction author: "Everything I publish is for my readers." These sentiments are echoed time and again by top-selling authors like Barbara Kingsolver, Ann Rule, Ann Lamott, W. H. Auden, and many more. John Cheever pointed out the impossibility of successful writing without an audience: "I can't write without a reader. It's precisely like a kiss—you can't do it alone."

As a literary agent who has worked with thousands of author clients over many years, I work daily to overcome any and all author resistance to platform building. Once I've chipped away objections, the questions I hear repeatedly are, "With no degree in marketing, promotion, or advertising, how does an author reach out to build an audience? Isn't that the publisher's job?"

It's true that the publisher will market your books, including catalogs, publisher websites, in-store promotions, news releases, and more. As an example, BenBella has done a fantastic job of creating our book website;

making our book postcards; listing our book on Amazon.com, in catalogs, and on their website; setting up speaking engagements and signings;
setting up online events for us; and much more. In fact, the reservoir of
knowledge and experience at BenBella connects us to every author success
story in their history, which boosts our own visibility. The problem is that
it's close to impossible for an author to get a publishing contract in the
first place without an author platform showing guaranteed audience following. In other words, an author platform—including an author website,
social media network, and traditional media presence—demonstrates to
a publisher that you already have a following that can be converted and
grown into an audience for your book. It's also impossible for authors to
understand and deliver content to their audience needs and preferences
without directly interacting with their readers. Your author website is
the place to centralize all of your platform elements, connecting these
under one roof for your readers to see your depth, breadth, and influence.

The web is a crowded place, and a strong author website that effectively targets and communicates with your audience is essential. As of
this writing, more than 2.4 billion people use the Internet for everything
from email, file transfers, and Skype to instant messaging. Close to a billion sites already exist on the World Wide Web since the digitally enabled
world makes it simple to connect with an online audience via websites.
And fortunately, Internet audiences search for real and tangible information, so that the more authentic the information an author shares, the
more meaningful the communication becomes between you and your
potential audience.

Why Your Author Website Is a Must

Many authors mistakenly skip building their author website—an essential
and central element of the author platform—or even worse, allow their
presence to be controlled by other entities, then regretfully find that their
Internet presence becomes fragmented and confusing for their audience.
If your audience can't easily find you or your book in the crowd of websites,
your book sales suffer.

Here are the main reasons to create your author site as soon as possible if you don't already have one:

- **Findability:** Readers find authors and books through websites by searching their names. If you have a scattered presence across multiple websites, you force potential readers to guess where to find "the real you." When confused, potential readers are likely to give up and look elsewhere.
- **Consolidation:** Combining the 14 steps of your author platform in a central location makes it easier for your readers to connect with you and raises your profile in all web search engines.
- **Control:** You own your website and maintain your author brand, content, format, and message. If your web presence is only on social networks owned by others, the rules that govern your presence may change on a whim. Don't give away the keys to your online presence when you are fully able to own your website.
- **Mailing list creation:** Your site allows you to collect names and addresses of your readers. Creating a custom electronic newsletter is by far the best way to announce your books and future events to an audience that has already expressed interest in your work.
- **Growth capability:** You alone determine the future of your site. If you want to add future webinars, links to YouTube channels, and the like, you don't have to wait for someone else to add a feature or change a policy.
- **Blog home:** In Chapter 2 (Step 2 of the program), we'll show you how to keep your website freshly loaded with new blog posts. Fresh content raises your profile with the search engines and keeps your audience returning to your website.

Your author website is your home base, so tie all of your online locations to this central hub for all of your author branding. Incoming links to your author website count, even from your other online locations. It's easy to create, and it's one of your best tools for tying all the steps of your platform together.

Plan Your Author Website Strategy

The time you spend now in setting up your site will influence and reward every segment of your author platform. Your optimum author strategy is to identify your unique, consistent, identifiable author brand. Create and present your brand and lead your audience to visit your site, where they can subscribe to your newsletter, follow your publications, favorably review your books, return for more and tell their friends, and, most importantly, buy your books.

So now take a deep breath, carve out a little time, relax, and give some deep thought to who you are as an author. Ask your friends and associates for words that describe you and then pick out the best ones. What value do you offer to your audience? Who are your readers? What are their terms and their vocabulary? When you start to record your planning into a workbook, you'll begin to see the component parts emerge into your author brand. Summarize your unique value addition to an audience you understand well. The solid definition of your author brand identity will help you coordinate your content on your site and will reverberate to all parts of your author presence and presentations. Don't allow your author presence to become a collection of online fragments! Follow these steps to plan your home central author website.

Define Your Audience

Before you can reach any audience or motivate anyone to buy your book, it's imperative to understand what your audience likes, enjoys, and, above all, what they need. A surprisingly common mistake many authors make when trying to pitch to me as an agent, or when pitching to a publisher directly, is not really knowing or understanding who they're writing for! Every publisher's book proposal form requires a thorough audience definition by priority, starting with primary audience definition, then secondary and even tertiary group categories. It helps to further detail each segment by creating "personas," that is, embody each audience segment in a single person whose characteristics you can pinpoint.

At the very minimum, start with a basic definition of your audience first and foremost:

- Who are the primary, secondary, and tertiary audiences of your book?
- What are the problems and concerns of each?
- What is your audience's point of view?
- Embody your audience in one "persona" for each segment of readers.

It's simply easier to define and understand an audience segment through a single reader or customer who you already communicate or work with. Define what draws that person into your community of readers. The more details you can add, the better you will be able to speak directly to your readers to create an audience-centric experience that leads to author platform success. If you don't already understand your audience in depth, a quick way to find out is by interacting with your audience through blog comment areas. You can also check out the blogs of others who write for your audience; read those comments for valuable insight about where they are coming from. Some best-selling authors like Ann Rule even complete manuscripts dictated by audience ideas and reactions, gathered from blog comments, polls, or direct emails. The bottom line is that the more you understand your readers, the more enabled you are to talk with them. Direct communication is a path to building an audience that returns to your author website, social media profiles, and every other aspect of your author platform.

Plan Your Website Self-Introduction

So take time to think through who you are as an author and why your experience is of value to your readers, and then write out this description as a guideline for how you present your author brand.

- **Develop your own brand tagline.** Keep it short and memorable. For example, my tagline at Jelen Publishing is "Hi, I'm Carole Jelen, Literary Agent/Author, Publishing Veteran." Why? Because this is what authors have told me that they are most interested in.
- **Choose a welcoming author photo** that you use consistently for recognition (more on these elements later). The photo counts because it's the first impression you leave for readers to "meet" you. It's a good idea to get second opinions on which photo to use from people whose opinions you trust.
- **Keep your online and live persona cohesive** so your audience will be able to identify you, recognize you, and then connect with you from multiple locations. Authors who reach out a friendly hand to introduce themselves front and center have the highest chance of connecting with their audience quickly and successfully. Introducing

yourself online, much like introducing yourself in person, leads to more interest in you. The online click that brings a browser to meeting you on the page is a first step leading to a first impression that grows into a lasting relationship.

Plan Your Site Landing Page to Keep Your Audience

Over half of us leave websites within seconds of getting there! We've become skimmers on the Internet, sifting through massive amounts of information. Give your audience at first glance the ability to find what it needs, in their vocabulary, with their problems, issues, and their interests addressed. People resonate with simple elegance in your message on your landing page: They want to see you, your book, your unique value addition front and center with ease of navigation to where they can read more. For example, my site at jelenpub.com shows three easy-to-grasp segments: my photo and tagline with friendly greeting, our book cover and its tagline connecting to our book website, and evidence of my following, which people can read more about and easily join. On the side are critical social buttons for more information, a link to my blog page, and a newsletter signup.

Plan Your Tabs and Component Parts of Each Page

Stay simple and well-organized; an easy-to-grasp, easy-to-use website holds a viewer more efficiently and longer than a site with too much information. The essential author website tabs are listed later in this chapter.

Plan the Static Text of Your Author Website

The static (unchanging) content of your site needs to be potent, so boil down your message to contain its essence, using keywords you know your audience uses. If you follow our advice to keep your blog on your own website, covered in Chapter 2, you automatically gain the changing, updating text that keeps your author site rich in content as you add posts and blog comments to form your community. You'll see more reasons in the next chapter why it's far better to blog on your author website than at another URL.

All the static content on your author website pages needs to be precise, well written and well edited, and aligned with your audience's interests. For models, review the websites of the authors featured in the success stories at the end of each chapter in this book, then customize to your needs.

Creating Your Author Website

Whether you are creating a new site or updating an existing site with more interactive content and efficient tools, make sure your brand and added value, described in audience-friendly terms, show up front and center.

People tend to gravitate to a simple, consistent approach: quality content, delivered to meet audience needs, plus consistent clear style, simplicity, and minimal design. Over time, these elements have proven to be attractive and compelling to readers, whether in book, magazine, or website format. Here are the steps we recommend in the initial stages of author website creation:

Find a model site and customize. Save time by scouring the web to find simple, quality author websites that resonate with you. In Chapter 11 we include a list of author sites we like. It's better to forget about sites that divert attention with bells and whistles, shapes and colors, and fancy moving objects! Choose an author website because you quickly see and resonate with who the author is and what that author offers you. Identify sites where you find the easiest, most familiar route to get the information you need and where you can interact with that author.

Review as many author websites as you can, whether or not they are best-selling authors like Stephen King and Dan Brown, and choose one or two that come closest to your purpose. Start a list of the website components that work best, then integrate and customize these to craft your own site.

Take careful note of your competition. As you browse, it's important to collect information on authors and sites who you consider to be your competitors. This will teach you about your own uniqueness as an author. In every book proposal form, publishers require authors to list the top three competing titles, indicating why your book would sell instead of, or in addition to, that title. It's worth the time to think through this step: evaluate your own value addition as a publisher would, and you'll be better positioned to grow your audience of book buyers. Look at what your competition is doing, define your value as different and unique to you, and enhance your website with that information.

Plan Essential Author Website Pages

While I was working on *The NeXT Book* (Addison-Wesley) I was able to watch the way Steve Jobs built his business; I was instilled with great respect for the universal appeal and power of simple, elegant design and equally clear, simple messages. We encourage you to keep to this philosophy of presenting simple elegance by including only the most necessary web pages on your author website. Here are the key author site pages to include.

1. **Landing page:** The initial page people land on when they click to your author website. First impressions are powerful! On this page, your readers should immediately "meet you" and see why they should take an interest in you and your book. We recommend that you use these first few seconds of your audience's attention to present the following elements:
   - **Your photo:** As you review author photos on a site like LinkedIn or on author websites and back covers of books, you will see that the professional-looking, straightforward full-face shots with shoulders work best as an introductory photo to your audience. Take a look at top author photos like Stephen King's. A clean, clear, confident, professional-looking shot works best, whether it's taken by a friend with talent or a pro photographer like Karen Sterling in New York who created Carole's photo.
   - **Greeting:** A "hello" type of greeting and a one-line tagline that tells in a nutshell who you are and what you're up to. Welcome readers with a type of "Hi, I'm . . . and I'm a . . ." or just four memorable words about you in large type. Add a "Read More" phrase to go to an About page to tell all about you.

- **Contact info:** Now readers need to feel they can talk directly to you, so it's best to show them how to reach you, on the footers of every page of your site and/or on a Contact page.
- **Book cover photo:** Include a few quick bullet points about the book's value and a Read More link. For examples, take a look at the author sites listed in Chapter 11. Mike's website includes the value points for *WordPress in Depth* (Que) such as "Become a smarter WordPress user!" and "Advice on choosing themes and plugins!" Then use the beauty of linking to get more information elsewhere; when readers click the photo image of your book, it should link immediately to your book website (Chapter 11) or to an About the Book page for more information, and include the all-important Buy Now button to take the user to Amazon or another website to purchase your book.
- **Navigation tabs:** Links that lead to your other website pages, listed below.
- **Social networking buttons:** Small buttons leading to your presence on Facebook, Twitter, Google+, LinkedIn, and all other social media networks where you can be found. These buttons demonstrate your social influence and allow your audience added interactivity.

2. **Blog page:** Covered in Chapter 2, your blog is the heartbeat of your author website. Your blog is your own online magazine, where you can spark engagement, interact, and build your author community. As an added plus, your blog builds new content to increase your findability, a big win all the way around. Keep your blog on your own author site; that way, you can keep your audience right where you want them.

3. **Events page:** This can also be called a Coming Soon page and includes a calendar of your author events online and in person, articles, current and future books, appearances, training, speaking engagements, podcast or video releases, webinar information, etc. When you keep your appearances and writing announcements under one roof, your audience can get a complete picture. Authors get boosted in visibility by making it easier for readers to find you and easier to follow you.

4. **About the Author/Praise page:** Start this page with biographical information. Tell your readers who you are and why you're qualified to write about your topic. Once you've begun to gather an audience, then add your audience's positive comments about you. After your

book comes out, create a separate Praise page. Use comments from all social networks for this section, along with other positive reviews. There are many ways to collect praise, but if you don't have a few positive comments already, wait to create and publish this page until you do. In the interim, find just one single positive quote from a satisfied reader or colleague to include on your home page. A single positive quote is powerful so you might want to keep one on your home page after you've created your Praise/Reviews page.

5. **About the Book(s):** (Optional) More information about your book if you are not planning to create a book website. As time goes on, you can include a catalog of your earlier work, too.

Create Your Author Site with WordPress

Now we come to the technical side of building your website. In this section, we'll give you the basics of putting initial content on your author website and publishing your site to the Internet.

Select and Register a Domain Name

Every website on the World Wide Web has a unique identifier, a uniform resource locator (URL). One of the best ideas of the web pioneers was to create the domain name system (DNS), which allows those URLs to have human-readable names like MyCoolSite.com. The thing is, that name also has to be unique, which, 30 years into the Web's history, can be a problem. But given that humans haven't run out of names for their children after tens of thousands of years, we're confident you can find a unique domain name for your author website.

Here are some ideas:

- **Your own name:** Use your own name—versus the name of your business or niche—if you have plans to write in more than one niche or genre. Using your own name is also helpful in establishing authorship, which in turn helps web search engines find you. Understand that you have to be first to register your name. Mike is always grateful that the former chief executive of Humana Inc. did not register

MichaelMcCallister.com before he did, but suspects that some of his visitors come away disappointed. You can always use a middle initial, or Author<yourname> as alternatives.

- **Your business name:** If you do freelance projects or have other business interests separate from your authoring niche, you may want to use a business name as your domain name.
- **Your niche:** If you've carefully defined the subject matter that you're expert in, you can register your niche as your domain name. This has the added benefit of coming up in "serendipity searches," when a user looking for advice on solar-powered lawn mowers types in those words without spaces—solarpoweredlawnmowers—and finds your site without consulting a search engine.

As time goes on, you may decide you have the need for more than one website—or, when you really hit the big time, your publisher may decide to establish sites named for your individual books. But for now, focus your energy on developing your author website.

Register Your Domain

Most hosting companies will register your domain as part of your hosting fee, but before you agree to that, read the fine print and confirm that the domain is registered in your name (not the hosting company's). If you don't own the domain you select, you cannot change hosts and keep the domain.

You can also register your domain directly with an accredited registrar. GoDaddy, ENom, and Network Solutions are among the more popular U.S-based registrars, but comparison-shop rates and inclusions before committing; you can find a comprehensive list of registrars at internic .net/regist.html. Typically, domain name registration costs $10–$30 per year, and once you sign up you're often offered incentives for renewing early or for multiple years.

Find a Host

Theoretically any computer on the Internet can be a host, serving up web pages to any browser that "asks" for them. In fact, we'll be showing you how to set up a web server on your home computer later in this chapter.

But if you don't want to host your website on the same home computer as your financial records, works-in-progress, and other personal information, you'll want to find a different host computer that will store your website, make it available to the public 24/7, and protect it from bad guys who try to take advantage of the openness of the web.

There are lots of companies out there who will provide hosting services, some more reputable than others. Many of these companies offer "free hosting" accounts, but if the server your site lives on goes down for whatever reason, you may have trouble getting help. Paying customers always come first.

Your Internet service provider (ISP) may offer you free or low-cost web hosting, and that may be the right thing for you.

Three things should factor into your choice of web host:

- **Amount of disk space:** When you shop for a computer, you probably look at the amount of space that computer has to store your data. It's the same for a web host. Fortunately, the text files that account for most of the content of a website are fairly small. Where you can run into storage problems are with graphics and audio and video files. Even so, with most sites, you can easily get by with three gigabytes (3GB) of space.
- **Bandwidth:** This is the size of the "pipe" that brings data to and from your site. What you use in bandwidth depends on the size of your files and the popularity of your site. As with disk space, audio and video files take up the most space, and if you're Stephen King or Stephen Hawking, millions will quickly download every bit of audiovisual material they can suck up. Hosting companies generally offer 25GB to 75GB of bandwidth every month. Some offer "unlimited bandwidth," and if you pursue this option ask them how they handle sudden spikes in traffic (as when someone with millions of Twitter followers posts a link to your site). You don't want the best day for your blog traffic to be the worst day for your bank account due to hidden charges or downtime as a result of a traffic surge.
- **Support for third-party software:** Many hosts offer automatic installs of popular web content management systems like WordPress and Joomla. If you use one of these systems (this book will focus on

using WordPress for your website management needs), you will also need support for the PHP scripting language and MySQL database management system. If you want to install WordPress yourself, you need to make sure that your host supports PHP and allows you to create and manage at least one database.

If you're not sure where to start looking for a web host, the WordPress site offers a few recommendations at wordpress.org/hosting. These hosts handle a variety of website types (not just WordPress-based sites) at a reasonable price.

If you want special attention to WordPress issues and want a host that can easily handle large amounts of traffic, you might consider a hosting site like WPEngine that only hosts WordPress-based websites.

Install Your WordPress Site

WordPress started out as another tool for blogging but has increasingly become a go-to platform for all kinds of websites. It really makes it possible for even the nontechiest of writers to create a professional-looking site, with zillions of choices available to you. Once you have your domain registered, a hosting contract agreed to, and some content ready to publish, you can have your WordPress site on the web and attracting visitors within an hour or two.

The fastest way to create a stable environment for your WordPress site is to select a host with an automatic, one-click WordPress installation tool. Many of the bigger hosting companies have this option. The trade-off for the convenience of having WordPress installed for you may be a lack of control. The host may limit the number of themes or plugins you have access to, or otherwise limit your ability to manage your site. Check into this before signing a contract.

In this section, we will show you how to set up WordPress on your host site; you won't have to wonder how much control you have, and it won't cost you a dime. If the very idea of setting up a database scares you, you may want to skip ahead to the section titled "Choose a Design Theme." But we mean it when we say the technical stuff can be done in about an hour. Give it a shot!

GATHER SOFTWARE

Before you set up your site on the host's computer, you will need to download some software to your own computer:

1. You need a program to upload your files to your host. FileZilla is a bit of free software that can handle that. Download it at filezilla-project.org.
2. You need the latest version of WordPress. Download it at wordpress .org/download. This will be a Zip archive, which you will need to extract into a separate folder on your computer.

SET UP THE DATABASE

WordPress stores much of the content of your site in a MySQL database. Before installing WordPress on your host site, you need to create a database that WordPress can access. Go to your web hosting site to manage this.

The following instructions are for the popular cPanel web administration application. Your hosting company may use a different application, but the process should be pretty similar:

1. Click **MySQL Databases** from the main screen. Under **Create New Database**, type in a name for your database. Technically, you can name it anything. While it's common to name this database "wordpress," you run a security risk in doing so. It's best to use a name that you won't forget on those rare occasions when you have to change a database configuration setting, but hard for evildoers to guess.
2. Click **Create** to add your database. Write this name down, as you will need it during the WordPress installation.
3. Under **Create New MySQL User**, use the drop-down menu to select your newly created database.
4. Add a name under MySQL User and type in the password twice. Make sure you use a very strong password, one that's easy for you to remember but hard for others to discover. All the Privileges should be checked.
5. Click **Add**. Write down the name and password of the new user, as in Step 2.

Your database is now set up. You can now upload your WordPress files.

UPLOADING WORDPRESS

FileZilla is a simple FTP client application that connects to your web host and uploads your WordPress files with just a few setup steps. When you signed up with your host, most likely you received information about uploading files to the host's FTP server. Given its cross-platform character and its lack of cost, you might even find that your host has step-by-step instructions for setting up FTP with FileZilla.

After downloading and installing FileZilla, follow these steps to set up the file transfer between your computer and your web host:

1. Launch FileZilla.
2. Go to File > Site Manager (or click the first icon on the left in the toolbar). A dialogue box appears.
3. Click **New Site** to enter your information.
4. Insert the connection information you received from your host. This includes the following:
   - **Host:** This is usually the same as your domain name, with *ftp* in front, for example, ftp.myWPblog.com.
   - **Server Type:** This should always be FTP.
   - **Logon Type:** For your website, this should usually be set to Normal. You use anonymous FTP when you visit a software download site, where the keepers don't really care who you are. The Normal setting requires a password to get to.
   - **User:** Your host should give you a username to access your files. Type this here.
   - **Password:** This is the place where you supply your password. It is usually identical to your site password.
   Your host might have you fill in the Account line, and you can add information in the Comments section.
5. Click the **Transfer Settings** tab. Then select the **Passive** button. In passive mode, the client sets up all the data flow. This is more secure, especially if your firewall stops any data trying to pass through it from outside the network.

6. Click the **Advanced** tab. Your host might want you to set a Default Remote Directory. This is the directory at the host server that appears when you log in. If you don't set this option, you will likely enter a directory with your username at login time. You could set up a WordPress directory as the default, too. Similarly, you might want to set your local WordPress directory as the default local directory.

7. Click **Connect** at the bottom of the screen. If your settings are entered correctly, you should now be connected to your host server, and you can upload files by dragging them on the screen from the source folder to the destination folder. (When you're ready to disconnect from the server, press Ctrl+D in Windows, Command+D on a Mac.)

8. Point the Local Site section of FileZilla to the location of the WordPress files on your own computer. Connect to your host (Remote Site) on the right side and navigate to the directory where you want to store WordPress. If you're ready to transfer all the WordPress files, press Ctrl+A (Windows) or Command+A (Mac) to select them; then drag them over to the right side to begin the transfer.

Now you're ready to install WordPress!

THE FAMOUS 5-MINUTE WORDPRESS INSTALLATION

Let's do the famous five-minute WordPress installation!

1. Go to http://<yourdomainname>. If you did everything correctly in the last set of steps, you should see a mostly empty screen with a **Create a Configuration File** button. Click it.

2. Some more introductory language appears, with a **Let's Go!** button. Click that button.

3. Enter the information we advised you to write down in the previous section:
   - Database name
   - Database username (which should be the same as the database)
   - The database user's password
   - The database host (you shouldn't have to change this from *localhost*)
   - Table prefix (you can leave this as the default *wp_*)

4. Click the **Submit** button. If all has gone well, you'll see the "All right Sparky!" screen. If all has not gone well, you will get an error message. Most often it will complain about an "Error establishing a database connection." If this happens, make sure that you entered the right information about your database. Remember these details about your database:
   - The database name should be spelled exactly the same in the Word-Press Installation Wizard as it is in phpMyAdmin. Spelling counts everywhere else, too!
   - The database username should be the same as the database name.
   - The database password is case-sensitive.
   - The database host information is *localhost*.

Get all of these items right, and you'll be all right, Sparky! Note that when you are filling out this form in your browser, you are actually editing the WordPress configuration file, wp-config.php, so go through the steps carefully. Once you've got the database connection finished, now comes the fun part:

1. Click the **Run the Install** button.
2. Fill in the three items on this screen:
   - Name your site. Since it's on your computer, you can be as creative as you'd like, or you could just choose something as boring as "My Test Site." You can change this anytime.
   - Give WordPress an email address for communication purposes.
   - Check the **Allow My Blog to Appear in Search Engines Like Google and Technorati** check box.
3. Click the **Install WordPress** button. WordPress creates the admin user and generates an initial login password for that user. This user differs from the WordPress database user you created in the previous section in that you will be logging into this account on a regular basis to administer your WordPress settings. Write this default password down or copy it to the Clipboard or a text file. You will need it to log in the first time. This information is also emailed to the address you listed on the Install screen.
4. Click the **Login** button. The standard WordPress login screen appears.

5. Type in *admin* for the username and the generated password from Step 3. Leave the Remember Me box unchecked. The admin account should only be used when you have specific administrative changes to make to your blog. You'll create a separate user account for your everyday content needs in a few minutes. Click the **Login** button.

6. Your administrative dashboard appears. The first time you log in, WordPress reminds you that you used the autogenerated password and asks if you want to change it. The advantage of keeping the auto-generated password is that it is more secure, and using it makes it less likely that someone will steal your admin password and wreak havoc on your site. The disadvantage is that it's usually harder to remember.

The installation is complete. You've got a content management system! Celebrate!

Choose a Design Theme

If you're going to skip all the other aspects of setting up and installing your WordPress site, the one part you'll likely want to have a hand in is probably the most fun, which is choosing your website's design theme.

WordPress and its amazing community of programmers makes it easy to define a standard look for your site. A theme uses a web standard called cascading style sheets (CSS) to define the general look and feel of your site, promoting consistency from page to page. Themes often provide additional functionality beyond just how your site looks, and an array of options to give you more control over your site's appearance just by checking boxes or clicking buttons.

WordPress includes a default theme with your installation and updates it every year. You'll see the theme listed on your dashboard. Click the link to visit the Theme Management page. You should see a place to install new themes. On this page, you can access the WordPress Free Themes Directory and install new themes from among the thousands available. You can also find the theme directory at wordpress.org/extend/themes.

Click the links at the top to view featured themes highlighted by WordPress developers, along with the newest or most recently updated themes. Use the search box to find themes you may have heard of or that have particular keywords in their theme descriptions. The Feature Filter lets you check a box to find a theme with a feature set you want to have.

Once you find a theme you like, click **Install Theme**, and in seconds the theme will be available for your use. Click **Activate** to turn it on.

You can read more about WordPress themes in Chapter 2.

Add Social Buttons

The new rules of website creation demand interactivity. You will be left behind if you don't include social media buttons and use them to your advantage. These include the Facebook Like button, Twitter share button, the Google+ share button, and the LinkedIn profile button. Ideally, these buttons will appear on all the pages of your website—and in the case of Facebook, Twitter, and Google+ will be easily clickable on every post you write; your readers are far more likely to share your content through social media platforms if you make it easy for them.

Some themes incorporate social buttons like this or will require you to download and install such WordPress plugins as Social. Let's walk through installing Social, which connects your WordPress site with your Twitter and Facebook accounts.

To install Social from the Add New plugin page, type *social* in the search box. This is a popular keyword, so you'll see a lot of listings, but you'll see this plugin at or near the top. Click **Install Now**. WordPress will download Social and install its files in the appropriate location. WordPress will then ask you to activate the plugin to turn it on. That's it!

Build Your Audience Through a Regular Newsletter

One of your primary goals should be to turn your site's visitors into your readers, and readers into fans. One of the better ways of cementing that writer-reader relationship is to correspond with them regularly. Your website should allow visitors to sign up for a newsletter to learn more about you and your activities. This chore has become a lot easier with the rise of mass email providers that don't deliver piles of spam into every available email box. Instead, after taking a reader's email address and later giving them a way to back out, you can deliver solid information about your writing, your events, and whatever else interests you.

Several companies offer mass email services, but we've gotten very comfortable with MailChimp. Besides allowing you to maintain a list of up to 2,000 subscribers at no charge, they offer simple integration with your WordPress site.

Signing up for a MailChimp account is pretty straightforward. Go to mailchimp.com and click the **Sign Up Free** button. Give them an email address, a user name, and a password. After you sign up, MailChimp will email you a confirmation link at the address you gave them. You then get to prove you're not a spambot by entering a batch of stylized letters. Then log in with your username and password.

When you've set up your account, go to your website and pick up the free MailChimp for WP plugin by Danny van Kooten. This plugin creates a Subscribe form on your site and allows you to add a Subscribe link to comment and registration forms.

Check out the Getting Started with MailChimp page for information on setting up your lists, forms, and "campaigns" (that is, your newsletter).

You aren't required to put out a newsletter on any schedule. If you blog regularly and want everyone on your list to see each post, you can email your list with every post. You can also simply write when something is worth passing on, like a release date for a new book. If you're giving a reading, or going on tour, MailChimp lets you create sublists based on geography.

Optimize Your Theme for the Mobile Web

In the past, all you had to worry about when creating a website was how fast it loaded and how it looked on a square monitor attached to a desktop computer. Today, people access the web from traditional desktop PCs, laptops, tablets, and smartphones. Your website will potentially appear on screen sizes ranging from two-inch phone screens to 100-plus-inch big-screen TV monitors.

To cope with all these changes and simplify both the maintenance issues and the user experience, the movement for "responsive" web design—that is, a design that will automatically provide the best user experience no matter what type of device you're using—has moved to the fore among the people who make the web. WordPress is no exception.

When you're looking for a WordPress design theme, look for responsive themes, as they will give you the best experience for less effort. Searching the WordPress theme directory for "responsive" generates a list of more than 200 themes, so there's no shortage of options. We recommend installing a theme you like and opening the site with a phone or tablet to see how your site looks. We've seen good results with the Responsive and Custom Community themes, along with the default WordPress themes. Depending on the theme, you may be able to adjust settings to get a better result. If you find a theme you really like that is not specifically responsive, you can also use plugins to achieve a better mobile experience. WPTouch works well for this.

> **Keep in mind . . .** WordPress, Blogger, TypePad, and Tumblr all have mobile clients for viewing and posting to your site on the go. Check your phone/tablet app store to locate and install them.

Adding Widgets and More Plugins

All themes in WordPress enable you to install widgets in the web page sidebars that run alongside the main content on your page. Some themes support one sidebar, others two. To experiment with populating your sidebars with widgets, go to the Appearance area and find Widgets. You'll see a list of available items, ranging from a calendar that helps your readers find your blog posts chronologically, to lists of recent posts and recent comments, to a tag cloud that offers a graphical assessment of the topics you cover. Just drag a widget from the list to the sidebar to add a widget to your site.

Don't confuse widgets and plugins. Widgets almost always relate to the aforementioned kinds of features you add to your sidebars. Plugins, such as the social ones described above, often work behind the scenes of your blog and can provide a nearly endless supply of search engine optimization (SEO) tools, spam fighters, event calendars, and contact forms.

WordPress provides two plugins by default. The first is a toy called Hello Dolly. Click **Activate** and you'll see a random lyric from the musical

Website for author client Victor Villaseñor, author of the *New York Times* bestseller *Rain of Gold*.

Hello Dolly appear on your administrative page. The other is more important: Akismet, a comment-spam fighter that is perhaps the biggest "must-have" plugin. Don't set this up on your test site, but be sure it's turned on for your live site. Akismet is free for personal use, and business licenses are inexpensive and worth every penny.

Adding new plugins is very similar to the process for adding themes described earlier. From the plugin management page, click **Add New** to gain access to the free plugin directory at wordpress.org/extend/plugins.

While there are tens of thousands of free plugins in the WordPress plugin directory, the popularity of WordPress as a web content management system means that commercial developers have produced hundreds more premium plugins, offering more complex functionality.

Some of our favorite plugins are listed on our companion website, buildauthorplatform.com.

Best Practices for Website Content

In setting up your author website, remember to optimize these two kinds of content:

- Static content is any content on your website that doesn't change or changes very little over time, such as your author bio, contact information, and what your book is about. The section you are reading here addresses your static content.
- Dynamic content changes frequently or is interactive and is great for searchability purposes. All you need is your blog entries and audience comments to form the dynamic content of your site. One beauty of keeping your blog on your site is that it reduces the necessity of bolstering your site with static pages; the dynamic blog keeps your site ever-fresh and highly indexable with Google and other search engines.

According to author client George Plumley, author of *WordPress 24-Hour Trainer* (Wrox, 2nd edition 2011), a key to maximizing WordPress content (and the same can be said of blog content created in non-WordPress sites, too) is to "keep your content split into the smallest possible pieces. That's also part of what makes blogs highly effective: Break up content into individual pieces for easy managing."

Website content works best when paragraphs and sentences are short and clear. Website usability guru Jakob Nielsen performed a study showing that usability increased by 58% by editing out extra words. Website viewers move quickly, so the value of your message must be condensed into the span of a glance. Since there is so much content on the web competing for our attention, we scan by habit, and web users tend to scan down the left side and read only a few lines to the right. If you understand the short attention span of viewers, you can appeal to this kind of speed reading in chunks. Here are the guidelines for creating effective author website content:

Get attention with your first words. Like a good speech, the opening impression of your website has to catch the readers attention and convince them to stay on the site, read more, and interact.

Get attention with attention-grabbing short subheads. Your viewers scan the headlines first, and many of them never get beyond reading the topmost half of the page.

Use lists. They help cut words and keep content scannable for the viewer.

Use only one single, readable font.

Leave enough horizontal space between sentences.

Keep ample margins on both sides. Remember to facilitate ease of viewing and reading. The reactive theme mentioned earlier in this chapter allows clear website readability on all sizes of mobile device screens.
Edit your content. Make sure your text is clear, jargon-free, and error-free.
Add an incentive to interact, such as an invitation to offer feedback, enter a contest or sweepstakes, or get something for free, like a sample chapter or excerpt from your book.

These techniques help lead your audience to an easy path to take action, that is, read your blog, engage and interact with you via your blog, look at the rest of your site, subscribe to your newsletter, and, ultimately, buy your book.

Use Keywords and Tags and Measure Results

When you identify your strategy and tie together the 14 steps of your author platform efficiently, your site continues to attract visitors for many years to come. The first nine months of your site's life are the most critical to establishing your presence, so ensure that your website is working as efficiently as possible during this initial stage. Test-drive your own links regularly to make sure they are working, that the site as a whole is functioning well, and that the interactivity that you set up on your site initially can work on autopilot in the future. After your site is established, it won't require spending as much time maintaining or refreshing the content.

Keywords: If you identify and use the same keywords your audience uses to search the Internet, they will find you in the crowded space of the web and you will get a higher SEO ranking and higher numbers of visitors. Ideally you want to be in the number-one slot or close to it when a user types that keyword into the search bar.

Metadata: Learn to create compelling metadata, which is the line or two of text that shows up next to your website name when it's found by the browser. If your metadata does not compel users to click that link to your website, then the best site in the world will be lost. By default, your search results display the first 156 characters on the page they searched. The Yoast WordPress SEO plugin allows you to write a 156-character meta description for every page and post on your site, giving you complete control over what appears in your search results. Use this option well! Be sure you describe what your readers are looking for to lead them to your site instead of a weak line or two such as "Like what you see? Please subscribe to my newsletter!" every time your site comes up in search results. Test this out when your website is complete: Google your keywords, find your website, and adjust your metadata to get the most powerful impact in searches.

GETTING HARD NUMBERS: GOOGLE ANALYTICS

Through the Jetpack plugin, WordPress gives you wonderful numbers showing you how many visits your site is getting, where your visitors are located geographically, and what pages and articles they visit while surfing there. Your web host also probably gives you a separate set of data. The gold standard for free information about your site's visitors remains the company that relies on such data to drive its advertising-based business strategy: Google.

You might be a little intimidated, but signing up for and using Google Analytics is pretty painless, even for the technophobe. All you need to know beforehand is the address (URL) of your website and how to copy and paste material from one part of the Internet to another.

Go to google.com/analytics (you'll have to log in to your Google account, which you already have if you use Gmail, YouTube, or any other Google property). Click the Admin tab, and look for +New Account. The new account screen appears.

You want to track a "website." Read over the features you'll get with Analytics, then scroll down to Setting up your web property. Tell Google the name of your site and the web address. Choose an Industry Category, such as Books & Literature, and select your Time Zone. Choose an Account Name, and choose who can see your analytics data.

When you've filled out the form, click **Get Tracking ID**. Google will generate a code that must be copied and pasted into the home page code of your website. The Google Analytics for WordPress plugin will simplify this process, so you'll want to install that.

Analytics is a very important measure of the size and reach of your author website. It's the best tool to show you how many people have viewed your site and to quantify your website subscribers, social media activity, and other data. Google Analytics also shows you search results for keywords and most-used phrases, responders to your contact forms, and more information that will help you target your audience further as you grow your site.

Your author website is your own online real estate, your central location to link to and plug in many pieces of growing media and networks, and your central place to tie your platform locations together. Don't miss out! Start creating or updating, and enjoy the draw of your author website.

Checklist, Step 1: Author Website

➤ Know your audience needs and your own value and plan your author site accordingly.

➤ Choose an existing author site model to customize for your needs.

➤ Map out your landing-page site strategy.

➤ List site pages and create a tab for each.

➤ Write static content for each page.

➤ Determine your website design.

➤ Publish your website—go live.

➤ Track and measure the users of your website.

➤ Include your live website URL in all networks, comments, articles, and every email signature.

Success Spotlight: Waterside Client David Meerman Scott
(davidmeermanscott.com)

- 8 books
- 30 languages
- 1,000,000 sold, including university sales
- *The New Rules of Marketing and PR* became a *New York Times* bestseller with 300,000 copies sold

Beginnings: Starting out as a student at Kenyon College, Ohio, as a liberal arts/economics major, David became a bond trader on Wall Street. He worked in Tokyo for six years, then held executive positions in the electronic news division of Knight-Ridder, at the time one of the world's largest newspaper companies. In 1995 David joined Desktop Data, which became NewsEdge Corporation, and then became vice president of marketing at NewsEdge until the business was sold to Thomson Corporation in 2002.

In our interview, David said, "I didn't plan on becoming a marketing strategist.... I came upon it accidentally." At NewsEdge, he and his team found that do-it-yourself programs based on creating useful content and publishing it online at virtually no cost consistently generated more interest from qualified buyers than expensive professional public relations programs.

How he came up with his best-selling book idea: David said that when he encountered Web 2.0, he started to see that thinking like a publisher was what seemed most helpful for people to understand it. He felt that it was important to share with others that online marketing is more like online publishing than traditional marketing, and that in order to be successful, traditional marketing thinking had to change. He felt that publishers:

- Know how to create and promote content;
- See patterns that others don't see; and
- Use the big picture for business.

The New Rules of Marketing and PR came together around the ideas forming in his head: Success on Web 2.0 is about content, about blogging, and about a great content-driven website.

Platform: As an author, David has successfully created his fantastic author platform covering all 14 steps outlined in this book, including:

- Getting reciprocal links on other websites
- Giving free info in the form of PDFs
- Maintaining his blog
- Making videos available on his site
- Using social networks
- Speaking, and much more

David went on to share another important finding: that his blog posts increased in popularity when he included things beyond his book topic, including links to related posts. In fact, David maintains, "That's when my sales doubled." He also placed his insightful articles on Huffington Post, which gained even more visibility for him and his books.

Every day, David said, he thought about how he could sell ten books with these questions in his mind: Where? How? And when? And never stopping. David believes that every single blog post he creates is another opportunity that can (and does) compel ten more people to buy his book.

David was sought after as a paid speaker before his book came out; he shared in our interview that later, when his book was out, he asked people to buy the book rather than taking a speaking fee. David continues to speak and teach seminars on marketing, and he constantly keeps his eye on how he can find opportunities to sell more copies of his books through these venues.

David's advice to authors: Have a vision/idea and articulate it; talk about things related to what you do, not just the book itself; and, most importantly, get out there and don't stop promoting!

David Meerman Scott's final word on author platform building: Now anybody can earn attention by publishing their way, using the tools of social media such as blogs, podcasts, online news releases, online video, viral marketing, and online media.

CHAPTER 2

Blog to Build Your Readership Community

"A blog is only as interesting as the interest shown in others."

—*Lee Odden, author of* Optimize: How to Attract and Engage More Customers by Integrating SEO, Social Media, and Content Marketing

IT WAS IN 2006 that we really began to feel the change in the publishing industry brought on by individual empowerment in the digital age. First the music business radically changed, starting with music downloads; and then the movie industry, starting with streaming video; and then publishing, starting with ebooks. Global business was shifting on its axis. It was in 2006 that *Time* magazine awarded the Person of the Year Award to "YOU" instead of to a single person as in the past. Lev Grossman's article in *Time* on December 25, 2006, said, "The new Web is a very different thing. It's a tool for bringing together the small contributions of millions of people and making them matter. . . . Silicon Valley consultants call it Web 2.0, as if it were a new version of some old software. But it's really a revolution."

The world has become sufficiently tech-connected to enable us to interact, collaborate with, and create a community around our interest with a global crowd. Marketing specialists consistently encourage bloggers to rise above this noise level, but what a discouraging concept! Imagine moving into the midst of a huge crowd and being told you must rise above it. How can you create a blog with sufficient pull among the 156 million+ blogs published on the web today?

- Tumblr has more than 101.7 million blogs with 44.6 billion blog posts
- WordPress.com has more than 63 million blogs
- LiveJournal reports having 62.6 million blogs
- Weebly states it has more than 12 million blogs
- Blogster has more than 582,754 blogs

Since the rise of blogging in the late 1990s, bloggers have discovered time and again that certain elements enable their blogs to successfully stand out from the crowd, and we share those elements with you here. This chapter shows how to draw your audience into your specialization in your genre, your unique value, and your subject matter expertise through blogging and outlines efficient strategies and best practices that will get you to your online community quickly and efficiently.

Your Blog Is About More Than Content

A blog is by definition a web log or web journal, but it's much more than that. A blog is your own instant publishing platform; your blog entries accumulate to form a body of journalism. When you attract and form an online community, they begin to interact with you and each other, which grows your book audience. Use blogging wisely to publish well, and you will find an audience ready and waiting for your book.

Your blog is your self-published online magazine, where *you* are the editor, writer, and publisher. Your blog's built-in powerful tool is comment-enabled social networking. Your blog showcases *you*, displaying your subject matter expertise, personal interests, and thoughts behind the scenes of your book(s). And here's the most powerful part: Once your blog readership numbers increase, it begins to exert an invisible pull of its own that attracts those who you didn't contact or expect to contact, but who are out there searching for you and the help, advice, and value add that you offer. The more effort you put into your blog up front, the stronger your blog's momentum will be and the less effort you'll have to put into it later on.

Your blog's drawing power contributes not only to your book's success but also to your overall success as an author. Authors can't see their whole readership, but they need to remember that a good-sized segment of the audience reading an online web journal includes media talent scouts in search of content, speakers, and more.

To mobilize the crowded web to work for you and to increase your book audience, first and foremost, direct your blog to the interests of your readers. Once readers see their needs and interests met, they feel a connection and take interest in you and then the best possible next step takes place: sharing this interest with their friends. This expands your readers' networks to add to your own. In addition, as journalists, radio and television talent scouts, literary agents, and publishing editors all hunt for subject matter experts with a large audience, we add our networks to yours. Start tapping into the networks of each individual who finds and likes your blog. What grows your blogging audience is not so much a special cleverness, an ability to sell yourself, or having special marketing tricks; it's how you maximize connections with others, showing authenticity, sincerely caring for and responding to your audience, and delivering to their needs.

At our literary agency, we scour the web daily to find authors who are subject matter experts and have a large following. Is that you? Can we find you? The same questions apply to fiction authors: if you are not findable, you will not be contacted by media scouts. As agents, we're hit with tough requirements in presenting authors to publishers, such as how many followers and readers the author has, what the author platform presence includes, where and how the author shows up in person, the possibility of video or audio, and how many followers they have in each venue. The reason publishers ask us to find writers who have an established audience applies equally to self-published authors: It's purely business. The larger the established audience, the better it's ensured that when the book is published, there will be buyers.

Authors expand readership by consistently increasing their own presence through blogs, then showing up in comments and contributions on others' networks. When I find you, a potential author to present to a publisher, I expand your audience by plugging you into our agency following, and then with the publisher who has their own following, and then with the bookstore buyers who have large book buyer databases. By starting a blog, you automatically begin to expand your reach by tapping into the reach of others; by commenting on others' blogs and exchanging guest blog posts, you expand your reach even further.

> **Side Note:** Over decades I've searched for and found many hundreds of author clients online now signed to book contracts, proof that publishing contracts can and do appear "out of the blue" for subject matter experts who can write and have an established audience. By following the 14 steps in building your author platform outlined in these pages, you are putting yourself in a position to become the next author discovery.

Blogging Is Beyond an Advantage, It's Essential

Recent surveys of book blog readers indicate that over half of all buyers buy books primarily based on the influence of the authors' blogs! Consider the power of doubling your own audience, that is, those who pay attention to author web journals, by connecting to who you are, your behind-the-scenes thoughts and preferences, what you think and feel, why you're a writer or subject matter expert, and the value add you are bringing to them. A major advantage to your blog, then, is the sheer fact of writing it, giving the inside scoop on you as the leading force of your book and opening the door to dialogue through comment boxes.

It's a fact that businesses that blog get more web visitors and interest than businesses that don't. Blogs create a loyal community of users that leads to higher sales, and businesses with blogs attain 20% more business than businesses that do not.

> The Edelweiss searchable catalog created by Mark Evans at edelweiss .abovethetreeline.com correlates book mentions on blogs with point-of-sale information and ranks the results. The correlation between blogs and increased book sales is dramatic.

Blog Strategy

Once you've created your author website as described in Chapter 1, the most important task facing you is defining your blogging strategy and execution. Your author blog, created well, is the single best promotion avenue to supercharge sales of your books.

In the first decade of my publishing career as an editor for two major publishing houses, I believed that idea is king and that every move should be predicated on just the integrity of ideas. It took more than a decade for the reality of the book industry to catch up with my awareness; publishing is an industry that creates a product like any other business. This was a blow to realize, and I have seen authors with great ideas get shocked that their book did not get published, or that once published, did not become an instant top seller! I'm hoping this awareness will boost your own author career: A book is merchandise in the form of bound pages and a glossy cover, with a price tag, and must sell in large quantities to be successful.

Your author blog jump-starts the proving ground: that is, the existence of your readership community; the readers who comment who are likely to buy your book and tell their friends about how great your book is; and the potential numbers in your expanded network of those who will buy your book. And just as a crowded restaurant looks more attractive than an empty one, community starts taking off on its own once it reaches a threshold size. In today's chaotic publishing climate, with increasing numbers of books being traditionally published and self-published, authors must attract a community, and maintaining a blog creates an important place to do it.

Here's a basic all-purpose author blog strategy to get started:

1. Start your hosted blog, following the steps in this chapter.
2. Choose a blog type from the list in the next section to suit your subject matter interest and expertise.
3. Commit to a blog schedule and stick to it. Do not stop. Daily blogging is excellent, but twice or even once a week is fine as long as you are consistent.
4. Encourage comments and respond to every single comment and question, the same day if you can. For us, our morning coffee is the optimum time for audience interaction.
5. Ask guest bloggers for added posts and become a guest blogger for others.

6. Promote your blog. Link your blog to every personal and web presence you have: sites, social networks, training, speaking, etc. Post your blog URL on your business card and in your email signature line.

Blog Types

There is a tremendous freedom in blogging in that you make every decision about what you want to blog about and you can use any format under the sun. That said, tremendous freedom can and does bring tremendous chaos. Create a method of organizing your blog and your blogging at the outset. Just as chapters organize a book, posts organize your blog and present best in a format similar to consecutive articles in a published journal. Whatever method you choose, be consistent with your formatting and the level of your interactivity.

Three types of blogs are used by most of our author clients or are used in combination:

Blog as "DVD extras." Movie DVDs carry a lot of extras: outtakes, directors' cuts, deleted scenes, that is, everything behind the scenes. The same goes for author blogs: Many of our author clients use this leading blog format to keep audience interest. The very successful blog by Waterside author David Meerman Scott can be found at webinknow.com. David's blog, titled *Web Ink Now*, is ranked in *AdAge Power 150* as one of the top marketing blogs, a combination of topics that his readers are interested in that does not directly promote his book. Waterside client Bill Evans also uses the DVD extra–type format for his blog at billevansbanjo.com/blog. Note that both of these blogs speak to audience interests in an interesting, consistent, and short format with accompanying visuals.

For fiction authors, the outtake is a great format for behind-the-scenes looks at the books and movies you like with accompanying reviews, information about your characters, plots, locations, and themes of your books. Or print a segment of your book on your blog and add comments along the lines of directors' cuts on DVDs. Mine your own database for original sources of writing you've done to post in your blog: letters, diaries, random observations, poems, or travel observations.

Blog as Question & Answer Forum. This format is the definite winner in terms of blog type, used by successful authors, in nonfiction and also in fiction. The Q&A format can be used not only to teach how-to's and skills but also has the benefit of reaching behind the scenes for readers to ask and find out the inspiration for a story, how the writing process works, what inspires a writer, etc. The Q&A format is a tool with major practical advantages for authors, including:

- Simplicity
- Ease of plugging in content generated by others in the form of questions, which leads to cooperative networking
- Built-in audience interaction
- Helping and giving deeper insight to others
- Establishing subject matter expertise, depth, and added dimension
- Consistently refreshed and 100% tailored content that improves search engine optimization (SEO) and, best of all, draws returning customers to find out what the next Q&A dialogue will be

Successful Q&A blogs are found all over the web and used by many of our successful Waterside authors, including Andy Rathbone (andyrathbone.com), who uses this format to respond to issues his audience encounters, and Dave Taylor (askdavetaylor.com), whose Q&A is the centerpiece of his author site's landing page.

A number of Waterside author clients write fiction as well as non-fiction, and these same techniques cross over to the world of fiction author visibility also. Fiction writers can check out Tee Morris' blog at teemorris.com, who writes science fiction, steampunk, and fantasy.

Collective blogs. Use power in numbers: authors with like interests have formed collective blogs, where various authors contribute to posting. Contributing to a collective site, authors are able to increase the size of their following by posting to their collective networks. This type of blog is fully loaded with content and is an announcement platform for upcoming dates, lectures, book releases, and schedules. One example is our author client Winslow Yerxa, who blogs at the collective site harmonicasessions.com.

Learn about Technorati (technorati.com), the search engine for rating blogs. It looks at SEO tags and the number of blogs that link to your blog to give you a blog rating. Technorati lists the top 100 blogs, a blog directory, instructions for submitting a guest blog, and much more.

Encourage Online Sharing with Your Blog

In their second edition of *Blogging to Drive Business*, author clients Eric Butow and Rebecca Bollwitt show how to foster your readership community through online sharing in your blog, suggesting that readers can have a sense of ownership within your blog space. Rebecca's blog (rebeccacoleman.ca) creates a sense of community by addressing customer interests stated in comments. The blog advantage is interactive content, so encourage a strong community to form around your posts. "In some cases Internet users will create groups, fan pages, or their own blogs dedicated to various products or services they like," Rebecca says. "Opening up similar access and playgrounds for discussion in your own online space can work to your advantage . . . the community might not necessarily be an actual page, forum, or comments section, but you'll find that your readers will become your blog's evangelists."

Encourage blog conversation starting with reading comments, respond to them in a way that continues the conversation beyond, and then allow and encourage readers to share your content with their own social networks. Ask what they think and what their communities think about an issue to solicit comments. Here are more blog sharing tips from Rebecca and Eric's book:

- To ensure tools are available, provide links and Share This buttons on your blog posts by using a service like AddThis. You can encourage readers to share your link through social bookmarking sites like Digg and Reddit and through Facebook.
- Use a plugin from Twitter such as Tweetmeme to abbreviate links for tweets.
- When readers share your content on their blogs, they can just link back to your post; you can make that link visible from your site.

- Remember that blogging is about public sharing that builds your author brand! Whenever your posts are shared, you win as the exposure for your author brand and your book increases along with your ability to be found

Start with a Hosted Blog

In the last chapter, we told you why you need to have a home base on the web, a site to serve as the magnet for all your writing endeavors. When you're just starting out, maybe you want to test the waters a little bit. See some proof of what we're talking about without going to the trouble (and expense) of finding a web host and registering a domain. In this case, often the best solution is to set up a blog on a hosted site like Blogger, TypePad, or WordPress.com. These are places where you can publish articles every day at no cost to you. The advantage of these particular sites for writers is not just the simplicity of setup and maintenance, but also the ability to reach many people through the communities around the platform.

There are many places on the web that will host your blog site, but we recommend choosing one of the big players: Blogger/Blogspot, TypePad, or WordPress.com. Where you choose to place your blog is largely a matter of personal preference. These sites will all help you find your audience through SEO and an existing community of bloggers. They are easy to set up and maintain. All of them have mobile apps that allow you to connect to your blog and post from a smartphone or tablet. Perhaps the availability of your preferred address on a particular host will be a deciding factor.

In this section, we'll show you the defining characteristics of three platforms: Blogger/Blogspot, TypePad, and WordPress.

BLOGGER/BLOGSPOT

The idea behind Blogger is to give anyone a drop-dead simple way to have a blog. All the software you need to create and maintain a blog exists in your web browser, and you don't have to install a thing. This has been true from Blogger's beginnings as an independent website right around the dawn of the 21st century, through its acquisition by Google, straight through to today. It is also one of the most heavily trafficked sites on the web.

Because Google owns Blogger, you can easily get yourself a Blogger account with your existing Google account. Blogger integration with other Google properties like YouTube and Google+ also offers several advantages:

- Linking to YouTube videos in your posts is a snap! In the post editor, you can search for relevant videos or link to your YouTube channel.
- You can automatically create a Google+ page for your blog that will share your posts with that audience, offering another way to interact with your readers.
- Perhaps most importantly, you can use Google AdSense and include affiliate links to earn money with your blog.

The downside to Blogger is mostly about control. Unlike WordPress and Movable Type/TypePad, you can't run Blogger as the blog page of your own site. You can link your existing domain to your Blogger site, but you should only do this if your site is just a blog. If, for example, you want to directly sell ebooks or other content, you can't do that on Blogger, though you can post affiliate links from other e-commerce sites.

If you like having lots of choices for how your blog will look, you'll find Blogger theme options quite limited, especially compared to WordPress .com. If you're one of those folks who complains about too many choices, however, choosing from the seven basic choices (with different color schemes) could be quite pleasant.

TYPEPAD

Whereas Blogger is for folks who just want to blog, TypePad from SAY Media is a specialized site host and content management system. It has been around a long time, and though it hasn't gotten the same media attention as its rivals in recent years, it's still among the top 500 trafficked websites.

TypePad's big brother, Movable Type (MT), was one of the first industrial-strength blogging platforms, starting right around the same time as Blogger. A few months after Google bought the company that created Blogger, the MT developers (called Six Apart) ended the practice of distributing MT for free. The hosted version started in 2003 and has always been a paid, commercial product. When noncommercial bloggers who still had to install MT and connect it to a database (no easy task in those days) had to start paying a fee to run MT, many fled to the upstart WordPress. Eventually, Movable Type 4 was released as open source software. Today you can install Movable Type on a server for free; TypePad costs around US$100 annually.

WORDPRESS

We don't have to tell you about the power of Blogger's connection with Google. What may surprise you is the reach of WordPress—more than three-quarters of all blogs on the web run on WordPress (either self-hosted or at WordPress.com)! WordPress is among the top 25 sites in terms of traffic.

You can use WordPress either on your own web space (using a hosting company as described in Chapter 1) or on WordPress.com. Sometimes you'll hear WordPress veterans talk about "self-hosted WordPress sites" or "WordPress-dot-org sites" to refer to WordPress running on a server. Self-hosted WordPress is typically updated with new features twice a year, with occasional smaller updates that are usually focused on plugging security holes. Depending on your hosting company, you may be responsible for keeping your site updated. The bigger hosts (and WordPress.com) handle this for you.

If you're serious about blogging, and really do want to try out blogging on a hosted system before creating your own website, we highly recommend starting out at WordPress.com.

Consider these advantages:

- Large and strong community of users and developers.
- Excellent technical support.
- More than 100 free theme choices (and more than a handful of premium themes). When you choose a self-hosted location, hundreds of free and premium themes become available.
- An easy way to determine how your audience is building through detailed statistics.
- Freshly Pressed on the WordPress.com home page highlights dozens of posts every day, giving you the chance to shine.
- Simple export of your dot-com site to a self-hosted WordPress site (even porting your audience to the new site for a small fee). WordPress can usually import posts from another blog system, too.

- WordPress.com users often get to see and work with new features before they are released to self-hosted users.

How to Create a Blog

Regardless of what vendor you choose, you will have to think about these things:

- What to name your blog.
- What address (uniform resource locator, or URL) to use to help people find your blog.
- Writing your About page.

Naming Your Blog

A few things to think about when naming your blog:

- Most likely, the title should reflect the primary topic(s) you expect to cover in the blog.
- Use a pithy title! Both Blogger and WordPress allow a subtitle or tagline that allows for more expansive explanations of your blog.
- If you are expecting to create a separate site for your book (see Chapter 11), avoid giving your author website blog the same title.
- Don't just toss off a title! Give it some thought, unless you plan to make the blog private while you work out your topic schedule and other details. While you can nearly always change the title of your blog, this is part of your brand. Often the title will also be reflected in your web address (which you can't change).

Defining Your Web Address

Consider these facts:

- Every site on the web has a unique, specific address.
- WordPress is the only vendor that talks about its size; they say about 100,000 new blogs are created every day.

The reality is that whoever you choose to host your blog, millions of blogs are already registered on your chosen site, so finding your unique address can be tricky. Always check first for your blog's title (or some shortened version). If you're focusing on a particular topic, look for an address that people interested in that topic might search for. You may want to start with your name, if it's not especially common. Have some backup ideas ready. You'll learn right away whether the address is available.

Creating Your About Page

No matter what topics you explore, your blog should always reflect your personality. Every blog vendor lets you create a static page that allows readers to find out what your blog is about. Often the first thing a reader does after finding an interesting blog post is check the About page to see if the blog is worth following or subscribing to. This makes your About page critical in finding and building your audience.

Use the About page to describe what prompted you to start the blog, the topics you cover, and as much as you want to reveal about yourself. Remember that you're making a first impression, so imagine what your reader wants to know about the person behind the words.

Now that you are set up with your blog, the next step is posting blog entries consistently all the way to your book's publication.

Best Practices

Start now: Timing is a critical element of your blog, so start your blog well before your book publishes, as ongoing buildup promotion is essential. Blog to jump-start the success of your book, as you're putting a hook into the pond of multimillions of web searchers who want to connect with you.

Look for model blogs: Before you create your blog, spend time reviewing possible models for your blog. When you see what's already working out there in the crowd for existing authors, you can create your own style based on those successes. Perhaps you've already identified the popular blogs in your niche. If you haven't, here are some examples of blogs that show author brand, personal touch, audience-interest-driven posts, and clear format:

- Tricia Goyer (triciagoyer.com/blog)
- Mary DeMuth (marydemuth.com/blog)
- Thom Hartman (thomhartmann.com/thom/blog)

Additional examples of preferred author blogs can be found at internet writingjournal.com/authorblogs.

Choose a template: Choose a format close to your favorite model blog and then customize it from there to save time. Review the different formats at blogsrater.com and technorati.com.

Choose a theme: Themes (aka templates) define the look and feel of your site. They take some of the pain out of choosing a color scheme, display font, and column size that can easily paralyze the average non-design-oriented writer. How you choose your theme differs depending on the site, but you can usually get a snapshot or preview of how your site would look with each theme applied. Click the picture you like best, and voilà! Your site will look like that.

This is where you can change your mind most often. Theoretically, you could change your site's theme daily (even hourly, but don't plant that in your brain), but that would drive away readers who come to expect that blog *content* is updated frequently, but that your style remains consistent.

While each blog host offers different choices for its themes, focus on these areas:

- **Number of columns:** One-column templates focus all the attention on your writing. Great for personal journals, not so great for building a community. A sidebar column with pointers to other areas of your site allows readers to navigate better, view the types of topics you cover, and perhaps see other sites that you visit (a "blogroll"). Add a second sidebar column for symmetry if you have a lot of sidebar content.
- **Column width:** You can usually specify a fixed width for each column. Often you can choose a "flexible" width that depends on your reader's screen size.
- **Colors:** As a writer, you want to make sure your content is readable, so choose your background colors and fonts accordingly.

Writing Blog Posts

We operate in a new paradigm of web-based promotion that requires thinking and communicating not from your own perspective, but from the perspective of your audience. This is a new community era that does not take well to selling. Instead, communities want everyone to share great things with them. It means joining your audience community, paying attention to and responding to comments, and giving solid valuable information instead of advertising. What does your audience want? What motivates your readers? What are their hopes, dreams, and needs? The more you know the answers to these questions, take them into consideration, and deliver solutions, the more you will build audience for your writing.

With valuable content presented in the way that buyers can connect to, they will be naturally drawn to your books. Remember, top publishers have always understood that audience definition is key to creating the success of any book.

Your first blog post is best created as an introduction to yourself in a Welcome post. Shake hands, tell folks what you're doing, and show that you are sharing and searching for friends with similar interests. Because the content of your blog is by its nature personal, readers want to see a flavor of the real person in the author.

Your blog post impact is a combination of content and presentation, so use these elements in each blog post:

- **Strong headline:** Use a great title and first sentence with SEO keyword tags.
- **Date of post:** This is typically added automatically by your blog system.
- **Blog post text:** Content ideas below. Shorter posts have become the norm, but maximum length is one short, edited intro paragraph, two or three body paragraphs, and one final short sentence, with second level subheads. Leave the last sentence as an "open for discussion" feel to attract the crowd, such as a question, a vote, or a request to comment.
- **Visuals are important:** Be sure to include photos in your blog. Images of 200 × 200 pixels are best for sharability. A related image or logo can work for this purpose. Use a file name and descriptive text caption.

Your camera phone or iStock photos are fine. Videos are also a big plus and discussed later in this book.

- **Links:** To your other author platform locations, to friends and associate blogs, related articles and posts, etc.
- **Comment boxes:** You moderate what comments will appear. Try to get as many comments as you can, starting with asking your friends and associates for comments, and sharing your own comments with them reciprocally. Responsiveness counts: Answer each and every one of them.

Permalinks: When you post, two things happen immediately: The post goes to the top of your site's front page, and a specific page gets created for that post. That specific page, called a *permalink*, breathes life into your post after it ceases to be new. One reason blogging is successful as a format is because it combines the immediacy of the always-current front page with the always-available archived posts. It is that *permanent link* that makes your posts available to search. So after you've written this amazing and informative post explaining the roots of the Great Depression of the 1930s to modern readers, that post does not disappear off your front page and into the dustbin. Search engines track these permalink pages to allow people to find them years down the road. After you've been blogging for a few years, you'll be surprised (and occasionally amused) by the amount of traffic your old posts get. If you either link to someone else's post for commenting on your blog or want to notify someone of a specific post of yours, don't point to the blog's home page; make sure you use the permalink, too.

Creating Content for Blog Posts

How do you tailor content to your audience once you understand the needs and interests of your audience? As an example, our author clients form a large audience for this book. I've tirelessly listened to authors' issues and concerns about platform for many years and am responding with the solution—this book. I know well that my literary agency clients generally don't have much time available after doing their day-to-day jobs and writing a book; these clients have demanded a complete, pre-digested, easy-to-follow formula for creating their own author platform. In deciding the table of contents and coverage, we have tailored the content of this book for that audience, which we understand well. That's why we included "best of" recommendations instead of endless choices, why we don't use marketing jargon, and why we're presenting a complete system under one roof instead of making our readers chase multiple tips that are scattered around the Internet.

Knowing the time constraints of our own authors, we're willing to bet that you don't have much time for posting original content every day, so try posting at least once a week, without fail, up until the time of your book's publication. To save you time, here are content and posting shortcuts.

The main thing to remember is that posting original, content-rich blog entries, however often you post, keeps your blog fresh so your readership will not migrate elsewhere.

Start posts with an interesting headline to engage readers and make your content more shareable. While your headline's foremost objective is telling potential readers what your post is about, editors know that informative headlines that grab a reader's attention in other ways are the most valuable. Be aware that WordPress, and most other blog platforms, use the post headline to create the permalink URL for that post. Your choice of headline matters!

> **Tip:** Include a copyright notice and permissions policy posted in small type so that your work doesn't show up elsewhere without your permission. Most blogs use a Creative Commons (CC) license for their content. See "What is a Creative Commons license?" in Chapter 10 for more information on CC's advantages.

Capture readership by writing in the first person in your authentic personal voice. As a book author, you have established that you have a lot to say through the written word. By sharing open and honest perspectives, thoughts, and observations that you know your readers will be interested in, you provide relevant and timely content that keeps your audience engaged. Here are some ideas to keep your blog fresh with minimum effort; choose from one or more of these types per week:

- Excerpts from your book, of course!
- Short excerpts from others' books that have helped you. Add a comment on reposts of others' work.

- Reviews of books/articles/blogs you recommend.
- Ideas relevant to your subject matter (and offer opinions).
- Personal story behind an experience you had related to your book.
- Anecdote: a lesson you learned from someone.
- A quote, plus commentary.
- Conversation or interview.
- Lists/resources.
- Reposts of articles you found on the web that are interesting and relevant and/or news and current issues related to your subject. We don't recommend this as your main posting strategy but as a fill-in to keep content fresh.
- An idea chosen from your book; express your opinion of it as the thought leader that you are. The crowd loves the controversial, so challenge an idea instead of playing it safe to generate more comments, sharing, and interaction.

Save time by setting up a monthly appointment with yourself to write multiple blog entries at one time and then schedule them. All blog platforms allow you to schedule your posts weeks ahead of time if you like.

As many authors do, use sidebars on all of your posts to show your book cover, upcoming publication date, and more information about the book's launch.

Getting Comments on Blog Posts

Comments on blog posts are a critical component of building a community around your writing. However often you post, you can get feedback just as often. Comments mean engagement, which builds community and attracts more visitors. In addition, comments not only add fresh content to your site, but also benefit you by adding to your findability through SEO.

Every blog platform by default offers your readers a chance to comment on every post. As an author attempting to build a community of readers, you don't just want to allow your visitors the chance to comment; you want to *encourage* visitors to comment. Here's how:

- End every post with a question, even if it's just to ask for comments and feedback.

- Take a poll or vote on some aspect of your post.
- Create a list and ask readers to add to that list.
- Give a prize for the best comment.
- Make a controversial statement.
- Show a weakness or vulnerability.
- Use a comment as a jumping-off point for your next blog post. When comments come in, welcome them this way:
  - Respond as soon as possible to each comment in a way that encourages a dialogue. Set up your blog platform to email or text you when comments arrive.
  - Praise the comment. You can still disagree with the comment, but thank the commenter for taking the time to engage, and ask for others' feedback.
- Comments are solid source material for your overall blogging content. If you are starting out, use comments from other social networks that you are a part of and then grow as readers comment on your blog. You can ask anyone who reaches out to you through email or online comments if you can use their questions or observations to start your blog entry. Savvy bloggers base their next blog post on a user comment from the previous blog post. When you reply to your blog comments, try this to increase future comments:
  - Instead of a closed-ended "thank you," offer the reader something, like a blog or book that would help them, or words of encouragement or further advice;
  - Expand your point further when you reply;
  - Ask yet another question;
  - Exchange comments with others bloggers.

Be sure it is easy and welcoming to comment:

- You shouldn't have to log in to comment (though your platform may offer some benefits to those logging in).
- The comment box should offer ample space and expand to fit the size of the comment.
- Join in with a new blogger community like Triberr.com or Bloggers .com.
- Join groups on LinkedIn/Facebook and ask for comments.
- Ask your network, friends, and associates for comments.

Regarding Trolls

Be prepared in advance that there are people out there who enjoy nothing more than ripping apart everything they encounter on the Internet. We're currently seeing a backlash to the "go for the jugular" approach to nasty comments. One example is BuzzFeed's announced banning of the negative book review (Garfield, "Banning the Negative Book Review" NYT 12/4/13). But trolls will persist, so you can adopt one of three policies regarding trolls:

- Ignore them, also known as "Don't feed the trolls." This is the only exception to the "respond to every comment" rule. If someone is clearly just trying to bait you into saying something stupid or regrettable, resist the temptation. If you want to be polite in ignoring the troll, just write "Thank you for your comment." If the person responds and escalates the conflict based on that response, that's a troll.
- Respond with a spirited defense of yourself and your ideas. Really only worth doing if others in your audience respond to the troll.
- Be so crushed that you never post again and rue the day you ever thought you could be a writer. An all-too-common response that only encourages the troll to try again.

The Blogger's Code of Conduct was proposed in 2007 by Tim O'Reilly for bloggers: To keep civility on a blog, be civil yourself and moderate comments on your blog. He suggested these ideas:

1. Take responsibility not just for your own words, but for the comments you allow on your blog.
2. Label your tolerance level for abusive comments.
3. Consider eliminating anonymous comments.
4. Ignore the trolls.
5. Take the conversation offline and talk directly, or find an intermediary who can do so.
6. If you know someone who is behaving badly, tell them so.
7. Don't say anything online that you wouldn't say in person.

Blog Shortcuts

In three decades of working with thought leaders, experience has shown that all have a lack of time in common. These leaders have difficulty finding time to write a book (which I believe is the responsibility of every cutting-edge thinker), and a blog is an added time burden. Here are the steps used to keep blogging time minimal:

- Work ahead and use the power of the web to automate posts.
- Write your month of blog posts on the first day of each month.
- Use Blogjet (Windows) or MarsEdit (Mac) to automatically schedule each post.
- Use an online newsletter service, like the free MailChimp, to tell your audience when you've added a post.

WORDPRESS POST TYPES

- **Standard**—Your normal, average, everyday blog post. This is the default styling for your theme.
- **Gallery**—Usually will show a thumbnail from the blog post, as well as an excerpt of what the gallery is about.
- **Aside**—Brief snippets of text without headlines that aren't quite whole blog posts. Useful for quick thoughts and anecdotes.
- **Image**—These posts highlight your images.
- **Status**—Short updates about what you're doing *right now.*
- **Quote**—These posts highlight your block-quoted text in a bolder way than standard posts do.
- **Video**—Just like Image posts, these posts highlight your videos.
- **Audio**—Just like Image and Video, these posts highlight your Audio attachments.
- **Chat**—These posts highlight snippets of memorable conversations you have with friends, both online and offline.

Author Blog Promotion Strategies

The last step to make your blog a successful magnet for your book is to promote your blog. You want to increase your audience size, keep the audience you already have, and encourage sharing your posts as much as possible.

Include Social Sharing buttons: Be sure to make it easy to share your posts and share posts of others to get reciprocal sharing. Include sharing buttons prominently at the bottom of each post to allow readers to share posts easily via email or other social networks, right from their mobile devices or laptops. Having these included in every post ensures (and reminds) others to publicize your blog for you!

WordPress.com offers this option. Go to Settings > Sharing. Scroll down to the Sharing Buttons option. Drag all the buttons down to the Enabled Services area. It doesn't matter whether you have an account at a particular social location; these buttons are for your readers. When you're finished dragging the buttons, review the other settings on the page, then click Save Changes. The buttons you selected should now appear at the bottom of every post. It should look something like the figure below. You can get the same effect in self-hosted WordPress with the Jetpack plugin.

Advertise your blog when you email: Include your blog's name and URL in your automatic signature line that attaches to the end of every message you send.

Link your blog to other blogs: Submit your blog to online directories. Post your blog URL on multiple message boards and check your page views.

Use RSS feed on your blog site: When people subscribe to your RSS feed, they are informed of updates and are more likely to read your posts. Your blogging platform should create this feed automatically.

Comment on others' blogs: Be sure to include the name of your blog and your website URL. People who like your comment will click back to your blog.

In settings, use Send Pings: Once you activate this setting, your blog will be added to recently updated lists on the web.

Get blog reviews: Link to the posts of other bloggers, and if they like your posts, they'll likely link back to you.

Guest blog: Find blogs similar to yours that share content. Look for similar blogs on your subject matter that have audiences that comment regularly. Search to find guest blogging opportunities by typing in words such as "submit a guest post" along with your subject matter keywords. Many book blogs have a guest post submission page that you can fill out. Contact other bloggers with praise for their blog and ask if they would be interested in your doing a guest post. Likewise, ask them if they'd like to guest post for you; exchanging guest posts allows you to cross-network with many other bloggers. My Blog Guest (myblogguest.com), a web community of guest bloggers, is a great place to sign up to find related blogs accepting guest posts.

Measure Your Blog Results to Understand Your Audience

Maybe you don't know this, but we hope you do: Every website takes note of every visit it gets and can report that information to its owner. When you own a website, that's a good thing.

WordPress.com and Blogspot provide you with assorted statistics related to the number of visitors you have to your hosted blog. You can see these statistics on your dashboard. WordPress offers even more detailed statistics at WordPress.com/stats. This table shows you each type of tracked information and how you can use this data to measure your audience.

You'll become engaged (and perhaps addicted) to checking these statistics every time you post, wondering whether your latest and greatest

Table 1: WordPress Statistics Categories.

Statistic	Description
Traffic/Visitors	The bar graph shows users who actually visited your site along with users who saw your post via a really simple syndication (RSS) feed. You can get this information for recent days, weeks, and months.
Views by Country	Where does your audience live? The world map shows where your visitors came from today and yesterday. You can also get summaries stretching back into the past. This information might help you determine whether you need to simplify your vocabulary to facilitate translation.
Top Posts and Pages	What people are reading. On the dashboard, you'll learn what's hot and what's not. Summaries covering the entire history of your blog are available.
Clicks	Have you got links in your posts? (You should!) See what links your readers are clicking to find out how many are interested in digging deeper into your topic.
Referrers	How did people find your blog? Through a particular search engine? From a link elsewhere on the web? This is how you find out if your site's search engine optimization (SEO) is working. You may also find other bloggers to connect with after they connect to you.
Search Engine Terms	If people visited you as a result of a web search, you can learn the terms of the actual search they used.
Tags and Categories	In WordPress, categories define the main topics you cover in your blog. Tags are the more specific topics included in each post. Think of categories as a table of contents, while tags are index terms. WordPress statistics shows you the most popular topics in your blog.
Followers	The number of subscribers to your blog through the blog itself. This number grows with every interesting post. When you get a sufficient number of followers, it's time to start a newsletter to keep them in the loop.
Comments	The people who have commented most on your blog.

entry is finding its audience. Did we mention that the WordPress mobile apps let you check stats with your phone without even looking at your site? Yet instead of seeing your statistics as just another distraction, you need to think about your statistics in a more long-term way. Ideally, the overall numbers grow, in terms of visitors, subscribers, and commenters. Statistics allow you to help give the people what they want and also determine if you're providing the service your audience needs.

Watch your Top Posts and Pages list for defining characteristics of your popular posts. If you've got a mix of practical information, link collections, photos, and opinion pieces related to your area of expertise, see if people read one type of post over another. If, for example, three-quarters of your posts are opinions, but all your top posts are instructional, perhaps you want to change that balance a little. People may respect the information you're giving them, but your arguments related to controversies in your field could be stronger.

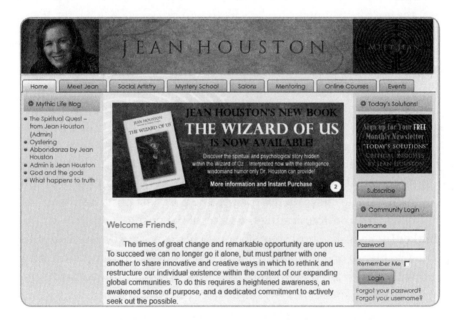

Blog site for author client Jean Houston, author of *The Wizard of Us*.

Look over the Search Engine Terms report. If someone was looking for a solution to a problem addressed in your book, could they find the answer in your blog? If not, perhaps you should add a post on that topic.

What posts generated the most commentary? Can you follow up with a summary discussion? If something happens to advance the discussion, be sure to schedule a post about the new development.

Link Your Blog to Your Social Sites

Always connect your social networks to your blog through linking! As you work your way through this book, you'll find explanations of social networking capabilities of the Internet you can use to supercharge your efforts. Without connecting via linking, you're not fulling realizing what online tools can do for you. So, as you build, be sure to link your blog to your social sites: LinkedIn, Facebook, Twitter, and Google+.

Twitter: Tweet a message (Chapter 3) with a link to your newly updated blog page. Share a link to your latest post each time you post.

Google+: Predictions are that Google+ will surpass Facebook in users in the not too distant future. Be sure to post on Google+ (Chapter 4) and provide the URL of your blog post along with announcements of your new blog posts to guide incoming traffic to your website.

Facebook: Also share your blog post URL on Facebook (Chapter 5) via your author Page and personal page to get more visibility for your blog, and then use the techniques above to solicit comments. Promote your blog post on your Facebook feed at high-traffic times to make sure people see it. An automated posting site like Hootsuite will choose these optimum times for you so you don't have to think it through. Use Facebook groups to post to a large number of people with a single click. Do not oversell the post, just post the link with a quick line communicating the value of the post.

LinkedIn: Be sure to post your blog post URL as a LinkedIn status update (Chapter 6) on both your company and your personal profiles, along with a very short description. Use LinkedIn groups to maximize exposure with a single click. Again, do not oversell it, just post a quick line, as you did with Facebook.

Email/Newsletter lists: Email a short summary of the blog with a link. Your targeted email list will likely yield a surge in viewership for your blog the day the email arrives.

Above all, enjoy the blogging experience as you connect with your readers!

Checklist, Step 2: Blog

> Create and link your blog to your author website, social networks, and email signature.
> Choose a model and customize your blog accordingly.
> Post original-content blogs consistently at least once a week.
> Add reposts of others' blogs or articles with a comment to add blog frequency.
> Write from the perspective of what your audience needs.
> Encourage comments and keep the conversation going via comments.
> Promote your blog.
> Encourage sharing via social sharing buttons at the bottom of each post.
> Learn more about your audience preferences on your blog with Google Analytics.

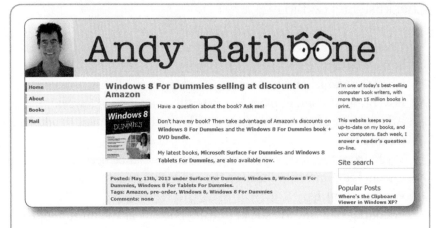

Success Spotlight: Waterside Client Andy Rathbone (andyrathbone.com)

- 50 books
- 20 languages
- 15 million in print

Beginnings: Andy started writing when he was a teenager at his high school newspaper, *The Clairemont Arrow*, as an extracurricular activity. As he got deeper into his newspaper work, Andy realized writing didn't feel like work. He found that he didn't just like writing, he loved it, and he followed his inner voice to do what he loved.

After Andy graduated from high school, he went straight to San Diego State College, studying comparative literature and journalism. He dropped out in the middle of college to work at retail jobs, then returned to college and graduated as an undeclared major with no job prospects. As college editor of the newspaper *Daily Aztec*, Andy learned about deadlines and how to "crank out a story whether I felt like it or not." That practical experience helped him to start freelancing for magazines, and he looked for magazine writing opportunities.

With that focus, he found the computer magazine *ComputorEdge*. An opportunity presented itself and Andy ran with it: CE opened a book division, so he wrote the first two books for them. He wrote a story on Waterside Productions that allowed him to start talking with the agency, which then led Waterside to create publishing contracts for his first major books. Another opportunity arose: Andy wrote the third title in the new For Dummies series.

At the time, nobody had an inkling that this new series was going to grow into a global phenomenon; the idea was turned down by almost every publisher. That is, until IDG books signed the first one, and the rest is history.

Andy became so successful in the sales of his books in the For Dummies series that as a top writer, magazines began to report about him! *People* magazine ran an article about his home, titled "The Home That Dummies Built."

Andy's advice to authors: It's important to continue to build your author platform even as a successful author. Your platform is necessary; build it before the book is published and work hard on it.

Andy Rathbone's final word on author platform building: "The most important work I do to build my author platform is constantly adding to my website. I offer the front page of my site to my audience and their questions, comments, and replies. It also creates a lot of great web traffic and a sense of a true, live community right on my site."

Andy also answers readers' questions each week, which keeps the site in public view, draws traffic, and connects with his audience in a personal way. According to Andy, "It's important to an author to gauge the level of knowledge and skills and defer to audience needs." Andy attributes his own success to the fact that he knows his audience very well and then is able to fill the need that his interaction helps him to define.

CHAPTER 3

Twitter: The Instant Handshake

"I particularly like Twitter, because it's short and can be very funny and informative. It's a little bit like having your own radio program."

—Margaret Atwood, best-selling author

WEEKLY PUBLISHING ACQUISITIONS meetings are unforgettable, especially the "Books Wanted" meetings. Written into my job as acquisitions editor for three major publishing houses was a constant pressure to originate a ready stream of great ideas. Publishers may call these dog and pony shows, or weekly "brainstorming" meetings, "blue sky," "acquisitions," or "new titles" meetings, but the point is the same: Sales, marketing, editorial, and sometimes production managers join together at the round table; editors on the hot seat toss out new ideas with enthusiasm, hoping not to get shot down. As an editor, my hope rose while pointing out new recent gems of topics of interest, imagining excited, unanimous approval and support to acquire contracts. Make no mistake: Nobody leaves the room in a meeting like this until greatness and originality are achieved; then and only then can cutting-edge lists emerge, and only then can new product be created. The Books Wanted process has remained similar over many years; book approvals are tied to audience desire to buy, also referred to as "the outstretched hand." To prove an existing readership potential, editors look for ownership of a product in large numbers; that is, publishers prefer book titles to be tied to

100,000+ sales of a product. The amount of anticipated readers has to be tied to a real-world measurement—say, numbers of readers of an article, or followers of a trending topic on Twitter or other social network. For a product example, a book on TurboTax is more likely to get signed than a general tax book because an editor can prove there are 100,000+ owners of that package looking for help on that product. Proof of audience is tied to the ability to measure its size.

Once the winning ideas are selected, then the second step to the Books Wanted process begins: creating the Authors Wanted list, now increasingly being measured by the potential size of an author's audience following. For example, these days, if you tweet about TurboTax and have 100,000+ Twitter followers, you're more likely to get signed for that book than a top-notch CPA without a following. To underscore this point, Kyle Looper, an acquisitions editor at John Wiley, advised us: "What moves the needle for us is Twitter followers. My advice: Become a Twitter 'influencer,' a person who gets retweeted. Those are the authors we're looking for. We're looking for more ways to get to exciting top influencers, as well as the emerging Twitter influencers." Kyle's advice to authors is "Develop followers, put out great information, make it easy to find, and then make it easy for them to share it."

As an agency, we have a passion for good ideas and a track record for sculpting ideas into top-selling books, and we find that many editors at traditional publishing houses contact us after their Books Wanted meetings to seek out the best authors for the titles that they want to add to their lists. Publishers now require agents to document the success of all our authors' platforms to demonstrate that there is a ready audience to buy their books. This is the killer fact, which led to writing this book: Often publishers will not even review a book proposal without first verifying that the author platform has a strong mix of presence on the web and in person! Without building a platform to add up the component parts outlined in this book, we face lower odds of winning that author client publishing contract. To put our clients ahead of the curve, we add the category of "Platform" to book proposals that we now send to editors.

Our author clients often ask why they should spend time creating a Twitter account when they are already busy managing their businesses and writing quality content. I hear "Bah!?" or "No way!" "Isn't it enough to be a subject matter expert?" The answer lies in this combination of facts: Currently Twitter is one of the ten most-visited websites worldwide, as ranked by Alexa's web traffic analysis; people continue to spend more time on social networks, including Twitter, than on any other category of sites; and Twitter averages almost 40 million tweets per day. In short, Twitter gets you and your work visible to your audience very quickly. Twitter, like all social networks, is not an advertising platform and it's essential to understand the difference. Turned off by advertising, people have come to value real, authentic messages and real people instead of actors and slick ad copy. On Twitter and social networks, you want to offer useful information, speak of your authentic experiences, and help others in the many ways available, such as retweets, covered later. Publishers include descriptions of your book on websites, at conferences, in catalogs, and in all interactions with selling your book to booksellers. On Twitter, you have an opportunity to meet and greet your audience and give people extra, useful information leading to your book.

In addition, in the new environment in which a socially enabled web operates, authors either embrace being in direct relationship with their audience or else face the prospect of obscurity. The initial use of the World Wide Web was naturally a copy of what we already knew: the passive viewer model we all understood via television. The first wave of dominant websites used the same technique as advertising on TV: pushing a message to viewers, end of subject. If you have a publisher, they will still create this kind of advertising message in their promotional materials. However, interactivity and dialogue have surfaced as the preferred way of doing business. In the audience-centric Web 2.0 environment in which we now operate, authors must connect with readers by presenting their own authentic selves and remain accessible to their following. Twitter is a quick and easy way to make direct contact with your readers via short messages.

This chapter shows you how to get up and running on Twitter, introduce yourself without self-promoting, enter a conversation smoothly, decide what and how to post about, and determine how to spend a minimal amount of time on Twitter to glean maximum exposure. You will also learn how to streamline multiple social networking sites to manage your social presence under one roof.

Why Twitter Is Important

Instant connection: Unlike radio and television, you're not a passive recipient of a controlled message on Twitter; you're a participant in a conversation. Twitter is the biggest social conversation on the Internet. Twitter postings are a super quick way to demonstrate your value and show you're in touch with your community. It's also a path to show your knowledge and thereby influence a conversation personally and directly.

Conversation: If you don't speak up, nobody will hear you. The more you demonstrate your knowledge of your subject matter in postings, repostings, and comments, the more likely you are to attract attention and gain the influence that grows audience and book sales.

Social authority: Twitter postings prove you are a credible, reliable authority that people are turning to increasingly. Twitter users love to be ahead of the information curve, whether that's getting instantaneous, on-the-scene reports of breaking news, new releases, or links to critical information and opinions about things they care about. If you're writing a book on any topic, you're probably already ahead of the information curve on that topic through your research, consuming and digesting articles and other sources, online and off. This puts you in a position to lead your audience to more information that will be genuinely useful to them, and they will tell their friends via retweets. Spreading the kinds of good information that your audience needs and likes will boost your authority even before your book is published. According to Inc. Technology's Brent Leary, "The turn towards experts and authorities seems to be coinciding with the rise of social media and networks."

Other parts of your author platform: Establish your social authority on Twitter and people want to know more about you. When you see a follower's tweet about your topic, it's okay to link to your blog post that directly addresses that topic. It's good practice to collect Twitter questions on your topic and then address them in a Q&A blog post. As questions continue to pop up on Twitter, you can address them on Twitter by linking to your post. As you create this interaction, take care to remain informative without veering into a stream of "buy my book" promotional statements.

Best Practices

Build up buzz. Start tweeting about your book and the topics it addresses as soon as you finish your manuscript. It does take time to build up awareness of your book. Craft your first tweets, taking care to stay in the "helpful" category; this may include links to your website, individual articles by you and others, and helpful blog posts. Your goal is to increase your presence, and by so doing, you start a drumroll for your published book.

Connect with new fans. Twitter gives you direct contact with readers who may have never heard of you or your book, with people who may have been searching for information about your topic, and with potential fans looking for new interests. When you introduce yourself and your subject matter to people already looking to connect, new connections, alliances, and cooperative situations arise quickly just because you showed up. On Twitter, potential fans can discover you when they weren't looking for you in the same way that shoppers find products they need and want while browsing for information related to their topic of interest.

Be authentic. An important practice on Twitter is to stay transparent, that is, without a motive, in order to build trust. It's that simple—build an honest relationship by staying true to your philosophy, viewpoints, and knowledge. It's the same rule that applies to making new friends in person: Reach out your hand in an outgoing way and know who you are, which ought to be a reflection of the author brand you defined in Chapter 1.

Make friends by complimenting others. Compliment people you meet on Twitter. The best way to do this is by retweeting and favoriting what they have written (more on those two tools later). You'll find you'll get complimented in return, which helps expand your network by tapping into the networks of others.

Be helpful. Show that you are genuinely interested in helping your readers by sharing advice and resources, including a steady stream of articles that you think would be of interest to your readers. Authors grow and succeed by trying to offer help and giving compliments on Twitter without asking for anything in return.

Remain courteous. And you will find your courtesy is returned. Remember: Twitter keeps a virtual public record of your good deeds and kind words.

Twitter Defined

Twitter is defined as a microblog, but authors use it in different ways. Some call Twitter a "cocktail party" where you show up when you feel like it, choose who you want to talk to, jump from conversation to conversation, and leave when you want. Some consider Twitter a mini website, ever refreshing with posts helpful to readers. Some authors just like to have conversations with readers that don't take too much time away from writing books.

Regardless, millions of guests sign in to Twitter that you can meet and converse with directly. Think of the possibilities for you as an author: readers and authors, as well as publishers, reviewers, journalists, talent scouts, and literary agents all available to you with direct contact. Networking by tweeting and reading tweets of others leads to new opportunities, for cooperation, for cross-promotion, and for sharing the latest developments in your book writing.

Everyone is invited into the public Twitter conversation, so it's best to simply introduce yourself and your work in a factual manner to connect your value to your audience needs, as usual, without excessive self-promotion. As you post, listen and show interest in others' tweets. Before digital networking via Twitter and its companion social platforms, editors and publishers spent tens of thousands of dollars on travel budgets to meet each other and build strategic alliances. We held and attended endless conferences and mixers, and trying to find the best minds unfettered by formality was never ending . . . and exhausting! And while in-person conversations and networking face-to-face at conferences are not quite obsolete, it doesn't match the ease, convenience, and low cost of connecting via Twitter. Now it's far quicker and easier to find common needs on agendas, align goals, and reap the benefit from alliances. There's less time and budget for massive in-person networking now, and thanks to Twitter, everyone is able to step into the inner circle.

Twitter Strategy

"The purpose of Twitter is to attract people to your content" by building trust relationships, according to Lynn Serafinn, client and author of

Tweep-e-licious (Humanity 1 Press, 2012). Lynn's advice is that 95% of your tweets should take people to your new blog posts, articles, newsletter, info videos on YouTube or Vimeo, audios, and articles written by others that you feel are valuable. If the majority of your tweets lead your readers to more useful information that helps them, solves their problems, and/ or makes them more successful, they will naturally be grateful and will want to find out more about what you have to offer. Lynn advises authors to use Twitter to give information, not to receive anything or advertise or sell. Helping others with useful information on Twitter builds trust and establishes your value to your audience. Focus on the quality of the connections you're making, not the big numbers, and not on making a pitch.

It's also important to connect with influencers, that is, those in your business or genre who have large numbers of Twitter followers and get retweeted the most often. According to our clients Brett Petersel and his coauthor Esther Schindler "... it's better to be followed by the 100 most important people in your business than by 10,000 strangers." Your own Tweets that go to your followers directly combine indirectly with your followers' followers, so you will receive more Mentions, Retweets, and Favorites for your Tweets.

Before You Send Your First Tweet...

Before you do any tweeting, take some time to strategize your Twitter presence by considering the following:

- **Express your author brand.** Review your author brand statement in Chapter 1 and be sure that your social networking statements are consistent with it.
- **Keep your goals in sight.** As an author, your connections with readers create the vehicle of a built-in audience to buy your books. Your connections with companies create alliances that lead to potential buys of multiple copies for their customers. Your connections with other authors like yourself can create combined networks to possibly double or triple your audience size.
- **Speaking of goals, don't just chase after followers.** Sure, it would be nice to have an audience of millions hanging on your every character, but don't succumb to the hucksters who promise to deliver thousands

of (fake) followers for a price. You want real people—real readers—to follow you and spread the word about your work and activities.

· **Plan how you will introduce yourself.** Review your audience description in Chapter 1 to focus on why people value what you offer as a writer. Consider what your readers want to hear most and then include that information in your first tweet.

· **Choose your Twitter handle.** Your name is best since it's easily identifiable, and authors are a "personality driven" brand. Alternatively, if you already use a handle that identifies you across the Internet, use the one that's most identifiable. Ours are @CJelen and @WorkingWriter. As with so many other services, be aware that only one person can use a particular handle on Twitter.

Choose what to include in your Twitter Profile bio. At 160 characters, you are forced to choose—what does your audience most value about you and how are you unique? Make it easy to follow you, and be sure to include room in your profile to provide a link to your author site. As you craft your bio, look at the many other different Twitter bios out there and notice what people choose to include, or not include, in this short description.

· Research who is on Twitter using Search and choose who you will follow—it's safe to start with organizations that align with your subject matter. Search by keyword and begin to follow those organizations.

· Upload your contact list and follow them all and be followed. We discuss how to do this in the First Steps section later in the chapter.

· Announce to your friends, associates, Rolodex contacts, and contacts on all of your social networks that "I'm on Twitter now. Here's what I'll be doing on Twitter . . . Here's my handle: @CJelen."

Getting Started on Twitter

If you're not already on Twitter, getting started is pretty straightforward. Go to Twitter.com and create your account by providing your name, email address, and a password, as well as create your handle. If the handle already exists, try again (just as you would if a username were taken in Gmail or any other medium).

One thing to keep in mind about creating your handle: Try to choose one that takes up fewer than 10 characters. As will become clear soon enough, the shorter the handle, the more easily others can retweet you without exceeding the 140-character limit. Mike (aka @WorkingWriter) wishes he'd had the foresight to think of this when selecting his "perfect handle" in 1995.

Customize Your Profile Page

Once you've created your account, the first thing you'll want to do is add your photo to your profile. With new accounts, Twitter initially posts an egg as your profile picture (Twitter, bluebirds, new hatchlings as it were). If you intend to get anyone on Twitter to follow you, get rid of the egg! You can use something other than your headshot photo, but a consistent image across your entire author platform is really the way to go. You can upload any image up to 2MB in size.

Your bio, as noted above, is a critical piece of your profile where you'll provide the most important things you want people to know about you. Since you know you'll have 160 characters to do this, spend some time crafting it offline, as suggested above, so you can just paste it into your profile when you first create your bio. You can edit your bio as often as you like.

As we also noted earlier, leave room in your bio to provide the URL of your author website so that it appears whenever someone sees your Twitter landing page or clicks on your photo when a tweet appears in their Twitter stream.

Other important settings include:

- **Mobile:** Get your official Twitter app for your smartphone and set up text messaging if you want to receive tweets as text messages, send texts to Twitter, and get password assistance via text message.
- **Email Notifications:** Twitter can keep you notified by email about a variety of things. Some things are really good to know as you build your platform (such as when your tweets get retweeted or favorited,

or when someone starts following you). You can turn these notifications on and off. Be aware that you can get this same information by
clicking the Connect tab once you're logged into your Twitter account.

· **Design:** Change the background of your Twitter page with a premade
theme or some other custom image. Anyone who visits your profile
page will view this design.

Whatever changes you make in your Twitter Settings, be sure to scroll
to the bottom to save the changes.

Plan, Write, and Automate Your Twitter Posts

Now that you've established your presence on Twitter, you're all set to join
the conversation. Use different kinds of tweets (discussed under "Tweet
Types," below) that link somehow to the subject matter of your book.

In the beginning, before you actually announce to your contacts that
you're on Twitter, start off with some retweets—denoted on Twitter and
abbreviated elsewhere as RT—to begin promoting the work of others and
building your network of followers.

Retweets are a powerful and easy way to create goodwill. If you've
helped to promote someone else—say, another author and his book—the
mention will be appreciated. Those you retweet will often reciprocate,
which in turn naturally leads to you and your fellow retweeters following each other. To start, retweet information that you enjoyed reading
and truly value, starting with colleagues, clients, and friends. As you gain
more followers and friends on Twitter, you may also want to send out a
Follow Friday tweet (including the hashtag #FF) that includes the handles
of authors, colleagues, friends, or anyone else you admire who you think
your followers should also be following.

When you retweet to your list of followers, you increase the audience
for the person you're retweeting. As time goes on, it's also fine to politely
ask people to retweet you, especially if you've done the same for them
enough times.

Some authors just Tweet links to interesting articles, as most news
articles now make it easy to tweet articles via a Tweet button (the same kind
of button that should be on your blog as noted in Chapter 2). Alternatively,

if there is no button, you can simply paste the URL of the article into the Compose New Tweet box. Just include the URL, the author's name, and a brief comment like "must read" or "great perspective." The more you retweet valuable information, the more you will be valued by search engines like Google, which will rank you higher so that your potential audience can find you online.

Other types of tweets include:

- **Mentions.** An acknowledgment of another Twitter user, indicated by tweeting their handle. For example, "@CJelen congrats on your new book! (link to book)"
- **Replies.** A public reply to someone's tweet. Everyone can see your replies, even though they are generally meant for one person. The first piece of text in your reply should be the recipient's handle: "@AboutPublishing thanks for the retweet!"
- **Direct Message.** A private message seen only by the recipient. However, you cannot direct message anyone who is not following you, and vice versa. For example, "DM @cjelen, when is your book-signing event?"

Start Posting on Twitter

The next step is posting original tweets, one to two per day if possible leading up to the publication of your book. No time? Do what many corporations and frequent Twitter users do: Set up your tweets in advance and automate their distribution, as described later in this chapter.

In general, let the tweets of people you admire inspire your original tweets. Some common tweet types are listed below.

TWEET TYPES

Vary your approach with a mix of tweets, picking from the following categories:

- **Alerts** to read your blog posts (which should include a link directly to the post) as well as news about book signings, launches, and other events.

- **Live tweets** from events you're attending, sent in real time.
- **News.** This can be a piece of breaking news or a trend tied to your subject.
- **Brainstorming.** Float an idea or concept and ask for others' reaction or opinion.
- **Requests for help.** Ask others to provide a missing fact or specialized piece of information. Or ask for opinions on a manuscript point or your cover design, providing appropriate links where relevant.
- **Questions.** Ask a thought-provoking question to provoke comments and get additional followers.
- **Links.** Offer links to helpful articles and events and anything else you think may be of interest to your followers.
- **How to.** Offer tricks, tips, and insider secrets.
- **Sharing.** Share online resources, book recommendations, information about events that tie into your subject matter, and any other information that likely will be retweeted.
- **Helping others.** Help promote other authors' book signings and events, book-related podcasts, etc.
- **Appreciation.** Thank people who retweeted you and/or helped you.

Automating Your Posts with HootSuite

Time is precious, and with platform-building tasks to perform, when do you have time to write? We recommend using HootSuite (www.hootsuite .com). This social media manager allows you to manage and monitor five social network feeds—including Twitter, Facebook, Google+, Linked In, and WordPress—in a single location. HootSuite allows you to auto-schedule postings across all your networks, which is a huge time-saver.

To get started, either sign up with your Facebook account or create a separate HootSuite password. You'll be asked to upload a profile picture, and you can add Bio/Description information to your profile.

Go to your profile page to add a Twitter account. Click **Add a Social Network**, and Twitter is at the top of the list. Click **Connect with Twitter**. Twitter will ask you to login and then will identify all the permissions that

HootSuite is asking for. Click **Authorize App** to complete the process. Add other networks from this same dialogue.

Once you've added your account, your "home feed" will appear in a tab, with tweets from everyone you are following. You'll also see your Mentions (folks who have referenced your Twitter name/handle publicly), private Direct Messages, and all your Sent Tweets.

At the top of the HootSuite screen, you'll see the **Compose Message** box. Click here to start typing. If you have a link to share, click **Add a Link**, and type (or paste) your link. To display a shortened version of your link, click **Shrink**.

To the right of the Compose Message box, you'll see Click to Select a Social Network. You should see all of the networks you have connected with in your HootSuite profile. Click on any or all of the icons present to post your message to that network.

Off to the right of the Add a Link box in the Compose Message box, you'll see four icons that allow you to enhance your post further. Use the paper-clip icon to attach an image to your message. The calendar icon, labeled 30, is the scheduling tool (more about this shortly). Define your location with the circular icon, and the padlock icon lets you define privacy options, if the network supports that (LinkedIn and Facebook do, Twitter does not).

The Scheduler lets you define when to post your message. If you're posting a link to something happening right now, you probably want to post it right now. Otherwise, you can schedule posts for a specific time of your choosing—or let HootSuite post at a more impactful time. AutoSchedule is off by default, so click the **Off** button to turn Auto-Schedule on.

HootSuite even offers a Pro version for a fee. This account lets you monitor up to 50 profiles, delegate your activity to another user, and access more detailed analytic reports to measure your success.

Tip: FollowerWonk.com is another source of detailed analytics of your followers. Without charge, they can tell you where your followers live, what time of the day they tweet, how many people follow your followers, and a few other statistics.

First Steps on Twitter

With your profile picture and bio in place, you're ready to see what's happening. In the real world, you'd go to a party, introduce yourself to the host at the door, and start looking for one of two things: people you know, or people talking about interesting things. Twitter (and its community) makes it fairly easy to do both. Click the **Discover** tab at the top of the Twitter window.

To look for people you know, click **Find Friends**. You can have Twitter search your webmail address books for people already using the service. Twitter connects to Google Mail, Yahoo, AOL, and Hotmail and quickly compares email addresses. A list of folks already on Twitter is displayed. You can then choose to follow any number of people. You'll also get an option to invite others in your address book to Twitter if they're not already signed up.

Note: Twitter uses a secure protocol to connect to the email service of your choice. It does not suck up your email password or record the names of your email correspondents.

If you already know some people on Twitter, you can search for them by real name or Twitter handle. You can also paste a list of email addresses separated by commas to invite to Twitter.

When you've imported some people, Twitter may take a stab at suggesting "Who to Follow" based on who you're already interested in, following the principle of "If my friend finds this person interesting, I might, too."

Now that you've found the people you know, it's time to find the people who are discussing things happening in your niche. You might find the other options on the Discover tab useful. For some broad suggestions, click **Popular Accounts**. You'll find celebrities and other top tweeters in an assortment of fields. The Books section, for example, links to publishers, literary magazines, and big-name writers active on the service. Tweets/ Stories highlights some things the people you now follow are reading, and Activity points you to what the people you follow are doing on Twitter— people they're following, tweets they are saving as favorites, and the like.

You have probably heard the phrase "trending topic" at various awards shows and other live and televised events. This is where it came from. Twitter has always recorded what words are popular at any given moment on the site. Trending topics appear in the lower left of your home screen under "Trends." Often the trending topic is prefaced by the # symbol, like #marketing or #threewordstoliveby. This is called a hashtag, and it provides an easy way for Twitter users to zero in on topics of interest to them. Pay attention to what's trending. If a subject related to your subject matter—or your actual subject matter—is a hot topic, you definitely want to be part of that conversation. If you are tweeting in response to a trending topic, be sure to use whatever hashtag (#memoirs, #authorplatform, #zombies, etc.) is trending in your tweet so that anyone else following the conversation will see your input.

Posting

Twitter works best if you post interesting news and relevant information in real time. Again, comparing Twitter to a cocktail party, it makes sense that you'll have a smarter, better-informed response if you can listen in on a conversation before contributing to it. Just as you would during a live conversation, get a feel for everyone's mood as well as how detailed the conversation is before jumping in.

When and how often to post. When you begin your presence on Twitter, be sure not to stop and start. It's important to build up your author presence consistently in the months leading up to your publication date and book launch, and as much as possible beyond. We recommend that every weekend you take about 30 minutes to choose your week's worth of tweets and then use the automatic scheduler in HootSuite.

Note: Another automatic scheduler is Buffer (bufferapp.com), which will schedule your tweets to hit Twitter on particular days and at particular times of day. By default, Buffer posts to Twitter four times a day (8:59 A.M., 11:49 A.M., 4:45 P.M., and 7:45 P.M. local time), to Facebook twice a day (at 11:02 A.M. and 5:46 P.M.), and to LinkedIn twice a day (11:03 A.M. and 5:59 P.M.).

The next step is a short daily review of the responses to your tweets and responding to every single one as soon as possible. It only takes ten minutes during morning coffee to answer feedback related to tweets you autoscheduled the day before. If you are responsive to your audience, they will also be responsive to you. Beyond tweeting itself, your interaction with your audience via comments is a vibrant and necessary part of the interchange that builds up your Twitter following.

Shorten your URL to allow for a longer tweet. As many URLs are too long for a short-form Twitter post and otherwise hog too many characters you'd probably rather be using for your message, such URL-shortening services as Bit.ly and Google URL Shortener were created. Type your URL into the box, and the service will give you in return a unique, short set of characters to use instead of the actual URL. One benefit of using a link-shortening service is that it keeps a record of every link you've shortened and will track how many times your link was clicked.

Note: Twitter and WordPress will automatically shorten links, useful if you only want to tweet the link.

Send Direct Messages

1. Click on the **envelope icon** in the top right.
2. You'll see a popup showing your direct message history. Click the **New message** button.
3. In the address box, type the name or username of the person you wish to send a message to.
4. **Tip:** You can only send a direct message to someone you're following if that person is following you (even though you can receive messages from all users you follow).
5. Enter your message and click **Send message**.

Use Twitter handles to start conversations. Try engaging someone you don't know by including that person's handle in a tweet. Unlike direct messaging, you don't need to be following the person (or vice versa) to engage them. For example, if you want to talk to me directly about how this book launched your career, start your post with @cjelen and ask me a question. I use my handle to check in and then will be able to respond to you easily. Try this approach on Twitter with celebrities, authors, journalists, and anyone else who is well known but perhaps not conventionally approachable and you might be surprised at how often you get a response.

Answer Questions. When you see a question you want to respond to, you can hover over the word "Expand" and you'll see options to retweet, favorite, or reply. If you choose the latter, Twitter automatically adds the questioner's handle to the start of your tweet.

Use Hashtags. Mentioned earlier, hashtags help you in two ways: either to follow a conversation or to start one. Hashtags are search devices, so you can search for or create a keyword easily. Hashtags make your tweets more easily identifiable, which will in turn increase your influence on Twitter. Check the Search box to find the most-used words in your subject area, then use them in your hashtags. You can also search hashtags to find thought leaders in your niche, links to related websites, and articles on your subject.

List any hashtags you create in all parts of your author platform; these keywords make it easy for your audience to find you and join discussions about you. When you launch your book, also create and promote special-event hashtags; this enables your audience to search that hashtag and connect with others who tweet about your event, which in turn builds excitement and enthusiasm for you and your book.

In the following chapters, you'll see how to add the other major social networks to your author platform to fortify your seamless and consistent author brand.

Hosting Twitter Chats

We've used the analogy of Twitter as a gigantic cocktail party. You can gather together a knot of people to talk about a common interest through hosting a Twitter chat. This is a live, typically hourlong conversation on a particular topic organized by hashtag. Typically, these happen on a regular, often weekly, basis.

Before hosting a chat, participate in some. Visit blog.tweetchat.com /calendar or tweetreports.com/twitter-chat-schedule to find lists of upcoming chats on a variety of topics. When you find a chat of interest, go to Twitter and search on the chat's hashtag (such as #WSChat or #MuckedUp) to view recent chats. The search allows you to see what sorts of topics the chat covers, and what sorts of people participate. Typically, Twitter chats take the form of a series of questions posed by the host to prompt discussion. Sometimes a guest comes to answer participant questions on their topic.

When you find an interesting chat, make note of the date and time of the next chat. Sign on to Twitter at the appointed time and search for the hashtag. Participate as the spirit moves you with information, links, and wit. If someone else on the chat responds to something you say, react politely.

ORGANIZING YOUR TWITTER CHAT

When you're ready to have your own chat, start planning. The most important thing you need to figure out is the hashtag for your chat. It needs to be unique and short. The name should suggest a general topic that people can discuss on a weekly basis. Also, remember that your hashtag is part of every post *in* the chat, so anything more than 10 characters will limit what your participants can say.

Set a time and date that works for you and your readers. Be conscious of where in the world your would-be participants live and work, and schedule accordingly. If you want a business-oriented crowd, you'll want to schedule during the business day. You probably don't want to schedule a chat for 2 A.M. in your target audience, unless your chat is about insomnia or night-shift work.

When you've got your chat planned, it's time to let people know about it. Post your chat to the calendars listed above. Announce your plans on your blog and other social networks. Invite and remind your Twitter followers often of the date, time, hashtag, and topic. Encourage your network to spread the word, too.

Finally, the day arrives. Ann Smarty of MyBlogGuest shared a great checklist for how to host a chat at Social Media Examiner (socialmedia examiner.com/twitter-chat-guide):

1. **Start with a welcome introduction** (a couple of minutes to let your chat participants introduce themselves and begin tweeting about your event).
2. **Announce your chat topic** (pick one specific idea for each of your chats to keep the discussion focused).
3. **Tweet your own thoughts and ideas** on that topic.
4. **Give at least 5 minutes for your chat participants to share their ideas** (retweet the best ones).
5. **Summarize the most important points** as you go along.
6. **Ask questions** (label your questions as Q1, Q2, etc., to make it easy for your chat participants to answer and encourage discussion).
7. **Retweet and summarize the best answers.**
8. **Share some related tools and links** and invite your chat participants to share their own as well (retweet the best ones).

9. **Announce the upcoming end of the chat** and thank everyone for participating.
10. **Tweet the chat conclusions.**
11. **Announce the next chat day/time and topic.**

Checklist, Step 3: Twitter

> Sign up for Twitter.
> Use your consistent author brand name and photo.
> Construct your audience-centric author profile.
> Emulate model tweets of others.
> Connect your Twitter account with your blog.
> Create and automate your Twitter posts.
> Respond to your Twitter comments.
> Respond to others with retweets and favorites of tweets.
> Follow others, especially influencers with a large following to create a broad network.
> Host Twitter chats to broaden and engage your audience.

Success Spotlight: Waterside Client Susie Cox (susiecox.com; @susiecox)

- 2 books
- 57 translations: *International Directory of Astrology*, two editions
- 46,000 astrological readings
- Astrologers Hall of Fame
- 945 tweets; 2,099 following; 2,309 followers

Beginnings: Susie Cox started her astrological career at the tender age of five. She read a monthly Dell Horoscope magazine and was instantly hooked. Susie was so dedicated that she taught herself astrology and started doing charts right out of high school, and astrology is all that she has ever done. She bought a metaphysical bookstore and learning center. After that, Susie studied astronomy at the University of Arizona. She now combines astronomy with astrology in all aspects of her career: her interpretations with astrological charts, classes, public lectures, media interviews, her newsletter, and her daily blog. Susie worked for 32 years as the Master Astrologer at the internationally acclaimed Canyon Ranch Health Resort, where she lectured regularly and also started the very popular metaphysical department. She has interpreted an impressive number of astrology charts, now over 46,000 readings.

   Platform: Susie uses Twitter as an excellent platform to reach out, with nearly 1,000 tweets to date to draw attention to the value she is bringing to her audience. She has also published an astrological newspaper, written numerous articles and columns, and currently writes topical articles about world events in her newsletter every month. Susie published two editions of the *International Directory of Astrology* (IDA Directory, 1992, 2nd edition 1995), which are alphabetical listings of contact information for astrologers from around the world. The *IDA Directory* was sold in 57 countries. Her recent book, *Susie's Sun Signs*, was bought by Sterling Publishers. Susie has had an astrology TV show on ABC for three years. She has been featured in the *New York Times*, *People* magazine, and the *Washington Post*, and on A&E, the National Geographic Channel, and the History Channel. Susie is listed in the Astrologers Hall of Fame.

Susie's advice for authors: It is important to understand that the passion it took to write your book will be needed to market your book. Only you have the passion for your work and the drive to see it through. Use a marketing plan or "road map," because the majority of the marketing is in the hands of the author. If you are not sure about marketing, then seek a specialist who can help you champion your work.

CHAPTER 4

Google+: More Than a Social Network

"Choosing anonymity is choosing irrelevance."

—Eric Schmidt, Google's Executive Chairman, author of
The New Digital Age: Reshaping the Future
of People, Nations, and Business,
cowritten with Jared Cohen

NEWS FLASH: Some of the top tech marketing experts (and authors and publishers) use the power of Google and Google+ as the centerpiece of their social media brand identity. Experts understand that Google itself is the most-used search engine in the world, and by tying into the search engine via Google+, search results can and do skyrocket. Google+ adopters, using the full range of tools, can and do reach a million+ by daily posting and reposting. Some use specific content directly related to their subject matter, which we highly advise; others post and repost more general interest, compelling content and then use that same audience to mix in personal and business announcements.

Google grew as it hired some of Apple's "brain trust" developers to create a "silent revolution." This was the term former Apple Technical Support Manager Scott Knaster used to explain Google to me years ago. Being one of the most talented developers and writers I've worked with, Scott's simple, cryptic comment proved spot-on accurate. Slowly, this leading-edge web search company has built global leadership by monetizing connectivity on the World Wide Web and by bringing large numbers of people to their business by offering a wealth of free products that many other businesses offered for a fee.

A challenge for you as an author is combining your online social persona with your professional brand without coming across as a shameless self-promoter. In response to this common concern, Google is leading the pack in making professional social networking effective and graceful, especially for authors and their content.

> For an example of how Google+ integrates into a social media platform, see the article "How Marketing Legend Guy Kawasaki Manages His Social Media Presence," revealing a complete social media marketing strategy that sustains mega-high numbers of followers (http://blog.hubspot.com/marketing /how-guy-kawasaki-manages-social-media).

Why Google Is Important to Authors

Google is the most-visited website in the world. In the most simplistic terms, Google's programs search documents all over the web for keywords. When the search is complete, the engine shows a list of websites with content where these keywords were found. Google runs more than a million servers in global data centers and processes more than a billion search requests in a single 24-hour period. On Alexa ranking, Google .com is listed as the most visited website in the world.

With brilliant minds working at this company, Google has grown and branched out, purchasing YouTube, Blogger, and much more, and creating its own social network, Google+.

Google+ is evolving into a leading interactive destination. On Google+, we can share in a wide spectrum of activities based on our interests, ranging from posting and collaboration to joining virtual communities and virtual conferences to connecting with industry and thought leaders and other influencers. Today Google+ has more than 500 million users and growing fast.

Google+ is a social network connected to Google search. Google+ is among the top social networks authors need to be part of, in addition to Twitter, Facebook, and LinkedIn. The + sign in Google+ signifies that on top of the social network itself, Google offers a significant search benefit. And for authors, this benefit is optimized by what Google defines as Authorship, the ability for you as the author to link your online content—anything you publish on your own website or blog—to your Google+ profile, which will significantly boost your visibility as an author.

Besides being an accomplished and very important influencer and employed at Google, Scott Knaster is an author of acclaimed books for such publishers as O'Reilly. While I was at Addison-Wesley, I was privileged to be his editor for the Macintosh Inside Out book series. Try a Google search on Scott Knaster's name to view a model for an approachable, very human online persona.

Scott suggests that authors understand that Google+ is not "just a social network." Google+ was created as a "foundation for Google, a sharing forum, a place where Google's search engines are enabled to tailor Google+ searches to individual needs. In integrating all Google's tools under G+, there is a consistency allowed when all apps are in one place, integrating into the social experience." For authors, Google+ is a showcase, a chance to rank higher in searches, and a place to share and connect with more of your audience.

In the following pages we'll discuss how to use Google to grow your audience—how to find them, allow them to find and follow you, and connect through meaningful content—and then how to use Google Authorship to connect all of your online content to your Google+ profile. We also present a couple of additional useful author tools from Google.

Keeping Control of Your Blog and Social Identity

Searching on Google is free, but the price that you pay for any browser is giving your search info to a company database to track where you search. Keeping your data "in the cloud" is also free, but another price you pay is giving your data to a company's large servers. Free email is stored in a company database, too. In using these services, you give away your anonymity.

However, the good news is that you don't have to surrender control of your online author brand, as defined by your website content and blog. While it makes a lot of sense to seamlessly use Google for everything, you'll have more control of your blog and website if you use a different

Anonymity vs. Privacy

We need to take a moment to address an issue basic to using Google and Google products. Because Google search and Google+ are fundamental to every author's platform, authors must know on which side they stand on the public vs. private issue.

Web browsers record our searches on keywords. Web services we sign up for online allow our information to go public. Online social networks record our typed-in information. Digital phone conversations are transcribed and recorded online, forever. If you use a computing device, you can't maintain privacy if you share information online.

Part of defining your role as an author is publishing and growing an audience, so you've already made your choice to go public. This includes your writing, photos of yourself, and in the new rules of the author platform, giving your audience ways to interact with you directly. Although we caution authors to keep their personal address and "real" birth date private, we advise you to make the move to your public persona sooner rather than later in order to grow your audience.

You will want to keep your online personal social life separate from your online business social network. Google+ has allowed for different "circles" of people in your life, but the good news is that if you're already sharing your vacation photos on your Facebook page like most of us, you're not required to change a thing. In fact, there are good reasons to keep your personal life on one network like Facebook and your business persona on a separate network like Google+. Later on you may want to consolidate your personal life with Google+, but the subject of this book emphasizes the author business aspect of audience building. You don't want to miss maximizing Google+ for its usefulness in building your author platform.

platform. That means buying your own domain, such as Carole did with jelenpub, and hosting your site and blog and its matching email addresses.

Google encourages the use of Blogger (which it owns) for blogging, but does not require it to rank you high in search results. Google does validate websites with matching email addresses higher than others and also gives higher ranking to sites owned for longer than a year; to Google, this length of ownership signifies that you are not a spammer out for quick bucks, occupying a domain for a year and then quickly disappearing.

Use Google+ and Google Authorship

Scott recommends that authors use a combination of Google+ and Google Authorship, as your presence is significantly boosted when you register for both. Authorship is how Google identifies the writer of any piece of online content.

The beauty of signing up for this two-step identity and identity authentication is that readers will more easily find your content. Google verifies ownership of your content and ranks your quality writing higher in Google searches. The reason is that Google intends to weed out spam and garbage content from web searches that will ideally move your quality author content more squarely into the spotlight.

With the combination of Google+ and Google Authorship, Google has created an unparalleled support system that works to an author's advantage. In using the combination of Google+ and Google Authorship, you are able to access a digital signature system through your Google+ profile and an identity "platform" through Google Authorship that connects your content with ownership via your "byline" and photo.

Therefore, Google puts a priority on Google+ results in searches. Authors who understand this powerful combination register in both of these places.

Waterside author client Jesse Stay is an expert in Google+, author of two books on the subject for John Wiley & Sons: *Google+ For Dummies* and *Google+ Marketing For Dummies*. As social media strategist for the Church of Latter Day Saints, Jesse's influence spans his circle of many followers as he develops social network best practices. For authors like himself, he strongly recommends owning your own author website "or you will suffer later" and recommends maintaining a consistent presence on Google+. Jesse's advice is to put emphasis on "making your profile personal and genuine, staying consistent to your subject, and posting to Google+ often."

Join Google+

You may already be on Google+. If you have a Gmail, Blogger, or YouTube account, you already have the login credentials. If you ever saved a Google Map, customized a Google News page, used Google Calendar, or linked up your copies of the Google Chrome browser, you have a Google+ profile awaiting your customization. In short, if you visit a Google property with the black navigation bar across the top, click the **+<your first name>** item and you'll arrive at Google+.

If you have avoided creating a Google account up to now, go to plus .google.com and sign up. As suggested above, the account will give you access to Google's other apps and programs, too.

Craft Your Google+ Profile

Your profile is an author showcase that goes well beyond your Google+ account. Go back to the plan you developed for your author website, where you considered and thought out the perfect identity for you as an author, and use this same information to create your profile. Stay true to what your audience needs and what they want to learn from you as you create your profile, content, posts, and comments.

Since your Google+ profile in your account and registration in Google Authorship connect you to all of your online content, the bio and photo you use in your Google+ profile will show up in Google searches whenever your content appears. As a quality author, you can use to great advantage the fact that Google introduces you in search results.

Think through what your audience wants to know about you and translate that into words on your profile. The first part of your profile is called the Story section; think about the story of your life and what story you want to tell your audience about you. Narrow down your unique skills to create an "identity" for yourself. For example, I've learned that people most care that I:

- Place authors in 100+ publisher/author contracts per year;
- Have 30+ years' experience in traditional publishing; and
- Build author platforms.

Boil down your list to the top three things.

Use SEO keywords. Your Google+ profile has its own page rank, so use all search engine optimization (SEO) techniques in writing your profile, including links and keywords. Dave Taylor, who you'll meet in the Success Story at the end of this chapter, uses his introduction to tell visitors he is a "Blogger, social networking consultant, online media expert, and professional public speaker for hire."

Develop a tagline that is memorable and shines a spotlight on your quality and unique service. Michael uses "Tech Writer, Linux Geek, Blogger, WordPress Author."

Choose your profile photo carefully. Be sure it is friendly and genuine and shows two eyes. You can either stay consistent with one professional-looking stock photo of yourself or you can do as many authors do—use slight variations on your photo from slightly different angles so that the composite that ends up showing on Google search shows the same easily identifiable person. Be sure that the size of your head and torso are the same in the various photos to keep a consistency, since they are often shown as a collage online.

Check for consistency. Your audience needs to be able to recognize you in multiple exposures, so it's imperative that your author brand and book be presented the same across all social networks. Use the same taglines and the same exact name with no variations or initial changes, so that all your bylines match up and are led back to your presence on Google+.

Use your plan. Keep the plan handy that you developed in Chapter 1 so that you use that same information on your author site, book site, social networks, etc. This repetition breeds familiarity and, with rich content, builds trust across networks.

Set Up Your Profile

When you are logged into Google+, point your mouse at the G+ logo in the upper left corner of any G+ page. Click **Profile** from the navigation menu. Across the top of the page, click **About** to see your existing profile. While you're looking at the top menu, check the **View Profile As**: choices, and make sure it says Yourself instead of Public. Your profile is divided up into several sections; click the **Edit** link at the bottom of each section you want to include. Some of these are personal, but the areas to focus on include:

Story. This is what people see when first introduced to you on Google+. When you post, readers hover over your name and see your **Tagline**. This is very similar to your Twitter description.

Introduction and **Bragging Rights.** The Introduction allows you to tell your visitors a little more about you. Bragging Rights is where you list your writing credits, awards, and other recognition you've received. You can narrow the universe of who can see this information, but as an author, you want the public to see this.

Work. Spaces here for Occupation (what you do for a living), Skills (things you can do; this will show up in search results), and **Employment** (you could include a résumé here).

Education. Be true to your school, with the ability to add your major and a description of the courses you took.

Basic Information. This is mostly the kind of personal information common to other social networks. Because Google+ enforces a "Real Names Only" policy for its users, "Other Names" (nicknames, maiden names, and the like) becomes a place to store any other online personas you may have, helping people find you.

Places. If your writing focuses on a place you have lived in or has relevance to your life in a particular place, be sure to include this. Otherwise, this is also optional.

Links. Three parts to this section. The Other Profiles section is critical for establishing Authorship (more about this later in the chapter). Be sure to link to your Twitter and author website. Click **Add custom link** to point to your website. We'll discuss the (also critical) Contributor To section later in the chapter. Feel free to include the other sites and blogs of fellow authors you like and respect in the Links subsection; this part is like a blogroll.

Contact Information: Your email address and phone number. You can define separate Home and Work locations and choose sharing options for each. We recommend making your Work information public.

Add Your Profile and Cover Photos

As with every other social media outlet, photos are the way to identify yourself on Google+. Your profile picture is part of your Google account and shows up as an avatar on every post you make on Google+ (or any other Google property). It will also be the photo that appears in your Google Search results when you have established Authorship. This should be the standard headshot you have used on your other sites. While we know we're being repetitive about this point, consistent visual presentation leads to added recognition for your contributions.

Google+ also lets you post a "cover photo" as a banner across the top of your profile page. By default, this is a generic nature scene pulled from a set of shots included in a gallery. You should customize this to show off your creativity, authority, and activity.

Your cover photo must be at least 480 pixels wide and 270 pixels high. You can just leave the striped background by default, use a single photo, or create a montage, developing a panel of a few related photos of you, in a professional head-shot style. These are for use on your social media sites and the back cover of your book and will also pop up globally on Google whenever your content appears, so think through your photos, as they will be recorded online, again, forever. Look at different Google+ cover photos to get ideas about models that you can customize. If possible, include photos of you speaking, participating in a conference, or otherwise showing you "in action" as an authority in your area of expertise as well as an image of your book cover.

When you have a good set of photos, use a photo editor like Photoshop, Paintshop Pro, or GIMP to create a panorama of your photos to display as your cover photo.

One technical note: In the settings we recommend that you keep all your posts Public for the specific purpose of building your audience.

Link Google+ to Your Author Website

Connecting WordPress sites to Google+ is easy with the Jetpack plugin. This plugin offers many of the features available to WordPress.com bloggers to the rest of the WordPress community. We discussed the Jetpack Statistics feature in Chapter 1. Once you've installed Jetpack on your site, go to the Settings > Sharing page from your administration dashboard.

Below the other social connections on this page, you'll see the Google+ Profile with a big Sign In button. When you click that, a popup window appears; sign in to your Google account, and click **Accept** to make the connection. This has two added bonuses: Any content you add to your site automatically posts to Google+, and Jetpack automatically generates a Contributor link from your site to your Google+ Profile (see "Connect

Your Content through Google Authorship" later in the chapter for more on Contributor links).

Scroll down a little farther on the Sharing page, and you can add buttons to every post, allowing your readers to share your posts on their favorite social networks, including Google+. Jetpack will also add a link to your Google+ profile to individual (permalinked) pages and posts.

Use Google+ Circles

One of the drivers for creating Google+ was the increasingly loud calls from Facebook users for better control over who members could share content with. Google+ proposed allowing people to create free-form groups called Circles. People could organize their social sharing in any manner they chose. By default, you get four circles: Friends, Family, Acquaintances, and Following (this last one mostly for pages). The theory here is that there are things you'd tell your friends that you'd be embarrassed to share with a random coworker or classmate. We recommend that you keep everyone in the same circle so that you do not have to keep track of this. Instead, keep your personal postings on your personal Facebook page.

Circles are an excellent method of communicating with your potential audience. You can post messages to any circle, be that a link to your latest blog post or an announcement of your impending book launch, Hangout (explained later), or other important event. Depending on their settings, you can drop a message into a circle member's inbox.

Circle People in Google+

The easiest way to get an overview of Google+ is by searching for who is already there, look at how they present themselves and their posts, find models to use and customize as your own, and choose who you want to circle (follow). When you are logged in to Google+, point your mouse at the G+ logo in the upper left corner of any G+ page. Click **People** from the navigation menu. Initially, you'll find "People you may know on Google+" based on all the information Google has collected about you. On the left side is a navigation panel that uses your profile to identify more people to add. These include current and former coworkers (if you've identified your employers in your profile) and alumni of your school.

Once you've gone through the suggestions, try using the Search for Anyone box at the top of this navigation bar. Start typing the name of a person, city, company, or school, and results will begin appearing in the window. In addition to personal profiles, pages and communities (more on these later) will also appear. The Search bar at the top of the Google+ window works the same way, so use this feature anywhere in Google+ to locate people and topics of interest.

Whether you use Search or review the suggestions offered, you'll see the Add button at the bottom of each person's mini-profile (consisting of name, photo, and tagline). Click the button and you'll see a chronological list of all your circles, along with a Create New Circle link. People can be in multiple circles, so you can classify a contact in any number of ways. For example, say you meet someone at a conference related to your niche, you can add them to your Acquaintances circle, plus a My Niche circle.

You can call these circles anything you like. The people in them will never know *what* circle they're in, only that they're in your circles. You can add people to multiple circles, so you can place them in one of the default circles and a custom circle. Thus, if you meet someone at a conference and exchange business cards, you can place that person in the Acquaintances, Conference-goers, and Conference-Subject circles. When you see a post by that person, you can refresh your memory by hovering your mouse over that person's avatar.

Of course, you are welcome to add Carole Jelen and Michael McCallister to your circles.

WHO TO CIRCLE

Carole Jelen's page shows a targeted following of thousands of authors, writers, and book reviewers. Everyone involved in her circles are direct connections pertaining to her audience, and the majority of which are in addition to the extensive Waterside database of author clients. This is a sound strategy in that everyone on this list will automatically be interested in postings connected to book announcements intended for and tailored to their interests. It's a powerful way to connect to readers to search Google+ for the right audience that has taken time to build up. It's well worth it! We are hoping that all authors will connect to Carole Jelen at Google+ to be included in this large and growing author community.

Choose only high-quality readers and associates to follow instead of just reaching for high numbers that don't apply to your audience. In Google's eyes, if you become associated with low-quality sites, your ranking can slip downward! Here are criteria to use to determine the quality of who you want in your circles: their number of followers plus their regular interaction on Google+, and how many people have shared (+1) their posts.

Since you're looking to use your established base and grow from there, if you're already connected to people on other networks like Facebook and LinkedIn, search within those networks and connect with those people at Google+. You don't have to entirely replicate your friends and connections from other networks, but you can naturally expect some overlap.

Remember that Google+ is newer than the other social networks mentioned in this book, but it is the one that has the largest impact because Google is also the global search engine leader. For purposes of building your author platform, you're using Google+ specifically to grow your author business persona.

Aside from harvesting your other social networks for ideas about who to add to your circles, also import your address book from Outlook, Thunderbird, or Apple Address Book. Your email client program should give you the ability to export your address book to a "comma-delimited text file" with a .csv extension or a VirtualCard file with a .vcf extension. You can then open that file with a spreadsheet program for editing, if you like. In Google+, on the People page, click **Connect Services** to add contacts via Yahoo, Hotmail, or your email client's address book to identify more people. Locate the address book file, and Google will display the list of those people who are registered on Google+. After the list of contacts already on Google+, you can invite others on the contact list to Google+. Unfortunately, on this page, you can only add them one at a time. When you add someone to a circle, Google+ will email an invitation to that person. Your circles should include:

- Your previous networks, which should include all clients, associates, and colleagues.
- Members of any author community that you can link to for cross-promotion of your books.
- College and institute members you're associated with; you can also search for new associations to include in circles.

Also use the following tools to fortify your circles and gather information:

- Google+ Search: In Search type in "share circle," press **View**, and click on who you want to add.
- Public Circles Database (publiccircles.appspot.com) shows lists created by others. You can find what public circles you've been included in by pasting your profile number into the box provided at the site.
- CircleCount.com offers free analytics of Google+ activity. You can learn who the most popular people are, based on the number of +1s, comments, and shares for each post over a given time period. Register with the site to see how your own activity fares. Use the site to help determine the day and time your posts are engaged with the most. Hours of entertainment and knowledge await.

OTHERS WHO CIRCLE YOU IN GOOGLE+

You are notified whenever someone adds you to their circles. Add all these people to an Audience circle. By definition, these are people who are interested in what you're up to. Target messages to this group as you get closer to your book release.

On Google+ people who share your interest in your subject matter will likely circle you, and especially those already linked to your subject matter expertise.

Join Communities

Check Carole Jelen's page for author, reader, and book review communities that you may want to join. Google+ launched a Communities feature, allowing anyone to create a community around shared interests. Hundreds of active communities are available for you to participate in, some with memberships in the tens of thousands. This allows you to post directly to large numbers of members of these communities, tap into larger networks to get the word out about your books, and create cooperative ways to promote.

Look for communities already organized around your niche on the Communities page (find that on the navigation menu in the upper left corner). Click the **Recommended for You** tab in the middle of the top navigation menu. Browse through the recommended communities on the page, or search for your topic with the Search for Communities box. Join a community if it appears active (with many current messages) and attractive (with many members, focused on your topic). Contribute when you can, and look for people to circle. Communities are prime targets for finding interesting people to interact with on G+.

CREATING A COMMUNITY

If you don't find a community in your niche or want to gather a group of collaborators for a particular project, it may be worthwhile to set up your own Google+ Community. Click **Create Community** on the Communities page to get started.

The first choice you get is whether to make your community public (where all content is searchable and accessible to the world at large) or private (where content is only available to members). You'll be asked to name the community and make an additional choice on availability. For public groups, you can force would-be members to go through a moderator before contributing content, or allow anyone to join. For private groups, you can choose whether your community is visible in the G+ search engine or is only for people you or other group members explicitly invite.

Your community (public or private) has a tagline, as with your personal profile. For public groups, this is the place to briefly describe what the community is about. Potential members will read the tagline to determine their level of interest. Add a more detailed topic description, along with any rules for posting and sharing, in the About This Community section.

Optionally, you can:

- Add a photo to represent your community.
- Define one or more categories for posts. If you were running a community about cats, you could have all your photos in one category,

veterinary concerns in another, breed choices in a third, and so on.

- Add links to relevant websites.
- Choose a Location, if that is relevant to your members.

Now your community members can post text, photos, links, and video to all the other community members. You can create events for people to attend, online or offline. Members can choose whether to be notified by email when anyone posts.

As the community creator, members will be looking to you to lead the way in posting content and managing all that goes on. You can delegate that authority to moderators, if you like. Communities, like forums and email discussion lists, can be an important way to connect with your audience, but can also be time-consuming. Only you can decide the value of community management based on your other time commitments.

Best Practices for Interacting on Google+

Keep all of your interactions professional and positive by showing that you value others. Circle them and comment favorably on their posts, and also offer to guest blog for others, leading links back to you. Here is where your existing community is extremely helpful, as when you are in a group who will do this for each other, everyone's ranking benefits by association.

Your mandate as an author is to entice people to follow you by posting (more on that shortly), using the +1 sign on stories you like, adding a comment to someone's post, and connecting with others' networks.

Show Approval: Three Levels of Enthusiasm

As you read through your feed, every post is interactive. You can highlight posts to your network in three different ways:

- +1
- Comment
- Share

(+1) A POST OR COMMENT

The quickest way to offer positive feedback is to use the +1 button, which simply shows you liked the post. When you see something worthwhile on Google+ but don't have anything to add or otherwise comment on, click the +1 button. You can +1 nearly any activity on the site, including posts and comments. To +1 a comment, move your mouse to the commenter's name; the +1 button should appear.

Many blogs and websites outside of Google+ also include a +1 button. These are collected on a tab on your profile page and can serve as a handy set of web bookmarks. By default, +1s are for your eyes only, but you can choose to share them with others if you like.

COMMENT ON OTHERS' POSTS

Remember you are looking to attract audience and seek reciprocal promotion opportunities on Google+, so your comment strategy is to leave a positive, welcoming impression that helps draw others to your work. Short one-word comments like "Wow!" or "Great!" can sometimes do the trick, or add longer comments with good feedback or more factual information and ideas you've discovered along the way. Remember that you're presenting yourself as a public professional and subject matter expert and that your comments are read by the whole circle around the person you're commenting on.

SHARE OTHERS' POSTS

Sharing posts is a high compliment to the people who posted them, as you're indicating that the value was so high that you're recommending this information to your friends and network. Click the arrow under a post (next to +1) to share. A popup appears with the original post in the main window. Above that, you should add a comment, explaining why you're sending it on. At the bottom, you define who to share the content with. By default, G+ includes the circle(s) you last shared with (you can change this default in the settings). You can choose to share with the public (that is, it appears in Google searches), specific circles, all your circles, or "extended circles" (just on G+, but including everyone in your circles, plus everyone in *their* circles).

In addition, you can share individual posts with communities, spreading the material outside your circles.

Strategy for Posting on Google+

"Involve your audience at Google+ while writing your book" is Scott Knaster's advice to authors. First create your author presence, and continue with the drumroll right up to the date of book publication and launch. Grow and involve your audience by getting readers invested in your work who will want to write positive reviews and buy your books. Google+ offers an easy path to sharing with your audience.

Once you've gotten a feel for Google+, try to post often in the months leading up to the launch of your book.

Here are some basic posting recommendations for your Google+ posts:

- **Update.** Most importantly, update your Google+ account with your recent blog posts with links that take readers to individual posts.
- **Post news items** related to your subject matter, using hashtags, which work the same way as in Twitter. Find these using Google Alerts on any topic.
- **Mentions.** When you +mention someone, that person receives an email showing your mention, which they will appreciate and most likely reciprocate.
- **Repost** others' posts with a comment. This also gives people an incentive to follow you.
- **Duplicate.** To save time, selectively repost your posts from Facebook, Twitter, and LinkedIn. People do not necessarily check all your networks all the time, so this is an acceptable practice.

Anytime you post or share content on Google+, you have the option to email your item to the circles you're sharing with. In the post/share window, select the circle(s) you want to communicate with in the To: box. At the bottom, check the **Also send email to X circles** box. Use this feature sparingly, as your circles may not appreciate dozens of emails from you on a daily basis.

Automate Your Google+ Posts

For every social networking platform you post to, you can save time by using a weekend hour to mastermind your posts for the week. Marketing experts not only duplicate posts across the big social networks like Facebook and Twitter but also post or use HootSuite to post the same thing multiple times to hit the various times of day when people are most likely to read them—morning and after work.

Google+ makes it more difficult than other social networks to automate posts. Pretty much the only way to schedule posts on Google+ is through an application only available with the Google Chrome browser: Do Share.

Do Share allows you to write your posts and select with whom you wish to share the post beforehand. Be mindful of two quirky aspects of Do Share: You must use 24-hour time (so to schedule a post for 5:00 P.M. your time, choose 17:00), and Google Chrome has to be running at the scheduled time or your items won't post until the next time you run Chrome.

Connect Your Content Through Google Authorship

Now that you are a member of Google+ you can go to the second step that Google has created to authenticate authors and establish ownership of content. Signing up for Google Authorship is critical, as it connects your Google+ profile to your individual pieces of content. This is a huge advantage offered at Google that isn't offered anywhere else on the web. At Google Authorship, you verify that you're a real person who actually writes the content that is attributed to you. When you do both steps, you're on the road to allowing Google to leverage your high-quality content.

Use your consistent name with byline on all of your content. Search engines can match exact letters of a name in a search, so be sure to use your name exactly the same way each time you byline your content. For example, if you use your first and last name in one place, don't use your middle initial in another.

Buy a website domain and email to match it. Google Authorship will list your name, photo, and byline next to your content when it appears in web searches. The main benefit to authors is that you get more clicks, you control your content, and you create a magnet for your audience. If you set it up right, when you contribute to others' sites, you'll get connected to the Google Author Rank to get found more in search results.

Google Author Rank

"Findability is the key to Internet success," according to Dave Taylor, Google+ power user and Google author. As of this writing, Google is discussing using writers' content reputation to increase their page rank in Google search results. The idea is to "grade" your writing to inform people how useful it is. If this initiative goes through, quality content will rise to the top of searches depending on how it is measured by shares and reposts.

Authors who contribute to high-quality websites will go to the top of the results in direct relation to how many people indicate that content is useful. When this happens, Google places your author photo next to your content in search results. The idea is that Author Rank will "inform" Google Page Rank. Your Author Rank would also increase in direct proportion to the increase in the number of your followers.

Setting Up Google Authorship

Setting up Google Authorship is a little complex, but it's worth the time and effort. You've already done the first part of the setup: You've created a profile on G+ and included a straight-on head shot. In the Links section of the profile page, review the Contributor To section of your profile. In this section, add links to every site on the web where you have contributed content. This starts with your author page and continues through any articles you've written for other sites (or print magazines with an online archive where your writing appears). Blog comments and forum posts don't really count here, but original articles count a lot!

WordPress Jetpack will automatically add a Contributor To link from your WordPress site to your profile. See "Link Google+ to Your Author Website" earlier in the chapter.

When you're done filling out the Contributor To section, look up at the top of your browser; in the address bar, you'll see your profile ID, your unique Google identity. It looks something like this: https://plus.google.com/<reallylongsetofdigits>*/about*.

Copy that URL through the set of digits. You may want to paste this information into a text file because you may need it down the road. For the moment, we're done at Google+.

Go to your author site, the only site on the web where you have complete control. Check that your photo appears somewhere on the site; the best spot is on the front page or the About page (perhaps both). Make it easy on Google's Authorship bots and use the same photo (or similar one) that you use on Google+.

Also, check that all your posts and pages have your byline on them and that the way you spell your name is identical to your G+ profile.

After you have inspected your visible site for these items, you need to go to your administrative page to tend to some behind-the-scenes tasks. The most important is to add a special HTML tag to every post and page. This "rel=author" tag is invisible to humans but important for Google's Authorship bots as they troll the Internet for content.

You can do this manually, but there's an easier way. Find a plugin or other tool that will work for your site framework. Many WordPress plugins exist to help you do this chore; we've gotten good use from the Google+ Author Information in Search Results plugin from WP-Buddy. See Chapter 1 for information on how to install plugins in WordPress.

If you use this particular plugin, in your site administration page go to Settings > Google+ Author Free. Paste your G+ Profile ID in the **Google Plus Link** box.

You should now have established Authorship for your website. To confirm this, visit Google's Structured Data Tools site, google.com/webmasters/tools/richsnippets. Type (or paste) the URL for your website into the **Structured Data Testing Tool** box and click **Preview**. In seconds, you should see your photo appearing alongside the name of the site you pointed the tool to.

Below the search results preview, you'll see additional information about Authorship on the site. If you've performed all the steps properly, it should say "Authorship is working for this webpage." Farther down the page, still more confirmation: "rel=author markup has successfully established authorship for this webpage." You can celebrate now.

For additional help before and after you set up Authorship, you should join the Google Authorship & Author Rank community on Google+.

You can use Google search as usual to gather information about your audience and your possible connections for cross-promotion of your books. It's worthwhile to take time to do this research online at the outset of your project. Many authors hire student research interns to collect online information in return for a small payment and acknowledgment in your book. Google search will help you to find lists about your audience and where to find them: Search for discussion groups (forums) on your subject, questions your audience asks, and at Google Groups (groups.google.com). Just type in keywords, or you can browse different types of groups.

> Google now uses a "social search engine" using the Google+ online community filtering to personalize search results. Part of Web 2.0 technology, the online community of Google+ interactivity allows interesting relevant content to be "tagged." Over time, developers expect improvement on search results for these keywords. If you're registered on Google+, you clearly indicate the people you trust. Then in searches, Google connects you so that you see content from these people in your search results. This is an amazing "plus" for authors as you can use their engine to increase your search results.

More Google+ Features

Google+ offers several features that other social networks lack. Here's a short list. By the time you read this, there will likely be other features to explore.

Reading and Posting Tools

On your G+ home page, the Stream carries every post from everyone you've circled. Narrow your focus to a particular circle by clicking any of the navigation buttons across the top of the stream. The four default circles display automatically. Any circles you've created are listed under the More button.

Click the left-hand navigation bar to view other ways to see what's happening on the site:

- **What's Hot.** This is a fantastic spot to find a mixture of fun and interesting tidbits to share on your Google+ page. Carole finds beautiful travel photos here to share, adding the label "Great Writer's Retreat" or Quotes that pertain to writing for fun intermission breaks from more serious posts. What's Hot shares publicly shared posts getting a lot of +1 and sharing attention on the site.
- **Search.** Besides the people search we discussed earlier, use G+ search to find posts (and people) relating to your topics of interest. Trending topics also appear on the right side of your stream. Click any of these to see what's up.
- **Ripples.** Another tool you can use to see how people have shared their posts. Click **the inverted triangle** in the top right of any post; select **View Ripples** and you'll see who has shared your posts with others. It can also show you who shares others' posts to get an idea of frequency of sharing and who is doing the sharing.

Google Events

Create and participate in real-life or online events with the events calendar. Events allow you and other participants to post pictures and video from your event, too. Schedule your book launch and invite everyone to attend.

Start by clicking the Google+ Navigation menu and clicking Events. You'll see a list of upcoming and past events you've been invited to. To get started, click the Create Event button on the right side of the page, next to the Plan a Hangout button; more on this in the next section.

Set the title, date, and time for your event in their respective boxes. If your event is not happening online, set the event location; when you start typing, a list of matching venues will appear for your selection. Add some details to help your guests decide to attend your event. Select who to invite in the To line, which works exactly as any other sharing button in Google+.

Under Event Options, you can decide whether the people you invite can invite others or add photos to your Event page. These options are checked by default. You can also choose to keep your guest list private by checking the Hide Guest List item.

Click Advanced Options > Show More Options to include optional URLs for the event website, YouTube channel, and your ticket seller. You can also provide transit and parking information for your guests.

Click Invite to send your invitations to your selected guests.

Your event gets a page on Google+ where people can RSVP, comment on the event, and get more information. Check in to the event page regularly to respond to any questions or issues and update any changes. You can change or update any of your event details at any time up to the event.

Google Hangouts

Hangouts are one of the main differentiators of Google+ compared to other social sites. These are live video chats. Basic Hangouts allow up to ten people to video chat at one time from their computers or cell phones. This is a great option for collaboration and small groups.

For authors, Hangouts on Air allows you to publicly broadcast your Hangout to anyone on the planet for free. You can host video podcasts and present interviews or other conversations. The video is recorded and stored on YouTube for permanent access. This group video chat is a perfect tool that can be used for your virtual book launch upon publication, covered in Chapter 14.

Click **Hangouts on Air** from the G+ Navigation menu to see a current schedule of featured Hangouts, along with the Hangouts on Air currently broadcasting.

Mobile App for Google+

According to Cisco, 2013 marks the year when the number of mobile devices equals the world population, and by 2017 there will be 1.4 mobile devices per person on the planet Earth. It's important to use the mobile G+ app on the go with your mobile devices. You can download the G+ app from either the Apple App Store or Google Play for your Android device. Open the app and log in with your Google account to access all of G+. You can also use a separate Hangouts app to participate in video chats.

Soul Wisdom: Practical Soul Treasures to Transform Your Life

books.google.com/books?isbn=1471105636
Zhi Gang Sha - 2012 - Preview - More editions
' And most importantly, you have the ability to heal yourself. Essentially this is the an introductory guide for all of us to learn practical techniques to help open our minds, empower, heal and transform every aspect of our lives.

Living Divine Relationships

books.google.com/books?isbn=1600230105
Zhi Gang Sha - 2010 - Preview
In Living Divine Relationships, Master Zhi Gang Sha, world-renowned physician, teacher, and author, gives you the keys to Living Divine Relationships with God, with your spiritual teachers and masters, and with your own soul.

Tao I: The Way of All Life

books.google.com/books?isbn=1439196516
Zhi Gang Sha - 2010 - Preview - More editions
In this process, healing, rejuvenation, and life transformation occur. In contrast to the ancient Taoist wisdom, knowledge, and practices, the new sacred teaching in this book is extremely simple, practical, and profound.

The Power of Soul

books.google.com/books?isbn=1471105644
Zhi Gang Sha - 2012 - Preview - More editions
This third book in his bestselling Soul Power series dives deep into spiritual mysteries and reveals ancient secrets and lessons that readers can apply to every area of the daily routine, clearing up negative energy, blockages and ...

Divine Healing Hands: Experience Divine Power to Heal You, ...

books.google.com/books?isbn=1476714444
Zhi Gang Sha - 2012 - Preview - More editions
Dr. & Master Zhi Gang Sha is a chosen servant, vehicle, and channel of the Divine to offer Divine Healing Hands to the chosen ones. Master Sha has asked the Divine to download Divine Healing Hands to every copy of this book.

Power Healing: Four Keys to Energizing Your Body, Mind and ...

books.google.com/books?isbn=0062517805
Zhi Gang Sha - 2003 - Preview - More editions
In this revolutionary guide, internationally renowned healer, teacher and speaker Dr Sha translates ancient healing practices for contemporary readers by combining four simple techniques - gentle stretching, breathing exercises, self ...

Soul Communication: Opening Your Spiritual Channels for ...

books.google.com/books?isbn=1416588973
Zhi Gang Sha - 2008 - Preview - More editions
Shares insights into the author's work as an integrative medicine practitioner, explaining how the applications of certain spiritual principles and laws can enable healing benefits in all areas of a life.

Divine Soul Songs: Sacred Practical Treasures to Heal, ...

books.google.com/books?isbn=1439129657
Zhi Gang Sha - 2009 - Preview - More editions
Contains singing, chanting, and meditation exercises designed to improve individual physical and emotional health and transform the surrounding world.

Soul Mind Body Medicine: A Complete Soul Healing System for ...

books.google.com/books?isbn=1577317742
Zhi Gang Sha - 2009 - Preview - More editions
A guide to physical and spiritual health blends sacred wisdom with practical techniques, and combines Eastern and Western medicine to illustrate healing strategies for more than one hundred ailments, from the common cold to diabetes.

Divine Soul Mind Body Healing and Transmission Sys: The ...

books.google.com/books?isbn=1439180873
Zhi Gang Sha - 2009 - Preview - More editions
This book offers you the most powerful soul healing available at this time; it is truly a breakthrough divine gift and treasure for humanity.

Google Books page for author client Dr. Zhi Gang Sha.

Google Services Beyond Google+

Everyone knows what a pervasive force Google is in our online lives. We discussed Blogger as a potential platform for your blog in Chapter 2. You'll learn a lot more about YouTube in Chapter 10. Here are some of the other Google services that can help you write and market your writing.

Google AdWords

Google uses ads from AdWords on their book search pages: google.com/ad/sense.

Google Alerts

An easy, free service: Go to google.com/alerts and sign up for Google Alerts on any keywords you type in: your own name (again, exactly as it appears in all other places), the name of your book, your topics of interest, etc. You'll get the latest news and posts mentioning your keywords automatically delivered to your inbox in digest form, which you can in turn repost on your Google+ page.

Google Analytics

Google's tool for measuring your website following is covered in Chapter 1. In Analytics, Google gives you free detailed statistics about your website visitors so that you can track and grow your audience by measuring the popularity of features and postings on your website.

Connecting Your Google+ Account to Your Website

As with every other piece of your social network puzzle, make sure to connect your Google+ account to your other networks.

Google+ developers have created a badge you can place on your website and blog to tell everyone "I'm on Google+" and invite them to add you to their circles. Visit developers.google.com/+/web/badge/ to get the code, then return to your website.

If you're using WordPress, the Jetpack plugin places a link to your Google+ profile automatically.

We're avid fans of Google's offerings, especially to authors, and have found a wide community of thousands of authors, writers, and publishers to share and interact with. As an author, you need to join Google+. We hope to connect with you there and we welcome hearing your comments and stories.

Checklist, Step 4: Google

➤ Create a Google+ Account.
➤ Include your friends, associates, and clients. Find people to follow in your niche, and repost others' works.
➤ Try to post once a day; automate posts to save time. You can duplicate your Facebook and Twitter posts.
➤ Post when you have a new blog entry and/or announcement.
➤ Use Google Alerts and What's Hot to find articles to post.
➤ Join Google Authorship.
➤ Join Google Communities.
➤ Use Google to hold "Events."

Success Spotlight: Waterside Client Dave Taylor (askdavetaylor.com)

- 20 books and 1,000 articles published
- 250,000 books in print, translated 40 times into 15 languages

Beginnings: Dave has been online since before the beginning of the Internet. He received his B.A. in Computer Science from UC San Diego, his Master's in Education from Purdue, and his MBA from University of Baltimore.

One of his professors encouraged him to get published, so he submitted an article he wrote to a professional journal, which printed his work. Then he got a call from *Computer Language* magazine inviting him to write for them and offered great pay. It turned out that there were a lot of markets for his writing. A few years later, Dave was called by John Barry at Sun Microsystems to write a feature for their in-house magazine, then later invited to turn that article into his first book, published by Springer-Verlag.

Platform:
- **Articles:** Published in the *Boulder Daily Camera*, the *Boulder Weekly*, *Linux Journal*, ScienceFiction.com, and *Colorado Business Magazine*.
- **Speaker:** Keynotes talks, moderates, and speaks on panels.
- **Teacher:** Variety of colleges and private institutions.
- **Podcaster:** Helps run two weekly podcasts.
- **Radio:** Former cohost, local phone-in computer show.

- **Blog:** AskDaveTaylor, focused on technical support and consumer electronics, along with fatherhood and parenting discussions on GoFatherhood, film reviews that he publishes at DaveOnFilm.com.

Dave's advice to authors: Every day, ask yourself, "What am I doing to make my book successful?"

The way to build an author platform is to know this first: Everything feeds on everything else you've done. Continue to bring people into the center of your network. Guest blogging brings in more people and sells more books. Articles bring people to your website. Think about it this way: A million arrows lead to you and your book. Your book is just a start that leads to a whole show; it's the beginning of a long-term relationship with your audience.

Dave Taylor's final word on author platform building: "The Internet is huge. HUGE! Successful books are about visibility and distribution. Do all of the steps outlined in this book! Write and publish small pieces on the web before anyone ever sees your book, add content to your blog, Facebook, Google+, Twitter, LinkedIn, Pinterest, websites, and more. These combine to create a magnet because findability is the key to becoming a successful author. Who wants to have a book where no one even knows it exists? Go out there, follow the author platform steps, and get the maximum possible audience!"

CHAPTER 5

Your Author Brand and Book on Facebook

"Every single service that you use is going to be better with your friends."

—*Mark Zuckerberg, creator of Facebook*

THE PUBLISHING WORLD IS EXPLODING with exciting and expanded digital options. Now every publisher acquisitions meeting includes decisions for publications that reach well beyond the printed book. Behind the scenes in these meetings, as electronic sales percentages increase, publishers discuss extending the reach of a print title through ebooks, mobile apps, online training, and more, which has expanded the consumer's ability to access content in different ways. Successful publishers maneuver by committee to reach out and find buyers in all of these arenas. It's simply more efficient to move bits and bytes than it is to move solid matter, so adding digital options creates a definite publishing win. Traditional publishers speed on well-developed avenues of global distribution that have expanded to encompass digital distribution, creating a difficult match for an author interested in do-it-yourself publishing.

Even so, self-publishing for authors who have felt they could go it alone has always stood side by side with traditional publishing, and over time a surprising amount of quality authors have decided to pursue publishing their own manuscripts. Examples of successful self-publishing date as far back as 1843, when Dickens self-published *A Christmas Carol*, later joined by self-published authors of perennial bestsellers like Strunk and White's classic *Elements of Style* and Richard Nelson Bolles' book *What Color*

Is Your Parachute? Printing successful books is tantamount to printing money because high quality sells content. The bestseller that will continue over time represents quality content that audiences universally want and need, so to cover the present moment and even beyond, traditional publishers' contracts contain clauses indicating rights to publish in "media not invented yet."

Along Comes Facebook

It was really MySpace and then Facebook that firmly put the term "social networking" into everyday usage. Consider your expanded reach for talking directly with people about your book: With the largest social network site, Facebook, you have access to over a billion people who use Facebook each month. Facebook can be addictive: The average user checks their Facebook profile 14 times per day! These check-ins are typically about two minutes long, adding up to approximately a half hour per user each day. This is an amazing online location to reach out to your audience (preferably for longer than two minutes), and this chapter is devoted to showing you how.

Facebook has already taught most people how to interact online with family and friends, and as a part of its growth and success, Facebook has expanded its network to include Facebook Pages. A Page is for a business, brand, public figure (such as a politician, author, or actor), or organization rather than a person. Once you have a certain number of people who Like your Page (30, currently), you have access to Insights data that gives you demographic information, available on your Facebook dashboard and emailed to you weekly.

Your book's Page expands beyond casual personal and social interaction while providing a gateway to huge numbers of people already on Facebook. Use your brand's consistent presence to in turn use Facebook to build your audience. In the next sections of this chapter, we'll show you a model strategy that you can customize for using Facebook as a vehicle to magnify your author and book brands.

In this chapter, we suggest the two-step Facebook strategy for authors: First, create an author brand presence as a header for your personal page; second, create a Facebook Page for your book and build the number of

Likes and comments on your Page. The beauty of the Like is that your posts will show up in your interested fans' newsfeeds, and your profile photo (of you or your book cover) shows up on the left side of each profile (or at least the Likes page linked to from there) for all *their* friends and family to see as your search engine optimization (SEO) increases.

The effort to set up your profile and Page efficiently is minimal compared to the power at work for you with Facebook. Keep your social network presence consistent as well as efficient by recycling the text you use for postings on your author and book websites, blog, and other social networks.

Why Facebook Is Necessary for Authors

Audience reach. At one billion subscribers, Facebook represents an unprecedented number of people available from which to find your audience. Authors have a great opportunity to present themselves directly, promote their books on Facebook Pages, and engage the audience personally. It is well worth your time to sign up for the Facebook Pages we recommend: your author Page—using your real author name, consistent with the rest of your online presence—and your book Page, using the name of your book as the Page name. (Note: Some customize the name to be the name of their existing company.)

We advise keeping postings to your family and close friends separate from your professional and book brands to ensure that your personal photos and information are not shared in public.

Social proof of audience. Publishers and readers look at how many friends and Likes you have on Facebook, so take time before your book is published to increase these numbers as part of your author platform. The larger your social network audience size, the larger your potential book audience size, but only if your Likes come from your potential audience. The trick is to find your target audience and build up authentic numbers of people interested in you, not a crowd of people who don't care. The best strategy is to grow your audience through Facebook groups, covered below.

Growing audience through groups. Large and small, in every range of interest, there are more than 620 million Facebook groups. You can join existing groups or start your own group based on your subject matter and interests. By announcing your book to a group, you are able to grow your number of Likes so that these followers will receive announcements automatically through their newsfeeds. Through Facebook groups you'll also find communities of authors who will offer reciprocal Likes. We have joined author groups because authors are our audience, and the Likes allow us to keep in direct touch with our targeted audience in regard to book updates.

Driving audience to your site/blog. Announcing new blog posts and sharing other information from your author website on Facebook increases your website traffic.

Building community via audience dialogue. When you post to your Facebook Page, your followers can comment and make comments on comments, and you can respond to create a written dialogue. When you comment on others' pages, you can open up even more dialog. The structure of Facebook makes it simple for people to talk with each other because all you have to do is read and fill in a box with a comment. In this familiar, friendly community, people comment often, so be sure to respond to each one to build interaction and engagement.

Buy Now button. Audience can buy your book through your Facebook Page. Awareness of any brand depends on an audience seeing it approximately eight times before they make the action decision to buy your book, and a Buy Now button can be included right on your book page.

Direct advertising. You can connect to even more of your followers by creating multiple Facebook ads to build a bigger audience for your Facebook Page. Facebook gives options to show your ads to only the people you want to reach, and also, the ability to try out and find which version of your ad works best. See "Buying Ads on Your Author Page" later in the chapter for more information.

Your Facebook Profile

We assume that you already have a Facebook profile set up for your personal, private use. If not, you can refer to our bibliography, which includes beginning Facebook titles that will take you through the steps of setting up a profile.

Unless you don't mind the public enjoying your private pictures and hearing your very personal updates, be sure to keep your personal profile separate from your professional Facebook Pages! That means you can keep your personal profile basically as is . . . with just a few modifications.

Considering that your own name is your author brand, and that anyone in public can look you up on Facebook, make sure your Facebook public photo on your personal profile is consistent with your author brand photo as opposed to a shot of, say, you partying on a yacht. Jesse Feiler, author of *How to Do Everything: Facebook Applications* (McGraw-Hill, 2008), suggests that you can keep your personal page private in the following way: "To build your audience for your books, adjust your settings on your personal profile; keep your author bio on the public view setting and the inside personal friend photos, posts, and conversations on the private view setting. When you showcase your public author profile for searchability in a way that presents your consistent author brand to the public, all search engines . . . will present you in the light you want to be seen by your audience."

As of this writing, your nonfriends, that is, the public, cannot see what conversations and photos you and your friends post on your profile as long as you use the private view setting. You have the option to friend only people you know, thereby protecting your privacy. If you get a friend request from a stranger, send them a nice note explaining your "friending policy," and pointing them to your Facebook book Page instead. That includes everyone whom you do not know who might be interested in further news about your book. As your family, friends, associates, and clients will likely be ready to support you in your book publishing endeavors, be sure to friend them all on Facebook and ask them to like your book Page so that they will receive your posts automatically in their newsfeed. Most, if not quite all, of your Facebook friends will want to hear about your writing projects and read your helpful posts regarding your subject matter and book.

Note: Your personal profile caps your friends at 5,000, whereas Pages allow unlimited audience followers.

Your Facebook Pages

Since public Facebook Pages can promote anything, including businesses, causes, or books, these Pages can be accessed by anyone on or outside of

Facebook. Pages have the added advantage of being indexed by search engines like Google, thereby increasing the ranking of your author brand and your books being found when people search on your subject.

Your author and book Pages on Facebook should mirror your website. We'll show you how to create both kinds of pages.

Set Up Your Author Page

From your Facebook profile page, you'll see **Pages** on the left sidebar. When you put your mouse on the Pages title, you'll see **More**; click that. You'll then see the Pages Feed, with the collection of all the Pages you've Liked since the beginning of time. Click **Create a Page** at the top of the middle column.

The first thing you'll see is a set of broad categories for your page. Click **Artist, Band or Public Figure**.

There's a drop-down menu called **Choose a Category**. Click **Author**. Type your name in the second box. Use the name associated with you as an author, regardless of what you use for your personal Facebook account: A pen name or nickname is okay, as long as it's the same as the name on the cover of your book. Review and agree to the terms of service. Though you may be used to ignoring software license agreements and website terms of service, you really should take a look at the rules for Pages, just so you know what is—and is not—allowed. Click **Get Started**.

ADD A PROFILE PICTURE AND DESCRIPTION TO YOUR AUTHOR PAGE

Your next task is to upload your profile picture. We recommend using the same photo as your other social network profiles for continuity of your brand. However, since Facebook has a personal aspect to it, a less formal photo can be used as long as it is as recognizable as your professional shot. The photo must be at least 180 pixels wide and not too big for the window Facebook provides. Then, click **Next**.

Note: Using slightly different profile pictures in your personal Facebook as well as your author and book Pages can act as a safety net of sorts. That is, when you post, you'll be reminded of which page your post appears on by a display of the picture from the page you're posting from.

It's a good idea to prevent personal life announcements from accidentally appearing in public!

The About page lets you add a description for your book and about you as author, and links to your website and other locations. You can do this later, but put something up now. Leave the description fairly brief. You can use more than the Twitter 160-character limit, but don't enter your complete biography here. Add links to your author website as well as your Twitter account to allow easy access to you. Facebook will ask you if you're a "real celebrity or famous person." If you check this box, Facebook will verify that you are in fact that famous person. Click **Save Info**.

The last setup page lets Facebook put ads from others on your Page. You must set up a funding source (credit card or PayPal) to pay for ads elsewhere on the site. This is optional; you can do this later. See "Buying Ads on Your Author Page" later in this chapter.

Your Page is now created! Facebook asks you to be the first to Like your page. You're then asked to invite your email contacts to Like the page, so they can start seeing your content in their news feeds. Next, post something—news if you have something to announce, or just a welcome message with information on what types of content people can expect on your page.

ADDING CONTENT TO YOUR AUTHOR PAGE

Once you have created your author page, you'll see that the top half of the screen is taken up by your Admin Panel. Among the first things to do is flesh out your profile information. Click **Edit Page** at the top, and your Basic Information page appears. This page should contain the category (People and Author) you set up with the page. Leave the Official Page line blank as its purpose is to tell visitors that the Facebook page is an unofficial page; that is, a page set up by fans or other people whom you don't know.

Next, you want to create a username for your page. This simplifies linking from your author website to your Facebook author Page. As with your website's domain name, Facebook creates a unique URL for every person and page on its site. By default, this is a really long ID number, so better that you can create a link along the lines of https://www.facebook .com/yourname. Be aware that Facebook says that "Your username should be as close as possible to your true name or the name of the business or person your Page represents (for example, John.Smith, Facebook)." Now if you happen to be John Smith, you can select author.john.smith or something similar, but don't choose a username lightly! You can only change your username once.

When you're ready to get a username, click the link and check the availability of your choice. If you find one, you'll be warned about bad behavior surrounding usernames and asked to confirm the selected username.

Check the name of your site again to confirm that you did not accidentally misspell your name (or that Facebook failed to get the capitalization right on O'Malley or similar). You can change the name of the page any time up to the moment the two hundredth Facebook member clicks "Like" on your page. This section of the settings includes the Start Date and Type. The Start Date is when Facebook begins the page timeline. Only use this if you intend to fill in important past dates in your professional life.

You can also leave the Address section blank and focus instead on filling out the last section of the Basic Information page, as it's where you can give your audience details about your book.

BUYING ADS ON YOUR AUTHOR PAGE

As Facebook's success is driven by advertising, you'll not be surprised that Facebook makes it very easy for Pages (that is, businesses) to buy promotional ads. Under the **Get More Likes** heading on your Admin Panel, click **Promote Page**. You'll see a Sample Ad with your Page's profile picture and the ever-so-clickable Like icon.

Set a Daily Budget from $5 to $20 per day using the drop-down menu. Facebook will charge you that amount every day until you tell it to stop. The more you spend, the more Likes you can expect. Monitor this closely while you run your ad.

You can define your Audience geographically. As an author whose works circulate well beyond any particular city or state, you'll want to select Countries as your starting point. If you're on a book tour or otherwise making an appearance outside your local area, consider targeting an ad announcing the event for that location.

Click **Promote Page** to commit to buying the ad. If you haven't yet defined a Funding Source (that is, where Facebook can get its ad money), you will do that now. Facebook takes credit and debit cards, PayPal, and electronic funds transfer (which they call Direct Debit). You can then make adjustments to the ad's copy and set start and end dates for your campaign. Once you've squared away the details, the Facebook Ad Manager has a nice dashboard that reports on the success of your ad on the site.

Set Up Your Facebook Book Page

When you create a Facebook Page for your book, the book cover and title are the star of the show. The elements of your book Page will be similar to those of your book website, covered in Chapter 11. You must have a book cover image before creating the book Page and should upload it as your page's profile photo. Here is the huge advantage of Pages: When your audience presses Like on your book Page, it will appear on the Likes page, and sometimes on the left side of their own profile page and they'll get your posts automatically in their news feed. When your book cover becomes a favorite appearing on each person's personal Profile, it will draw their interest and can easily be shared.

BOOK PAGE PHOTO AND BANNER

On your book Page, the larger banner photo best includes a larger version of the cover photo, to reinforce the image of your book cover. Many best-selling books use this doubling of photos as a strategy to strengthen the branding of the book image. Before creating the Page for your book, see what's out there, assessing other Facebook book Pages. Some excellent examples are Malcolm Gladwell's *Blink* (Little, Brown and Company) and *The Tipping Point* (Little, Brown and Company) and Neil Gaiman's *The Ocean at the End of the Lane* (Headline).

POSTINGS ON YOUR BOOK PAGE

Your postings can be minimal but consistent on your book Page at Facebook, and as noted can duplicate postings about your blog and any other announcements you make on Google+ and Twitter and your other social media channels. Continue to invite friends, family, and all of your clients and associates to follow and Like your book. Later in this chapter, you'll find recommendations on additional types of posts appropriate for the Facebook community.

BOOK PAGE DESCRIPTION

As with your author Page, click the **Create Page** button. Choose **Entertainment**. Select your category: **Book**. On the first registration page, add a Description that matches the one on your book site. Facebook then asks you whether this is "a real person, book/magazine, or venue" so it can give you a custom address. Finally, they want to know if this page is the "Authorized and official representation of the person, book/magazine, or venue on Facebook." This tells them that you're putting up an "official site" and not just a tribute site created by a fan (or critic, for that matter).

BOOK PAGE LINKS

This is also the place in the registration area where you can link to one or more related web pages outside Facebook: Link to your author site and, if you have them, your book site and publisher site, as the more opportunities people have to buy your book, the better.

Add the book's profile picture (your book cover) while registering as well. The rest of the registration box covers the same items as your author page: your custom Facebook Web Address (they suggest your book title as the address; change if necessary) and whether you want to Enable Ads on the page.

Your book Page will duplicate much of the content of your book's website, as it will serve as another showcase for your book. The type of audience exposure you offer on your book Page should be consistent with the work you already have done.

By default, your book Page includes an About section, including the book's ISBN and publisher, along with the website(s) you listed when you registered. If you're up for a little adventure, you can customize your Page with tabs and buttons. The easiest way to do this is to install the Landable Hosted iFrame app in Facebook. This app lets you add custom tabs to your pages with your own content. You can even paste HTML content directly from your website into Facebook to add content to your Welcome page.

If you go this route (which is not common), we recommend setting up two tabs besides the defaults:

A "Welcome" Landing Page Tab with a professional book cover and:

- A short, bulleted list of "back cover" book copy: succinct items that speak to your audience needs; you can find models of back-cover copy on the books in your library: short, catchy, enticing, descriptive.
- A front cover–type "praise" quote from a notable person or someone who found your book helpful.
- A photo of you the author as a person who is accessible to the readers, with information on how to contact you.
- A short, bulleted list of your qualifications. Also add a Read More button connected to your About page.
- Audio or downloadable sample excerpt from your book.
- Video book trailer (Chapter 10).

> The Landing page content is the basis for your main book Page. You can also include a link to your book's website for the Media Kit material.

A Press/Media Kit Tab that includes:

- High-resolution photos of the author(s)
- A schedule of appearances (real and virtual)
- Contact information

Also consider adding these buttons:

- **Buy Now button.** This leads your audience to the action you want them to take in purchasing your book.
- **Like button** with a chapter giveaway in exchange. Set this as "Non-Fan Only Content" in Landable.
- **Opt-in signup button** for your newsletter, as your author mailing list is crucial to building your audience. MailChimp is a popular newsletter service. Its Facebook integration allows people to sign up for your newsletter from your Page. MailChimp is free until you hit 2,000 subscribers; you can send up to 12,000 emails per month.

Book Page Connections

If you create more Facebook Pages for your books, be sure that all your pages Like each other. You can also add links to your other Pages on your About tab.

Your About tab should link to your primary author website, and at least one content element on your Facebook Page should likewise link back to a blog post or other content on your author website.

Developing Your Facebook Strategy

All parts of your author platform fit together to create an overall impact in growing your audience over time. As you create each part, go back to your plan, audience definition, and author identity as recommended and outlined in Chapter 1. As always, keep your author persona consistent with the intent of your book, so your audience becomes more familiar with you, leading them to trust you.

Post to your book Page in the same style you post to your personal page. We recommend book Page postings that are about you and your project, tied to your audience interests like announcements, progress, tips, signings, and, of course, notifications about new blog posts. It's best to keep your posts written in the first person as much as possible to keep the Facebook community feel. If you repost an article, be sure you include a personal note regarding why you're sharing it. Keep a personal tone and try to start conversations through comment boxes.

Encourage Likes with your audience of potential readers. Your author Facebook presence on your book Page will become linked to many others' profiles as a favorite when they click Like, so for starters, ask your friends, family, and associates who are interested in your writing to Like your page. Offer to exchange page Likes with others in your network and within communities where you find your readers and other authors.

Note: Once you get 30 Likes on your page, Facebook will send you a weekly email message with "insights" into your Facebook fans, the number of active users per month, Likes you've received, and how many visitors came to the page compared to last week.

Foster sharing between friends. There are many ways to start conversations that get people to share and interact, and you'll find that many conversations naturally develop around the information you're posting through the comment boxes.

Posting to Your Pages

The best strategy for posting on Facebook is using your own natural enthusiasm, that is, "Hey, read all about it!" when it comes to what you're working on. Always think from the perspective of your friends in regard to what news they most want to hear about your book progress, your next book, and all announcements related to the communities surrounding your subject matter. Facebook isn't the place to post too often or automate lots of posts, so your posts should be crafted in a way that aligns with the small-town news-feed attitude of Facebook. Post about yourself and what you're doing in your book workshop, and those posts will be interesting to your friends and fans.

Remember to announce events like:

- Your book's pre-publication progress, including book cover, book decisions you've made
- Events: when you're speaking, where you might be appearing (along with locations and times)
- Any media appearances
- When your book will be available
- Book signings
- Conferences related to your subject matter
- Other types of content you should share on your pages include:
  - Facebook groups you're in and the things being said there
  - Articles related to your area of expertise; always add a comment about why you think people should read them (One easy way to find these articles is by entering keywords about your subject areas on Google Alerts.)
  - A question or a poll on what your audience thinks, either serious, like "What color should my book cover be?" or lighthearted, like "What is the best food for a writer?" Enjoy the dialogue and keep

the conversation going, as this engagement is linked to Facebook's measurement of "Number of People Talking About."

- A line quoted from your blog as a way to announce and lead readers to a new post; be sure to provide the live URL

Note: If you decide to create a professional Twitter account, you can link that to your Facebook author or book Page so all your relevant tweets appear automatically on that Page.

EMBEDDING FACEBOOK POSTS IN YOUR BLOG

You can also embed Facebook posts in your author website's blog by cutting and pasting some code. The posts will look exactly the way they do on Facebook, including the number of Likes, shares, and comments.

After posting in Facebook, click the icon in the upper right corner of the post. Click **Embed Post**. A box will appear, inviting you to **Copy and paste this code into your website**. Copy the code into your clipboard.

Open your author website and create a new blog post. Paste the Facebook code into the editor and publish.

Facebook Best Practices

Facebook was built on the basis of people enjoying and extending their relationships with each other, so courtesy and a sense of enjoyment go a long way when it comes to building an audience on Facebook. Best practices in interacting on Facebook are:

- **Appreciation.** When someone leaves a comment praising you, reply with a comment thanking them, or at the very least Like their nice comment. React favorably to other people's posts with kind comments like "Wow" or "That's great!"
- **Personalization.** Add photos to your posts to make them more compelling and memorable.
- **A sense of humor** also goes a long way on Facebook, as it does elsewhere.
- **Like and comment on the Pages of others and ask for a reciprocal Like.**

Side Note: Always Like a page from your personal page, not your professional Page as only the personal Like adds to the quantity for some reason. As you Like the pages of others, their icon will then appear on your own page. If you do not want to see posts from the pages you Like to show up in your newsfeed, you can turn off postings at the same time you press Like. Just hover over the Liked button, and you'll get the menu to uncheck Show Notifications.

Join Facebook Groups

With the staggering number of Facebook groups already on the network, it's our recommendation that you join existing groups first before starting your own.

Take time up front to:

Find and join Facebook groups that align with your specialty area. Use the standard Facebook search to find groups of people with common interests. You can go to facebook.com/bookmarks/groups to see groups you have joined, along with some groups Facebook recommends you join based on your Likes and groups your friends have joined. For example, here are a few common interests in groups connecting to the subject of our book *Build Your Author Platform: The New Rules*: Authors/authoring, Authors promoting authors, How to publish a book, International association of authors.

Comment favorably. Within the various groups, Like others' posts as you would elsewhere on Facebook, liberally! The Likes that you post do grow reciprocally over time.

Create a Facebook Group

It can be a more difficult task to create and maintain a successful Facebook group, but the benefits for your platform can be tremendous. This is especially true if you are filling a need for discussion and activities around an underdiscussed activity or niche. In this section, we'll walk you through the process of creating a Facebook group.

Set Up Your Group

Click the **Create Group** button either from the Groups sidebar on your home page or from the Groups page.

Name your group, add at least one friend to the group, and define how people outside the group can relate to it. You can change the privacy settings at any time.

Open groups: The group is in Facebook's directory, and nonmembers can see who is part of the group and can see all posts.

Closed groups: This is the default setting. The group is in Facebook's directory and nonmembers can see who is part of the group, but they can't see posts.

Secret groups: The group is not in Facebook's directory, and only members have access.

Click **Create Group**.

Share with Your Group

With the group created, you can now share content with all of its members. This works like any other Facebook post, but posts only go to members of that group (and appear in their news feed). Share links, make comments, and ask questions to stimulate conversation. Besides simple status updates, you and your members have many options to generate content. You can:

- Add photos and video. These are stored in the Photos tab.
- Take a poll of the group. Click **Ask Question** to poll your group about an issue, or to set up a face-to-face meeting. Click **Add Poll Options** to give people multiple choice answers.
- Post documents directly from your computer or from the Dropbox cloud storage service. Your file can be up to 25 megabytes (MB), and you can add a comment describing the contents of the file. Group members can download the file but not edit it directly in Facebook. Documents are stored in the Files tab.
- Share posts from your author and book Pages or even your personal page (when appropriate) within the group.

How to Be a Group Administrator

Click the gear icon to adjust the settings for your group. These settings include:

Membership Approval: Who can add members to the group.

Group Address: Use this setting to turn your group into an email list. Members can post to <yourgroup>@groups.facebook.com when you tell Facebook what <yourgroup> is.

Description: If your group is in the directory, you can add a description to attract new members.

Posting Permissions: By default, only members can post. You can further restrict this to only the group administrators.

Post Approval: If you're having trouble with spam, you can channel all posts to the group through you.

If you want to add another member to your administrative team and allow that person to make changes to the group settings, click on the **Member list** to see the current list. Click **the gear icon** to display a small box. Click **Make Admin**.

Planning an Event

As with Google Events, Facebook Events can happen in real life or online. Click the Events tab to tell people about them.

If you want some help deciding when to have an event, use the Poll/ Ask Question option described above to throw out some possibilities. Members can vote among the options you present or choose their own preferred date and time.

When the details are nailed down, click the **Events** tab to tell people about them.

1. Click **Add Event**.
2. Title the event.
3. Add details to describe the event.
4. Tell people when and where.

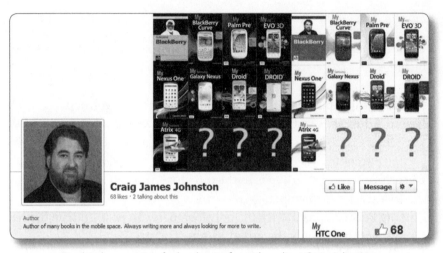

Facebook promotion for book suite for author client Craig Johnston.

5. By default, only group members know about the event. You can make it more public if you want.

6. Check the **Invite all members** box to message each member in Facebook (and, depending on the member's settings, their email inbox, too).

Once created, make sure to promote your event by posting regularly.

Mobile Apps

People use their mobile phones to update their Facebook status all the time, and the service has always accommodated that use. Facebook's mobile apps for Apple's phone and tablet mimic the website completely. You can view and update your Pages on the go. Facebook has also beefed up the functionality of its Android apps. Regardless of what mobile platforms you use, the easier Facebook makes it for you to transact business on the go, the more efficiently you can maintain your author platform.

Be sure to explore and then join the large and growing list of authors who have created fantastic author and book pages, already building communities on

Facebook. It matters not whether you are a best-selling, new or tradition-ally published or self-published author, you'll find a supportive and friendly group on this social network. Like our Facebook page at https://www .facebook.com/JelenPublishing?ref=hl and leave the link to your book page for a reciprocal Like to get you started.

Checklist, Step 5: Facebook

➤ Create a personal profile.
➤ Keep your author photo and name consistent across your author platform.
➤ Write your profile bio for public eyes.
➤ For your personal profile, keep as friends only family and those close to you.
➤ Create and customize a book Page consistent with your book website.
➤ Post updates and events to your book Page without advertising.
➤ Respond to comments on your book Page.
➤ Encourage Likes on your book Page.
➤ Join Facebook groups with common interests.

Success Spotlight: Waterside Client Kellyann Petrucci (drkellyann.com)

- 5 books, including *Living Paleo For Dummies, Boosting Your Immunity For Dummies* (4½-star Amazon reviews, available in some 20 countries); *Paleo Cookbook For Dummies; Paleo Workouts For Dummies;* and *Fast Diet For Dummies.*

Beginnings: As a little girl growing up, Kellyann was the one who could be found in the center of a group of neighborhood pals, tablet or pad of paper in hand, talking and jotting notes while all looked on in wonder. Her mother would tell you today that Kellyann has always been passionate about education and the written word. Her genre of choice—then and now—is the whodunit mystery; she is always the one to crack the case.

As Kellyann grew into her studies and career, she developed a passion for health and wellness. You could say her focus turned from "whodunit" to "whatdunnit." This led Kellyann to study advanced nutrition in both the United States and Europe and to develop a successful nutrition-based family practice and consulting business.

How she came up with her book idea: The busy mother of two recognized early on in her practice that she was in a "solutions" business. In essence, Kellyann spent her days effectively finding solutions for her patients so they could be as healthy as possible, whether that meant losing weight, boosting immunity, fighting the aging process, healing various ailments, or performing better. Her passion spread to her nutritional knowledge. Her client audience insisted she write a book, so publishing became a top priority. Her happy childhood memories of contentedly writing and "reporting" came flooding back when she wrote her book proposal. At that pivotal moment, Kellyann recognized that for her, the *process of writing* was an absolute extension of her very being and what she was meant to do. Kellyann discovered that passion for an idea often fizzles, especially in the frustrations of the publishing world, so she decided to get agency help with Waterside. Kellyann went from a struggling, hopeful author to a woman with four books under contract.

Platform: Kellyann built her author platform in much the same way she pursues any major process or program—with a strategy and a great deal of effort, learning the habits and practices of authors with winning platforms through seminars, workshops, coaches, and books. Kellyann uses social and broadcast media, with over 20 local and national television shows under her belt.

Kellyann also focuses on expanding and maintaining her online presence as e-commerce and social media outlets continue to evolve in the marketing arena. She is developing online products to create additional lead generators. Working with bloggers is key to her author platform; Kellyann worked with 11 popular bloggers to leverage her email list and says her list grew "like wildfire" from this method. Per Kellyann, "Joint venturing, collaborating, and doing guest blog posts was the tipping point for me. My list size tripled after that."

Kellyann's advice to authors: "I can't stress enough my 'Big 3' success generators: Purpose, Determination, and Focus. Keep those elements top of mind—they will keep you going—even when the wheels feel like they are coming off your wagon!"

CHAPTER 6

Using LinkedIn: Not Only an Online Résumé

"No matter how brilliant your mind or strategy, if you're playing a solo game, you'll always lose out to a team."

—Reid Hoffman, creator of LinkedIn

CAROLE'S WORK EXPERIENCE at Addison-Wesley publishing was invaluable in developing the concept of building "strategic alliances." In the era when Silicon Valley was exploding in tech innovation, we aligned publishing efforts with cutting-edge thinkers. We also aligned with a common set of goals to create one profitable corporate press book series after another, leading the pack in book title sales, revising biannually into brand-new editions, and continually growing volume by volume. With or without the Internet (we were only moving atoms back then), it was an effective strategy to link with others who had a built-in audience, addressing their needs and exchanging specialized content.

As publishers we were able to reach a wider audience than corporations could, with approachable prose in book form, well before the era of LinkedIn and online social networking. And it's just as critical today that authors develop and explore mutual goals with a broad list of contacts throughout the manuscript process and after the book is published.

Definition of LinkedIn

LinkedIn is the largest online professional network, starting out with the concept of professional résumé posting and growing well beyond and achieving a global networking reach. Reid Hoffman launched LinkedIn in 2003 based on the idea of "Six Degrees of Separation" and that every human being is actually connected to every other human being by no more than six intermediary people. Once you join LinkedIn you'll see the power in using this concept.

Why LinkedIn Is Important to Authors

One of the major unseen benefits of LinkedIn is that talent scouts are looking for you. Agents, acquisitions editors, TV producers, radio show hosts, and many other talent scouts search LinkedIn in the same manner as employers seek job candidates. In addition to subject matter expertise, we in the publishing industry search for an ability to communicate and reach a large audience, as well as cultivate a dedicated following. This magic combination has always been hard to find, but thanks to LinkedIn, finding talent has become far easier.

Now agents and publishers can find and contact potential authors, discover a single person or organization, and find subject matter experts by just typing in a keyword. This chapter shows ways to use LinkedIn as a magnet for unexpected opportunities, a valuable online location for your author brand, social authority, and professional presence, and a place to gain ground in growing audience and building co-branding affiliations.

The new rules on the web require that to be noticed, you need to be actively engaged in the business of reaching out, growing your author brand, and showcasing your book. As a professional network, LinkedIn is a fantastic platform for growing awareness about you and your writing. It's also free (for basic membership) and easy to use and provides these additional advantages:

Network with millions. More than 259 million people use LinkedIn. It's a well-established and well-recognized global professional network for every type of author. Connect with other authors to announce your book, to share ideas and communities that will support your writing goals, and to find out about events and opportunities.

Connect with more than 100,000 moderated LinkedIn groups. Through membership in groups targeted to your subject matter, you can easily post your book announcements to a large number of professionals who have expressed interest in your subject matter. Your informational posts, discussed later in this chapter, will reach all members in targeted interest groups. Post about your book publication manually, or, as we recommend, through an automated service like HootSuite to automatically send the same post to every relevant group you belong to. This is especially helpful to announce a new blog post quickly and easily. Members of your group generally respond with kudos, advice, and information, and by telling their friends, they can help you reach a larger audience in ways you hadn't imagined. A viral message to friends will expand your announcement far beyond your initial list of contacts.

Connect to organizations and businesses. Many businesses purchase large numbers of books for their employees or clients. People who are connected to you on LinkedIn may be tied to particular companies or industries in ways you're not aware of. For example, a book on using preventative measures to take control of your health could be a perfect title for an insurance company to distribute to their members to help them keep their health-care costs low. And the company could potentially be looking to buy hundreds or thousands of copies of that book.

Rank higher on web searches. Try a Google search on your name from a friend's computer. If you have posted your profile to LinkedIn, your presence on the site will appear near or at the top of the search. The reason is that LinkedIn is a well-respected and trusted site, and therefore its profiles rank highly on search engines like Google.

Control your updates. When you make a change to your profile, such as adding information about your upcoming book, you can use your settings to broadcast this to your whole list of contacts, automatically. All new viewers of your profile, regardless of whether they're in your contacts, will see your book announcement! Your connections will notify you of updates in the same way.

Showcase you résumé. Of course, LinkedIn showcases your experience and accomplishments on your résumé. Your LinkedIn author profile promotes your author brand as a storefront, along with your book image. Your public photo, author profile, and book description add up to essential multiple exposure to your audience.

Collect public "endorsements." These are the short words taken from the "skills" area of your LinkedIn profile. Your contacts are automatically encouraged by LinkedIn to endorse you for special skills you have. LinkedIn also prompts you to endorse others, so every chance you have, endorse others generously and you will find that others do the same in return. The more public endorsements you collect, the more your social authority rises by virtue of the fact that others see power in numbers.

Share public "recommendations." Recommendations on your LinkedIn profile are the best recommendations you can get, as they are posted in public and often show up on searches on your name. Positive recommendations equal their weight in gold in terms of their importance to your author platform. Satisfied clients are generally happy to write a short recommendation for you, so it's appropriate simply to ask for these. Recommendations should be short and have a boost for you right in the first sentence, as people tend to scan these. And when people recommend you, reciprocate.

Creating and Optimizing Your LinkedIn Author Profile

If you are not already among the 259 million people in more than 200 countries who have posted a résumé or biographical description on Linked In, it's easy to start, as we illustrate below. And if you already have a profile on LinkedIn, you can rework it so it's aligned with the author profile and brand you've established on the rest of your platform. It's also easy enough to add information about your book.

LinkedIn is straightforward, and our primer will get you started, but if you wish to read more as you go, top LinkedIn reference books have been published, including books by our clients: Joel Elad's *LinkedIn For Dummies* (Wiley Publishing, Inc.) and Eric Butow and Kathleen Taylor's *How to Succeed in Business Using LinkedIn: Making Connections and Capturing Opportunities on the World's #1 Business Networking Site* (Amacom).

It is critically important to fully complete your LinkedIn profile. Complete profiles appear in more search results on LinkedIn itself, and it's a professional necessity to communicate to your potential audience, colleagues, potential booksellers, agents, editors, and publishers a complete picture of your background and subject matter experience to establish your authority in your field.

Getting Started

When you open your LinkedIn profile page by clicking the Profile tab at the top of the LinkedIn window and selecting Edit Profile, focus on the following:

Photo. To ensure consistency and recognizability, use the same author photo that you included on your author website in Chapter 1. Linked In claims people respond to profiles with photos seven times more often than those without.

Name. Use your name the same way you do in other parts of your author platform: first and last with no variations. Searches depend on the exact same set of letters, so be careful to keep this 100% consistent.

Headline. Your headline is your advertising for your author brand, so be sure to include the identifying term of "author" somewhere in your headline. For example, on LinkedIn, Carole uses the headline "Literary Agent, Author Platform speaker, author and consultant" under her name. You can use Author of [BOOK TITLE], Publisher, or any short form as long as it includes your identity as author and, ideally, your book title. Front and center, your headline is tagged to your name. Your headline appears in search results, on your comments on LinkedIn, in your use of Answers, and everywhere else on the network. Your headline is a signature line that becomes part of how your audience knows you as an author and it also entices and motivates people to go further in reading the content of your profile.

Summary. If your headline is the catch-phrase description of your career, your summary is the quick overview of your career, showing who you are, what you do, and what you've done. It's acceptable to duplicate content you already used in creating the author biography on your book and author websites.

Experience. This is the detailed résumé section of your profile, and you have an opportunity here to go far beyond the traditional chronological list of your employment history. Include everything that proves your subject expertise, including nontraditional roles and projects that do not fit in a conventional résumé. For example, create job titles that fit nonemployment segments of your professional timeline. I often use the self-created title of "Idea Magnet" to show my interest in cutting-edge thought. List your position as author, and then go beyond using some of these possible job titles for yourself:

- **Contributor:** If you regularly contribute to your blog, or other publication or website, include these in the separate position spaces and add a description of your articles and/or posts that you wrote for these.
- **Journalist:** If you write a popular blog.
- **Student:** If you have spent long periods researching or studying a particular topic.

  You can add portfolio items to each entry in the Experience section to enhance your authority. Link to pictures of your book covers, YouTube videos, network television interviews, and presentations. Every site you regularly post to should be included in your profile.

  As in every other part of your author platform, be sure to include your industry keywords in your summary and experience entries. People use keywords to search, so be sure your keywords match *what* people search for. For example, if you are an expert scholar of the Gilded Age of United States history, and you want a publisher to find you, don't refer to "the period after Reconstruction," or simply list the date range of your interest. Include the phrase *Gilded Age* in your description.

List of Publications. Be sure to list all of your publications, including articles. For each publication, you can include:

- Title
- Publication (for articles) or publisher (for books)
- Publication date (month/day/year)
- Publication URL: A link to any useful site on the web for information about this publication. This could be a link to any article

you have published online, your book site (if you have one), or the Wikipedia entry for your bestseller. You can only list one URL here, so make it count!

· Authors: You can recognize any coauthors you have here, especially if they are already on LinkedIn.

· Description: You'll want to have a ready overview paragraph, known as a "blurb," about your book. This can be the descriptive copy your publisher used on Amazon or other online book vendors.

Projects. Consider how you can expand your list of projects to include everything you've worked on that might be relevant to your areas of expertise. Consultants have the freedom to list individual clients one by one, and you can take a similar approach if it presents your work in the best light. Each book, article, and course can be listed as a project. The more projects you list, the broader the perception of your social authority. To add a project, click **Add** at the top of the Projects section. If it makes sense, connect each project with your Occupations; use the **Occupation** drop-down menu. LinkedIn, true to its name, allows a lot of linking between your profile and other parts of your author platform, so be sure to link a project to all relevant websites.

Contact Info: Website and Twitter Links. At the top of your profile, between your headline and summary areas, is a small Edit Contact Info button. Use this to connect your Twitter account to LinkedIn. It also allows you to create three website links. Use the drop-down menu to select from Blog, Personal Website, Company Website, RSS Feed, Portfolio, and Other. We suggest using the Other option to create compelling headlines for these links, encouraging your audience to "Learn About My Book" and "Buy My Book," leading to your Amazon purchase page. Also use one of the links to bring your audience back to your author website where your complete author presentation is fully showcased.

How to Increase LinkedIn Connections

You may already have begun building your LinkedIn connections. If not, search through and invite all colleagues, clients, friends, and associates from your address book. If you have not already uploaded your address book to LinkedIn, it's the best way to build up your LinkedIn connections quickly. In addition, search through others' contacts to find additional people to connect to on LinkedIn.

The sidebar on your LinkedIn home page shows the current size of your network and lists your direct (1st degree) connections and also tells you how many people you theoretically could link to, sometimes numbering in the millions; that gigantic number represents your 1st degree contacts, all the people whom your direct contacts know (2nd degree), plus all the people that your second-level connections know (3rd degree).

Be aware that LinkedIn restricts communications a little bit, depending on how many degrees of separation exist between you and the other person. For connections beyond 1st degree, you will need one of your connections to introduce you (using the LinkedIn Introductions feature) before communicating directly. Or you'll need to introduce yourself, in which case we recommend personalizing your invitation email instead of using LinkedIn's standard invite. As you connect with your peers, consider and suggest opportunities for cross-promotion, such as guest blogs. Build as many connections that are meaningful to your writing as you can.

Finding People on LinkedIn

Building a professional network on LinkedIn is not difficult. With the millions of people already using the network, you won't have to look very far to find your colleagues and friends. LinkedIn makes it easy to locate them.

List all possible places of work or other group affiliations to find people you may know. As you fill out your profile, LinkedIn reviews its database to locate your current and former coworkers, college friends, and the like. Every time you log in, you'll be greeted with the names and photos of three "people you may know," with a link to connect with them.

Email import. Click the **Add Connections** button in the upper right corner of any LinkedIn page (next to your name). The first screen you see is the Address Book import screen. As with many of the other services we've discussed, the import service supports most web-based mailboxes: Gmail, Yahoo Mail, Hotmail, and AOL. They will also pull in Microsoft Outlook address books. Select the people you wish to connect with and send them a note. The import will also identify email addresses that aren't on LinkedIn, and you can invite their participation as well. The weakness of this method is that you cannot customize the invitation for each user, but the convenience may outweigh the less-than-personal greeting. You have the option of following up personally with another message.

Advanced People Search. If you're looking for a single individual you know (or would like to know) on LinkedIn, typing the person's name in the search box at the top of the LinkedIn screen works just fine unless it's a common name with multiple listings. Advanced People Search can help cut through the clutter. If you're looking for a specific contributor for a project, click the **Advanced** link next to the Search box to open the Advanced Search page. Three columns of search criteria appear, but only two columns are available to basic (that is, unpaid) LinkedIn members.

Say you're researching Martian gravity and want to know who might be the best subject matter expert to connect with:

- For title: Type "astrophysicist" in the field. A drop-down menu will appear, labeled Current or Past. Change this to **Current**.
- Relationship: Free members can send messages to people they know (1st Connections), people your first-level connections know (2nd Connections), and members of LinkedIn groups you're part of (see later in the chapter for more on Groups). If you want everyone (not just people you can contact directly), check **3rd + Everyone Else**.
- Industry: Check **Defense & Space, Higher Education, and Research**.
- Click **Search**, and quickly you'll get a pretty big list, ten to a page, sorted by their relationship to you. From this screen, you can view each individual profile and send a message to each person. You can further filter the list with the fields on the left side of the list.

What about those fields in the third column of the Advanced People Search? The gold icon clues you in that you'll need to send LinkedIn some cash to access these fields. Premium membership (discussed later on in this chapter) can be obtained for monthly or annual fees.

For a search like the one described above, you might also try finding people who participate in groups discussing issues in your niche.

How to Join LinkedIn Groups

LinkedIn groups are forums of people with a common interest, and groups are the places on LinkedIn where people post articles, blog updates, advice, and comments. Maximize your presence by joining all groups related to your subject matter; it's easy, free, and bumps up visibility of your author brand and book. Be sure to join groups that reach the target audience related to your book. Visit Carole's LinkedIn profile to see her list of author and publishing group memberships for ideas about which groups to join. Find more groups for your subject matter by searching LinkedIn profiles of people you are already connected to in your field. Among the thousands of varied groups on LinkedIn, find at least a dozen to join and introduce yourself to the group. Generally if you are new to a group, other members will contact you immediately, as everyone is on these groups for the same purpose: to network. Remember, most groups have rules limiting promotion, and the general rule is to introduce yourself and what you have to offer with a book "byline."

Keep the following things in mind when joining and participating in LinkedIn groups:

- LinkedIn limits free members to a maximum of 50 group memberships. Given that you may not know which groups are going to be the most active or fruitful for your activity, you'll want to scope things out. As you edge closer to the 50-group limit, consider what groups you may just want to monitor for activity. Most groups are designated as Open, which means anyone (including the general web-searching public) can visit and read what's happening in a group, but only members can post. If you're already a member of 50 groups and try to add a new one, you'll get a message that you've reached the maximum number of groups. At that point you can choose to leave a group by clicking on the group name within the Groups page and then click the Member button within the group page.
- Once you have joined a group, you can post to it through a single click, forming an immediate audience that helps people to find you and your book. Try to seek out connections for any and all parts of your author platform, including guest blogs, interviews, and guest appearances on others' podcasts. The best strategy to get support is

to give support, that is, show how you can contribute to the success of others' publications or platforms.

- Groups include professional organizations, educational organizations, and businesses, most likely all of which are also seeking co-promotion opportunities. If any of these contacts are willing to buy some quantity of your book to use in courses or support, that early adoption will increase sales and future publishing opportunities for you. These can also lead to custom corporate writing opportunities, as all organizations now seek out strong Internet content writers. You can also ask your groups for names in your area of specialty to review and write an endorsement or foreword for your book.

- Your own postings to your groups should include only professional announcements, such as book release information, reviews, and interviews. Convey information—not advertising, which is considered "spam."

Are You a Top Influencer?

If you want to make an extra commitment to creating your LinkedIn presence, you can become a LinkedIn Top Influencer. This means your discussion has generated the most engagement with members of your groups. If you want to become a master at creating discussions that others comment on, look for models that other Top Influencers use. One example: Reposting a hot current news story about a topic everyone is interested in. In the San Francisco Bay Area, for instance, the America's Cup race tended to be big news. So if your subject pertained to this topic somehow, connections could be made by reposting an article about the race with a meaningful comment showing insight. The article and your comment post attract people who are likely to comment on that news story through your post. Then invite comments that engage people by including added links to other posts that validate your opinion. However, note that the LinkedIn Top Influencer status is fleeting: It's wiped out every Sunday at midnight. If you pursue this option, try to post on Monday mornings. If you want to remain a Top Influencer, you must continuously engage others in discussions in as many groups as possible. Consistently appear as a Top Influencer, and you may get invited to contribute to Pulse (see "Articles to Repost" later in the chapter).

- Be sure to join groups that discuss the topic or product or service your book pertains to. Then be as active as possible in discussions by asking and answering questions. However, don't push your book when you ask or answer questions. Let people see you as an expert and be intrigued enough by your expert comments to click over to your profile. Once a LinkedIn user visits your profile, you have a better chance of steering them to your author and book websites and your LinkedIn company page, which you'll learn more about later in the chapter.
- Use groups to find other writers and experts on the topic, product, or service about which you wrote your book. If you find someone in the same group you want to connect with for potential cross-promotional opportunities, consider adding that person as a connection and/or contact that person through InMail, LinkedIn's internal mail system.

Update Your LinkedIn Profile Regularly

Remember that LinkedIn is a professional network, not a personal one like Facebook, so update your profile and post status updates regularly to keep your search ranking high. Post links to new posts on your blog, repost links to articles (with short comments about their value), write short original posts related to your subject area, and report on events, media mentions of you and your book, speaking engagements, reviews of your book, and guest blog posts. Be sure to post updates as you write your book and keep posting as you launch. Authors generally cheer for other authors, and you'll find LinkedIn author communities to support you, which will become more valuable as time goes on, especially when you need buzz and reviews for your book to be posted on review sites.

> **Side Note:** You can create a LinkedIn company profile page as an option for added exposure. A LinkedIn company page for your book can connect to your book's website. A company page is not a necessary part of your LinkedIn strategy as an author; it's just an "extra" that will show up in Google searches along with your book website.

Articles to Repost

Pulse has replaced the former LinkedIn Today to bring you a customized set of headlines relevant to your career and industry. These stories are a rich source of information for reposting to your author platform. When you repost articles that are of interest to your readership, you become a "curator," sharing valuable information that your audience wants to read and people will thank you and share them. This is a great way to increase your posts beyond what you write in your own words. Reposting information like lists of resources will generally elicit appreciation and yield reposting. The Pulse news feed is also a good way to keep up with your industry and see what your LinkedIn connections are reading and sharing.

You can customize your news feed to select news in additional and related industries of importance to you and also check on the people who are sharing these articles. Here's how:

- Under the Interests tab at the top of your LinkedIn page, click **Pulse**. You'll come to Your News, a batch of stories customized for interests, companies, and industries you are already connected to. Notice the other tabs at the top of this page; reviewing them will further customize Your News.
- Click **Influencer Posts**. Pulse displays the top posts of the last day from their set of contracted celebrity bloggers. Many of these people are household names, others are famous in their niche. Click the All Influencers tab to see who they are, even the ones who didn't post today. These posts appear like business cards, following the same format. There's a featured graphic for the post at the top, followed by the name and photo of the poster. Click the **+Follow** button if you want to see every post from this person. After the post title and date, you'll see the Channel it's in (more on this shortly, but it gives you a sense of the broad category the post fits under). At the bottom of the card are the Social buttons: Page views (in thousands), Likes, Comments, and an arrow to let you share the post with your network.
- Channels are broad categories of Influencer posts and news stories. Channels include perennial topics like Finance and Banking, Higher Education, Law & Government, and Professional Women. There are

also channels like My Startup Story, Big Ideas & Innovation, The Book That Changed Me, and What Inspires Me. If any of these match your interest, click the + sign to follow.

- The All Publishers list is an alphabetical list of news sources for Your News. Look for your trusted sources, clicking on each source name to review its stories before clicking the + sign to follow that source. If you have the time to scan the whole list, you might find some interesting places to write for as well.

Note that before LinkedIn bought the company, Pulse was an independent social-news outfit with mobile apps for Apple iOS, Android, Kindle Fire, and the Nook tablet. These are still available.

LinkedIn Strategies

Our author client Eric Butow, coauthor of *How to Succeed in Business Using LinkedIn*, has summarized the best strategies that authors can use to expose their books to the professional audience on LinkedIn. Note that Butow's strategies, below, involve interactivity among your LinkedIn contacts.

Status reports. When you get updates about your book, such as a speaker event or a link to a great review of your book, be sure to write a "status report" post about it as soon as possible and share it with all LinkedIn users. By sharing with all users, you increase the chances of someone searching for your book topic to find your LinkedIn update and clicking through to your profile.

Create your own group that discusses your book. You may want to do this after you become familiar with LinkedIn and start to get more interest from people in groups you already participate in. Be sure you invite your connections and do things in your group to help promote exclusivity, such as posting articles and links that readers can't find anywhere else. Name the group with the subject matter of your book, then send out a group email as a blind copy to everyone in your address book, giving reasons for joining. Keep members engaged with weekly announcements and fresh discussion questions.

Ask for recommendations from people who say they enjoyed reading your book. With Eric's books, he's found that some people who want to connect with him say specifically that they want to do so because they enjoyed one of his books. Help your connections in turn by recommending them. Remember, recommendations count more than simple endorsements. Your credibility is enhanced by each reader saying something you've written has impacted his or her life in a positive way.

LinkedIn Ads

Use LinkedIn ads to promote your blog and the publication of your book. You'll notice rectangular boxes in the right sidebar, labeled "Ads by Linked In members." You can create these types of ads for any purpose and target an audience in several ways.

- Geography: By continent
- Job Function: a somewhat shorter list of occupations than in the Advanced People Search, but some good choices
- Seniority: target everyone from entry level to the C-Suite
- Industry: another broad range of choices

Before your book is released, you may want to sign up potential media reviewers and academics to use your book in classes. Create your base ad, then come up with various text and image combinations that you can use to customize the base ad and reach your targets (LinkedIn allows up to 15 variations for the same campaign). The ads are simple to create: a 25-character headline and 75 characters for description and call to action. You can point them to your website or a page on LinkedIn. Add a thumbnail image of your book cover to draw the eye.

On the next page, you can target your audience on the categories listed above, and even more narrow groupings: school (as specific as you like), skills, gender, age, and also specific LinkedIn groups.

LinkedIn will charge you only each time a LinkedIn user clicks on your ad, or based on visibility (per 1,000 impressions). This ad can link to another website, such as your book blog. Costs vary depending on the budget you want to set for each advertising campaign, and as with Facebook (described in the previous chapter), you can set a time limit on your campaign or run it indefinitely. You have the option to collect leads, where people who click on the ad can opt in to a follow-up contact from you.

Get more information by moving the mouse pointer over **Business Services** in the menu bar and then clicking **Advertise** in the menu.

Best Practices of LinkedIn Networking

Introduce yourself with a factual brief statement. People are inundated with information, so the concise introduction has become critical. Find a way to condense who you are and what you do into a minimal number

LinkedIn page for author client Mark Goulston, author of #1 internationally best-selling *Just Listen*.

of words. For example, many people don't understand what a literary agent is, so by saying "I connect authors to publishers and publishers to authors," the lightbulb turns on. Present yourself with your name, URL, high point of your career background, and mention one successful or upcoming project. Then the door is open to ask your question or state what you're seeking.

Post useful content to groups. Make sure that your public postings are informative and open doors to knowledge that is useful. The best way to get a reposting of your work is to find valuable lists, insights, or facts that further the knowledge base of your readers. As long as you include other information, it's okay to tell people what you are doing, too (publications, events, and the like).

Express appreciation to those who help or comment favorably. Always send an appreciation message to people who've given you their time in any way or who may have referred you to one of their contacts. Remembering someone in a "thank you" keeps you top of mind and increases your value when someone asks about you.

Find ways to help others. Always be on the lookout for how you can help someone, that is, when you hear of opportunities that might interest them, and you'll often find they'll reciprocate.

Benefits of LinkedIn Premium Accounts

Your account at LinkedIn is free, but paid upgrades are also available. The added features aren't necessary for basic author platform use, but here's a note on added features:

InMail. Send messages to anyone on LinkedIn without asking for an introduction.

Profile Organizer. Organize profiles in folders, add contact info and other details to profiles.

Unlimited advanced search. With a free account you can only search up to 100 profiles. With a Premium account, you get access to more profile information when you conduct an Advanced People Search.

Access to the full list of Who's Viewed Your Profile. Author client Joel Elad, author of *LinkedIn For Dummies*, which includes step-by-step tutorials on the basic and advanced uses of LinkedIn, suggests having access to the full list of people who have viewed your profile, noting that as an agent, the "list is useful to me to contact authors who are actively searching for agents. If someone views me and I'm interested in their profile, I will always contact that person who viewed me."

Checklist, Step 6: LinkedIn

➤ Join LinkedIn.
➤ Optimize your author brand profile with photo, name, and keywords consistent with all parts of your author platform.
➤ Upload your address book contacts into LinkedIn.
➤ Grow your contacts list and post updates.
➤ Join groups and post your news.
➤ Seek joint book-marketing opportunities.

Success Spotlight: Waterside Client Ed Tittel (edtittel.com)

- 100+ trade books as writer/contributor
- 1,000,000+ copies sold

Beginnings: As far back as junior and senior years of high school, Ed enjoyed writing. Then after graduate school, he entered the workforce in high-tech, circa 1981. At Hart Printing in Austin in 1986, they took over a Macintosh-oriented magazine they'd been printing. Ed's pride and pleasure started with, in his words, the "princely remuneration" of ten cents a word. They agreed to his writing articles, at the rate of a couple articles a month for the *Macazine*, and then *MacWeek, LAN Times, ComputerWorld*, etc.

His employer at the time offered a bonus for each article that appeared in any computer trade publication. He placed 18 articles that first year with 18 bonuses. The next year, the company amended the program to limit the bonuses to one per quarter and required that articles include mention of their products and services.

His books: By the early 1990s, Ed coauthored with Bob LeVitus their first project together, *Stupid PC Tricks*, which became a bestseller for its publisher, Addison-Wesley. Ed notes, "Our project editor for that book was Carole Jelen, who would go on to become my lifelong friend and literary agent today."

After six more books, by 1993, Ed was writing For Dummies books. He was working for Novell, who decided to close their Austin operations in 1994, so Ed decided to become a freelance writer.

How he came up with his book idea: In 1996–97, luck struck for Ed while developing courses for the American Research Group. In preparing those courses, Ed realized that IT professionals who already knew and understood IT certification didn't need the huge doorstop-sized books that are so typical of full-length study guides. The lightbulb went off when he realized that a product was needed that was short and focused. From this insight, the Exam Cram series—now the second best-selling computer book series ever, behind only For Dummies—was born. The series was launched as shrink-wrapped "Core Four Pack" books; these initial offerings sold like hotcakes (over 10,000 copies a month in their heyday). Coriolis Publishing started the series, and then Pearson bought it and continues to publish the series to this day. Ed's all-time best-selling title is *HTML For Dummies* (coauthored with Chris Minnick), now on its 14th edition.

Platform: Ed is the consummate networker on LinkedIn. He also blogs eight times a week, writes dozens of certification-focused articles, creates custom publications, publishes corporate white papers and technical briefs, conducts webinars, and remains involved with the For Dummies series.

Ed's advice to authors: "Start with a great idea you believe in, write your manuscript, and use all 14 steps in *Buildng Your Author Platform* to build your platform and audience! My own platform is based on using the social networks in this method in addition to blogging, training, writing articles, and more. All of the pieces add up to an author's successful presence in a busy publishing climate."

CHAPTER 7

Inform, Educate, and Entertain: The Power of Personal Appearances

"Listeners like lists. . . . The rule of three is a fundamental principle in writing in humor and in a Steve Jobs presentation."

—*Carmine Gallo,* Forbes *columnist, author of*
The Presentation Secrets of Steve Jobs

S TEVE JOBS BECAME THE BIGGEST INFLUENCE in Carole's professional life when she worked as the West Coast editor acquiring books for Addison-Wesley in the late 1990s. It was amazing to have the rare opportunity to go inside Apple headquarters in the early days and witness Steve Jobs' mesmerizing presentations in the Apple headquarters auditorium in Cupertino, California. It was a visceral experience of the power of speaking to an audience with emotional force and tapping into the dreams of each person. There is an immediate and powerful force that was built into the speeches of Steve Jobs. He carried the inspiring message "follow your dreams" on the body of ideas and technology. His personal charisma and drive, combined with a well-crafted message with the audience's needs foremost, was destined to shape the wired world we live in now. Luckily you, too, can witness these inspiring talks, now available to everyone to watch on YouTube.

Before he even reached the stage, the audience could feel the power of anticipating Jobs' spoken presentations at Apple. Through the premium auditorium sound system, a song like the Pointer Sisters' "I'm So Excited" would vibrate the huge room long before Steve even walked out. By the time he took to the stage, the cheering was so loud it drowned out the music. Jobs' speeches had entertainment and drama; they drew in an audience far and wide. Today the effects of these speeches are legendary.

All of these now-famous speeches had a well-thought-out and practiced method, all of which are beautifully documented in Carmine Gallo's book *The Presentation Secrets of Steve Jobs.* In this book, Gallo points out a little known fact, that Steve Jobs was nervous when he started out as a speaker in 1978. Jobs understood the power of personal presentation, believed in what he did, and then honed his speaking skills, practiced many times, and stayed with it, until he became regarded as one of the most charismatic and persuasive modern business leaders.

All of us who have a passion for what we do and take the time to think through the quality of how we communicate it are also able to reach out and touch our audience in a memorable and meaningful way. In interviewing the Waterside author clients for this book, it became clear that the most striking traits that all of these successful authors have in common are a passion for their work and a commitment to work tirelessly at building an audience for their message.

Short Talk vs. Long Speech

The good news for authors is that the era of necessity for the long lectern speech is over. Now people don't generally expect or desire an hour-long speech. In fact, with attention spans ever shortening, most audiences now prefer short talks. Most people are not naturally gifted public speakers, and audiences generally only remember about three points from a speech anyway. As a result, the construct of a short talk is preferred and has gained widespread acceptance.

The proof of the wide popularity of short talks is found in the rise of TED talks. TED was founded in California as a series of conferences owned by the nonprofit Sapling Foundation, whose slogan is "Ideas Worth Spreading." TED started out collecting short speeches about Technology, Entertainment, and Design, but that sapling has grown to include more than 1,500 short talks with a widening range of topics. You can watch any of these talks on the TED website (ted.com). The TED conferences have given rise to a new art form, the well-crafted short speech, in the process bringing cutting-edge authors and thinkers to ever-wider audiences.

To get an idea of the power of this type of talk, search ted.com by topic or by speaker (the 2005 Steve Jobs commencement speech, "How to Live Before You Die," has over 11 million views). It's likely you'll become mesmerized and inspired by how memorable a single idea presented well can be. The common trait among these speakers is passion, spoken by a range of people, from the famous to the unknowns.

Apply to speak at a TED conference and your name, talk, and video could appear alongside many famous people. Among our author clients who have given TED talks are David Meerman Scott ("The Need to Explore") and Gaurav Tekriwal (TED-Ed "Why India Should Be Proud of Vedic Math"). These talks give speakers instant global social authority and an almost celebrity-type speaking status.

For local speaking, check into the TEDx program (.ted.com/tedx), which gives you the same visibility on a smaller scale. Here locally, we have a Bay Area TEDx conference, so check your local TEDx speaking opportunities and apply to speak at them. Our author client John C. Havens delivered an October 2013 talk for TEDxIndianapolis called "Shift the Impact of Modern Technology." TEDx events are created by local organizers independently of TED.

The good news is that you don't need to speak at a TED conference to give a TED-caliber talk. As an author you can use TED talk guidelines to create a model speech to give at any event; our client Lynn Johnson created her talk "Igniting a Passionate Revolution" in the TED style. Ranging from 5 to 18 minutes, a TED talk is based on a stone tablet of "TED Commandments":

1. Thou Shalt Not Simply Trot Out Thy Usual Shtick
2. Thou Shalt Dream a Great Dream, or Show Forth a Wondrous New Thing, or Share Something Thou Hast Never Shared Before
3. Thou Shalt Reveal Thy Curiosity and Thy Passion
4. Thou Shalt Tell a Story
5. Thou Shalt Freely Comment on the Utterances of Other Speakers for the Sake of Blessed Connection and Exquisite Controversy

6. Thou Shalt Not Flaunt Thine Ego: Be Thou Vulnerable; Speak of Thy Failure as well as Thy Success
7. Thou Shalt Not Sell from the Stage: Neither Thy Company, Thy Goods, Thy Writings, nor Thy Desperate Need for Funding. Lest Thou Be Cast Aside into Outer Darkness
8. Thou Shalt Remember All the While: Laughter Is Good
9. Thou Shalt Not Read Thy Speech
10. Thou Shalt Not Steal the Time of Them Who Follow Thee

Audiences love this style, and it is well worth creating your own TED-style talk on video as a valuable addition to your author platform. In addition to your own sites and networks, there are a wide range of places on the web that house author talks, some of which are mentioned later in this chapter. Video opportunities are also covered in Chapter 10.

In this chapter, we show you how to broaden your author platform by speaking, covering options from speaking in person to teaching and training, along with some basic principles to integrate into the classic short, memorable book presentation.

> Look up Mary Roach (maryroach.net), a writer whose speaking strategy is well worth checking out. She weaves an unusual blend of humor and popular science into her books and has spun out a stellar author platform. She makes multiple personal appearances right before each of her books is published, even securing spots on *The Daily Show with Jon Stewart*, in an unusual category of pop science books.

Personal Appearance Options

In working with more than a thousand authors over the last several decades, it's become clear that some authors love, crave, and show talent for public speaking and some do not. The in-person appearance transmits your enthusiasm for your subject matter as the most memorable way to connect with and gain followers. Thanks to the rise of a huge Internet audience, authors can deliver short talks in a number of audience settings, from in-person to online video. If you have the excitement and passion to appear personally in public, we highly recommend this! If you do not, the options below are also very powerful, so choose at least one of the options offered. Your audience needs to experience your persona along with your knowledge, insight, and expertise, and the only way to connect on this level is for your audience to see you speak.

With a crowded list of published books, your author platform is what makes your book stand out and your author brand thrive. Successful authors prepare a personal appearance strategy in advance, and a whole subcategory of author publicists has sprung up to assist with this very need. There are great publicists available if you have the cash, but many authors understand their work and audience well enough to avoid spending thousands of dollars on these experts.

Advantages of Live Personal Appearances

Personal appearances are a proving ground for your authority and carry immediate rewards. When you appear in person you can make eye contact and meet and greet your audience before and after your talk, making more of a personal connection than you would via an online webinar or video. Among the other advantages:

Create viral interest. When you touch your audience speaking in person, you increase chances of creating conversations about your book.

Ready audience to buy your book. Your upcoming book sells better when there is already an audience in place, interested in you and what you have to say. That's why publishing companies search for authors who already have a teaching, training, and/or speaking background, preferably with large audiences.

Learn the needs of your audience. There's no better way of hearing what your audience likes, needs, and wants than hearing it directly from them. Interacting with the people you're writing for, whether you're teaching, training, or simply speaking, helps you write a better, more targeted book.

Build up your mailing list for future book announcements. In connection with speaking events, it's customary either to ask attendees to sign in with their email addresses or advance register for your talk online with email addresses.

Increase your chances of additional media. Speaking in person increases your chances of being photographed, filmed, or quoted across a variety of media. This can go even better if scouts are in the audience. As a part of my acquisitions editorial job at Addison-Wesley, I attended industry conferences and speeches on a regular basis and stood in line to make direct contact with the speaker, which often was the only route to meeting that person.

Sell copies of your book. After talks, most authors tell the audience that books are for sale at the back of the room. Alternatively, some authors fold the price of their books into the price of their talks so that each attendee finds a copy of the book on their chair. Of course, books that are signed live by authors at the end of a speech are especially in demand. Just attend a Book Expo America (BEA) conference in New York to witness lines as long as a city block for signed books!

Pay nothing. Live speaking does not cost the author anything except time and travel, and teaching and training can generate money enough for some to make a living.

Record/repurpose video. Your personal appearances do triple duty: engaging your audience, creating buzz, and using the opportunity for videotaping for future use on all locations of your author platform. Some events and panels are streamed live online, but most are recorded for showing evidence of your enthusiastic audience, so be sure that the recording shows applause and engagement.

Personal Appearances Strategy

Start making your personal appearances one-on-one. Don't wait until you are in front of a group; start to tell everyone you know and meet about your book! This is not a sales pitch; it's an expression of enthusiasm, telling people what you are writing about and showing how you are impacting others in their lives, and it's great practice for group speaking.

Get people excited, including friends, family, clients, associates, colleagues, coworkers, and online contacts, and they will likely tell their friends. Word of mouth, as we all know, has the biggest influence of all. People love telling about something that helped them or a story that entertained them.

Authors and what they are writing is pretty fascinating to people, so mention your writing freely—at events, on the road, even while standing in line. For example, I personally love what I do, and my enthusiasm for helping authors build a platform has now gotten the interest and attention of my friends in retail, sales, and just about any profession. The reason? Everyone with a message now needs to build a platform or risk anonymity. If you find that universal interest or need in your audience and meet that need with unique information or coverage in your book, you'll find ready listeners.

Next, target a group to present to, either in person or online. You can start small and then work up to a larger audience at your comfort level. Below are the options that most of our author clients use for online and live speaking and training. We recommend a mixture of options that fit your natural instincts so that you are at your most confident during all appearances.

Personal Appearance Opportunities

Teaching, online or in person. As noted earlier, publishers seek talented subject matter experts among teachers and professors, many of whom are under "publish or perish" pressures. Interaction in the classroom and exposure to the questions and problems expressed by students creates an instant window of understanding your audience needs.

Speaking, online or in person. In live presentations you can underscore the value of your book by presenting your knowledge in real time. When you appear in person, you also have the option of including your book as required reading for purchase or including it in the price of admission.

Many businesses, organizations, and associations, when seeking speakers for conferences and meetings, look for published or soon-to-be published authors with a proven body of knowledge. Seek out speaking engagements at the following places:

- Panels at industry conferences. Search the Lanyrd, Plancast, and Conferensum websites to investigate potential speaking opportunities at conferences and events.
- Local consulting/speaking at businesses.
- Schools and colleges.

- Book club groups.
- Trade shows. Your publisher can arrange for you to speak on a panel and/or appear at an in-booth signing. Look into BEA, held in New York each year.
- Writing and publishing conferences.
- Bookstores love to bring in authors to speak about their books either in-store or off-site in an auditorium.
- Local service clubs. Rotary, Lions Club, Toastmasters International, and Chambers of Commerce all seek speakers for meetings.
- Business networking groups, such as Le Tip, Business Networking International (BNI), and Local Business Network (LBN).
- Trade associations. The National & Professional Trade Association Directory shows conventions, meetings, and trade show dates for thousands of trade associations. Also consider the Directory of Association Meeting Planners.
- Speaker Services that charge a fee to find engagements include speaker services.com and speakerzone.com.

TV and Internet Interview Opportunities

Major broadcast television is ideal exposure, of course, but other potential appearance opportunities await on television and the Internet. Following is a list of some of the many options our author clients use in building their author platforms.

Book TV interviews (booktv.org) is on C-SPAN2 and covers BEA. Ideally you or your publisher can arrange a book signing at BEA, so there would be a chance of appearing on *Book TV*, too.

Local TV interviews. Check your local stations for interview opportunities at local talk shows.

BookTelevision (booktelevision.com). This Canadian specialty channel broadcasts shows relating to books, literature, and other media.

Fresh Fiction (freshfiction.com/GMT) has a listing of local TV stations that interview authors.

American Library Association. For a listing of librarians who interview authors on television in a variety of cities, check out ala.org/tools /librarians-who-interview-authors-television.

For more resources, search on keywords "books and TV" and "television author interview" to find local listings that apply to you, and contact these venues to build up your televised speaking list.

Online "Events." Often people organize "virtual" gatherings when they have shared interests. Google Hangouts is great for this, and you may consider starting an event of your own as we plan to do for the launch of this book. (See "Google Hangouts" in Chapter 4.) As you join groups on Facebook and LinkedIn, watch for announcements on events and join in. Check for meetings or events by location and topic and geographic location.

For more speaking possibilities, see our chapters on audio (Chapter 9) and video (Chapter 10).

Best Practices for Teaching and Training

The most fundamental step in building your author platform is intrinsically tied to the success of your book: Know your audience! Audience needs and preferences drive interest and sales of your book, so it makes basic sense to try to direct decisions based on reader preferences. The more time you spend researching and understanding your audience, the better. In fact, a good revenue source from our agency's published author base is training, and for good reason: Authors who are teachers know best and deliver on audience needs. Experts who teach also have organized their content into lessons that correspond to chapters.

Some training organizations require a college degree, but most require no credentials, other than a proven ability to communicate effectively. Many of our author clients who are also trainers agree that the easiest way to create a course—to teach either online or live in a class setting— is to use the steps below, starting with short courses and then building from there.

Create a single short course. Use the subject matter of your book to create a series of numbered segments. Your book's chapter titles can serve as an outline for a single course. For example, we've organized this book into 14 discrete steps to build your author platform, each of which we will teach as an expanded unit for a course, webinar, teleseminar, or talk.

Write out the presentation points with visuals for each. You can use the subheads of your chapter organization, then find visual slides to accompany each point, preferably that utilize very little text. Avoid boring presentations that simply require you to read slides! Liven up your points with interesting visual background to give your audience a fresh point of view. The term "edutainment" summarizes how to get to the heart of an audience. For example, we like to flash the visual "Don't Be Anonymous," showing why authors need to care, before showing them any how-to steps. One effective visual I use is from a Sourcebooks button I got at BEA, with a rock band drawing of Shakespeare and the caption "Authors are my Rockstars."

Vary the presentation. As you run through your points, make your presentation as dynamic as possible. Use anecdotes, insert short videos, ask a live group for a show of hands, or do an exercise.

Make your opening and closing remarks memorable, so that you'll be quoted in the media and social networks if possible. Ensure you end your presentation with some take-away about your subject matter.

Rehearse and rehearse again. Ask your friends for feedback, and if needed, use your iPad or iPhone as a streaming teleprompter if you're prone to forgetting lines. Use Teleprompt+ for iPad, Android Prompter, or one of the many other teleprompting apps available for tablets and smartphones.

Publicize your course. Get the word out on your author website. Our authors add events plugin calendars to their sites, since it's the clearest way to show events dates to mark on your own calendar. The Events Calendar or Event Organiser displays your course events and links to registration. See Chapter 1 for information on installing these WordPress plugins.

Teach a short course. Your options are wide here, as you can teach a course on your own by choosing from the options below. Or you can teach for an online university, course provider, or your publisher with a seminar branch, such as Hay House hayhouse.com/event_search .php?format_id=19,31&is_browse_search=1&search_or_results=results &searchType=browse (hayhouse.com). Some authors teach on author-related cruises as well.

As a news producer for Associated Press Television, John Carucci conducts studio and live interviews for red carpets and news events, and writes and edits television scripts. He also works on webinars, webcasting events, and PowerPoint presentations. As someone who has watched a massive number of online classes, John warns against creating a boring, underproduced course. He says the best courses get to the point quickly, use a time limit of about 20 minutes, and have a clearly laid-out structure and format: "The success of a webinar depends on holding your audience's attention. So have a structure and keep time to a minimum. As a speaker, it's important to stay on point. Make sure you adhere to the time constraints and understand that you can't teach them all you know in that short time."

Our client Nigel French is a designer, author, and trainer who suggests choosing models of speakers you like and emulating that style (he likes the styles of BBC Radio 4 and *This American Life*). Nigel suggests that you "bring a new angle to your topic and make the content as real-world as possible. For a how-to, start at the end so that you can demonstrate what will be achieved so that your audience knows it's worth the effort."

Some fiction writers teach on the topic of the writing process and publish books on this topic. See Stephen King's book *On Writing: A Memoir of the Craft* as an example.

The Simple Course Format

Here's a practical, basic format that our author clients use whether teaching online or in person.

Before the Presentation

- Show up before your audience for a sense of control and confidence, and to test any equipment you're using for your presentation.
- Take time to make personal contact with a simple hello as people arrive.

During the Presentation

- When you introduce yourself, make sure everyone is able to hear you. Tell your audience your talk will be about 30 minutes, including accepting questions for the last 10 minutes.

- Deliver your talk, with your three major points. Speak slowly, leave time for pauses, and if possible project visuals on a screen behind you. Remember to use stories and anecdotes to illustrate points.

After the Presentation

- As you close, offer follow-up information or show how to get access to your slides. Many authors offer a slide at the end of their presentation showing how to follow up and often provide a link to an online survey. A simple three-question survey can give you valuable insight into making your course better as well as positive testimonials to post on your website.
- Remain at the back of the room to sign books while a separate person handles the purchase transactions.

Teaching and Training Strategy

Start small. Even if you create a couple of short courses, your author platform will be enhanced. Ideally, try to present material either online or live during the months leading up to the publication of your book.

Get Speaking Practice

One easy way to start cultivating a live audience is by joining meetup .com. On this site you can find local face-to-face meetups, bringing together enthusiasts of many different stripes to talk about a common passion on just about any topic. You can join existing meetups or easily start your own. For each existing group, contact the group organizer or first attend a meeting to meet your audience.

If you're in or near an urban area, there may be dozens of small Toastmasters groups (Toastmasters International: toastmasters.org) within a few miles of home. Check their website to find a chapter of this nonprofit organization that brings together people for the purpose of helping members improve their communication and public speaking skills.

Types of Online Teaching and Training

Webcasts, teleseminars, and webinars are the primary ways to deliver online teaching and training.

Webcast. A webcast is an Internet broadcast that uses live-streaming video technology to reach many simultaneous listeners/viewers at once. You can record a webcast to replay and repurpose throughout your author platform. The disadvantage is that you won't be connecting directly with your audience.

Teleseminar. A real-time telephone seminar that includes interaction with students. The advantage is that a free conference call line enables you to interact with your students and have a robust question-and-answer session. The disadvantage is that while you can link to recordings of a teleseminar, you lose the interactivity—unless you have the energy to repeat the seminar!

Webinar. A webinar is a web-based seminar. Hundreds of these are posted every week across a variety of subject areas. This is the best online teaching option because webinars offer live, real-time interaction with your audience. Your webinar can also be posted after the fact on all parts of your author platform. Setting up a webinar is a little more complex than creating a webcast or a teleseminar, but the process has been made far simpler with software created to organize your webinar, as you'll see below.

Creating a Webcast

You can create your own live webcast from home by using technology similar to what's used for concerts and large events. A webcast is a much smaller event that employs a free live-streaming website and a digital or web camera. Before choosing to create a webcast, check out various webcast channels and find ones that have the look and feel of the final result you want to have.

What do we mean by "streaming"? In the early days of web audio and video, you had to download a complete file before any of it would play on your computer. So you would click on a three-minute video clip, wait for it to download . . . and then you could see it. Streaming technologies allow media to start playing almost immediately while the rest of the file continues to load. Live streaming allows a speaker or musician to perform in one place, with camera and microphone connected to the Internet, and be seen by anyone with a web browser.

Once you're ready to move forward, the first step in creating your custom live-streaming website account is to log into a live-streaming website like Justin.tv, Ustream.com, or Livestream.com, as of this writing the three leading Webcast sites. On these sites, you are directed to create a channel where your audience is able to see you and your live webcasts. Visitors to the site are able to find information about your webcast, such as updates about your schedule, and see your archive of previous webcasts. You'll be asked to include a title for your channel and a description of you and your broadcast, as well as some keyword tags. When you have your channel ready, publicize it by adding your webcast link to all parts of your author platform.

Choose a location in your home with a neutral background and good lighting and do a few dry runs in front of the camera to get comfortable with how you look and sound. When it comes time for your live webcast, log in to your channel and press the **Go Live!** button at the top right corner of Justin.tv or Ustream (or **Post** if you are using Livestream). At all three sites, your live broadcast can be recorded and linked to from any other site. Each service also provides pretty good help in how to get started, though the UStream videos (like this live demo: ustream.tv/recorded/16851190) may be the best.

As you do more webcasts, you can opt to add interactive features, such as live questions and answers, polls, tests, and surveys.

How to Create a Teleseminar

The teleseminar is by far the easiest way to connect with your audience in real time. With a telephone and a free conference line such as those offered at freeconferencecall.com, you can teach your course as a telephone workshop in a live audio-only format. Teleseminars are perfect for having the interaction of a live audience while eliminating the time and costs associated with classroom instruction. A teleseminar also gets you maximum impact in 30-minute blocks.

Students attending your teleseminar only need access to the teleconferencing service and, of course, a phone line. This is a medium that works fine for telephone conferences alone, but you can also use your computer to monitor who's attending the conference.

There are a lot of services available that will allow you to host a tele-seminar on a free conference line but will charge for webinar hosting, sometimes with charges tied to the number of participants.

How to Create a Webinar

A webinar gives you the most control, interactivity, and reuse options, so we highly recommend using it as one of the tools on your author platform. The webinar requires a few more steps than a webcast or a teleseminar but is well worth the effort for how it engages your audience. Webinar participants need an Internet connection, a computer, and access to web-conferencing software, and they can dial into the webinar through their computer or phone line.

GoToMeeting is a web-conferencing service that costs around $49 a month, with a 30-day free trial. It's well worth the cost to use this service in the three months leading up to the publication of your book. Afterward, you can make extra money with paid webinars. You can have up to 25 people connecting to your webinar. If you expect many more connections, you can upgrade to a $99-a-month package that permits 100 people to connect.

For a webinar course, we recommend the short course at 30 minutes. Remember to schedule your webinar when your audience is most likely to attend. Business-oriented webinars often take place around lunch hour, while consumer-oriented topics run after dinnertime. Generally, you'll be talking into a headset while slides are being shown on the web. Practice your delivery and timing well before making your first webinar. We cover this further in the video chapter (Chapter 10).

Publicize your webcasts, teleseminars, and webinars on your author and book websites, and social networks, and through your targeted email lists of followers to draw as many people as possible.

Types of Live Teaching

There are as many options in teaching live as there are in teaching online, from short courses to long, from local venues to large auditoriums. If you are not already teaching in person, begin with one small course and grow from there. It's always easiest to start with local opportunities. Check with continuing education courses, community centers, coaching and consulting opportunities at professional organizations, book clubs and bookstores, and corporate and training companies.

A couple of online businesses can help you organize classes, and you can even get paid for teaching them. Both of these sites offer writing-related courses, among a variety of topics:

Dabble (teach.dabble.co) is about one-time, live classes in your hometown. For students, Dabble is a low-cost, informal way to learn about topics they are interested in. Instead of investing a lot of time and money taking a college-level master gardening course, they can come to Dabble and talk to someone who can help them assess whether they have what it takes to start a backyard vegetable garden. As a teacher, you can propose a class to Dabble and set your date, time, venue, and fee. When your class is approved, they will list your class on their website, handle all the registration stuff, offer you some ideas for developing your course, and transfer the fees to your bank (they will, of course, take a percentage of the total fee). Whether you want to establish yourself as an expert, bulk up your résumé, or get new clients in the door, Dabble can help.

Speakers bureau listing for author client Aaron McDaniel, author of *The Young Professional's Guide to the Working World.*

Skillshare (skillshare.com) is more focused on "project-based" video courses online, but also hosts live classes (mostly in New York City). For example, you can take an introductory web design course for $40 that consists of 56 videos, ranging in length from 6 to 40 minutes. According to Skillshare, "Anyone can teach. It's a great way to share your knowledge, build your brand, and make your community a better place." As a teacher, your main task is to prepare a "project guide" or course curriculum, get it approved, and then record your videos. Skillshare offers recommendations on software and equipment, and also offers guidelines on class development. Skillshare also provides a discount code to include on your website; students who enroll in your course with the referral code sign up for less, and you get 85% of the fee (otherwise, you get 70%).

Live Speaking Strategy

Speak live to groups as often as possible to grow your audience before your book is published. Our author client Ray Anthony, coauthor of *Killer Presentations with Your iPad: How to Engage Your Audience and Win More Business with the World's Greatest Gadget* (McGraw-Hill), suggests that regardless of where you give your speech, the following format gives polish and a professional framework to any author's talk and can be customized to fit your needs.

The Simple Author Short Speech Format

Visuals: Two foam boards, 2′ × 3′, one with photo of author, one with photo of book, both on easels. Before and during your talk, the visuals serve as visual reference, frame, and backdrop.

Introduction. Have someone who knows you and your book introduce you, holding the book up in her hand as she mentions some key points or tidbits in your book that won't be duplicated in your speech.

Presentation. Your author talk should focus on three points in your book without focusing on yourself.

Relate each of the three points to someone else who helped you with the book, which makes you very likeable rather than self-aggrandizing.

Highlight the book without pitching it. An example of doing that is to say, "My good friend Sally Q gave me excellent insights that I incorporated into Chapter 4 that covers . . . Here are some powerful ideas she shared with me that I put in my book . . ."

Periodically refer to something in the book that is a key part of your presentation.

Reference someone whose comments were quoted in the book.

Give great insights into the writing of the book behind the scenes.

When you talk about your book, you do so in an indirect way that communicates specific, useful ideas, strategies, and information that the audience will appreciate.

Closing. The same person who introduced you should make a closing remark suggesting that the audience meet you and "pick up" the book in the back of the room (don't use the word "buy"). If there is a discount or freebie it should be mentioned here. If it's a nonprofit, it should be mentioned if a percentage of the sales are going to that organization. You can also raffle a copy or two of the book. As the speaker, you should delegate the handling of the money, focusing your attention on signing purchased copies and speaking to people

Regardless of the type of personal appearance you choose, be sure to connect with your audience on a one-to-one basis in person or through teaching courses for maximum impact.

Checklist, Step 7: Personal Appearances

➤ Organize your subject matter into teachable lists.
➤ Plan your mix of live and online personal appearances in advance of your publication date.
➤ Create and deliver a short course or series of courses.
➤ Record and videotape each appearance for placement on sites and networks.
➤ Give live talks and connect with readers afterward.
➤ Attend industry conferences for networking.
➤ List your personal appearances in your media kit on your websites and on all parts of your author platform.

Success Spotlight: Waterside Client Jay Elliot
(jayelliot.net)

- 2 books: *Leading Apple with Steve Jobs: Management Lessons from a Controversial Genius*, and *The Steve Jobs Way: iLeadership for a New Generation* (coauthored with William L. Simon)
- 28 languages
- 1,000,000+ copies in print worldwide

Beginnings: Jay was raised in California on a dairy ranch on the Monterey Bay, milking cows twice a day from age eight on, which was not very exciting as a teenager. Says Jay, "Being raised on the ranch coast of California didn't qualify me with a mastery of subject most people have." Jay attended a state college with a scholarship for sports accomplishments and graduated with a mathematics major. He went on to get accepted to Boalt Law School at UC Berkeley, where he took his first computer programming course. By surprise, he realized he had an aptitude for math and got an A++ on a test. Immediately he was recruited as a software programmer by IBM.

Jay met Steve Jobs in a café in Los Gatos, California. They started talking and Steve almost hired Jay on the spot. Jay went to work for Apple as Vice President of Administration, where he managed all the company's administrative functions (real estate, planning, HR, education, IT), reporting directly to Steve Jobs for five years.

Immersed in new ideas for the future, Jay helped formulate Apple culture. His group became the most creative group in the company because he realized he was creating a corporation of the future, one that had never existed before.

Jay says, "I had a passion and energy for start-up culture. Back in 1988, I was asked to write a book on Apple full of insight." He later went to Waterside, where his books were launched into global success.

Jay had "no idea" his book would become a bestseller and was shocked at how well it did. In 2010 he was invited by Adobe to give a speech on entrepreneurship. He was shocked and surprised that he was mobbed by audience members after the talk! Hundreds tried to get to him after the talk to meet him personally.

Jay's advice to authors: Create passion doing what you love, and deliver a message you want to tell.

Jay Elliot's final word on author platform building: "I respond to each email immediately. Once you write your book, if a reader contacts you, that is the most important person in the world. Apple was about users. Ask [your readers] questions. They are your users, and it's why Apple was so successful, since you have a user platform. It's all about the user experience."

CHAPTER 8

Create Your Article Bank: Original, Excerpted, Repurposed Variations

"New media is like a megaphone. It amplifies your ability to reach more people."

—*Mark Batterson, author of* Soul Print *and* The Circle Maker

IT'S NO SURPRISE THAT SOME of our successful author clients began careers by writing for traditional print magazines and newspapers and then grew into top-selling book authors; it's a natural progression and sound strategy to grow from writing shorter to longer pieces. Some clients are book authors as an adjunct to a successful syndicated newswriting career, and some write for smaller publications with huge audiences like our author client Eva Shaw does in writing articles for the Costco magazine that include her byline. Regardless of where your articles are published—online or on paper—your author platform is expanded. In fact, some top writers on the web have earned a type of celebrity status, and people often follow the trail of the best writers through articles in various publications. Now readers will quote the specific writer in a paper like the *New York Times* instead of the publication itself.

We've also seen authors use every kind of Cuisinart approach to writing: slicing, dicing, excerpting, spinning off, quoting, even combinations of new writing sandwiched with existing excerpts. The beauty of writing is that all pieces work together to form a larger body, and written pieces of any size lead back to your author brand and your books. Quality writing appearing in different locations establishes your voice, connects you to your readers, creates opportunities for feedback, and broadcasts more and more mentions of your name and book title via your byline.

Like a bank account gaining interest, your written articles add up and accrue valuable readership over time. Success is built with multiple exposures, which works beautifully and naturally for authors building a platform on the web.

The problem for most authors is that they have little or no master plan or strategy behind their article-writing efforts. With the new digital landscape, the publishing real estate available for articles involves a huge territory and continues to expand, as new publications seeking content pop up continually. It's our hope that all authors will choose from the vast array of choices for articles, use the master plan described in this chapter, and start a database of articles to use strategically as an extension of their author brand.

This chapter shows how to use these many new expanded locations to publish articles to promote your books, how to create articles efficiently, and where to place them to start people talking about your articles. Useful information in articles generates audience interest that leads to that content being reposted, quoted, and discussed by others via comments and social networks.

Everyone Is Now a Journal Publisher on the Web

With new Web 2.0 tools, top blogs are recognized as authentic news and opinion sources. As one example, when you sign up for a Google Alert for a topic at google.com/alerts, you'll find a list of articles with your topic among magazines, newspapers, and yes, blogs.

In the new digital landscape, there is no barrier whatsoever to uploading your own articles. Our author clients harness the web as a tool to propel their content to a wide audience, instantly. As if this weren't powerful enough on its own, it's almost as easy to write articles and place these articles on others' websites and blogs while linking back to your website. Every website needs solid content, and quality writers know how to deliver these written goods. Beyond the ease of self-publishing your articles and publishing on associates' sites, online content destinations are advertised in many places on the web as described in this chapter. Finally, content will always be sought after in the many traditional print magazines and newspapers with online versions.

It's both an expectation and a plus, in publishers' opinions, that authors should write articles about their book topics to spur audience interest. To help enable authors, some publishers have even developed websites to house their authors' articles, such as dummies.com.

Advantages to Writing Articles

In a Web 2.0–enabled world, "content is king" because people are seeking authentic, solid information from a trusted source instead of advertising claims written with a motive to sell products. That means the more you deliver solid, useful information to your audience, the more you build their trust to return to you for more. Authors with this kind of visibility and credibility build a large audience for their books. Some of the advantages to including article writing in your author platform include:

Short-term web traffic. Get people over to your author platform websites by making sure your byline on all your articles includes your website URLs and book title.

Long-term web traffic. Well-written articles stand the test of time. Your articles stay posted online and your audience can reread and reference them as time goes on. Articles attract visitors to your sites months and years after you post them. The term for this is the "digital footprint" you leave behind, forever.

Cost-effective. Writing an article is a free way to increase visibility and get people to find out more about you on your website. As a plus, articles can become revenue generators for authors.

Easy and short. Articles are easily generated from your book excerpts and manuscript outtakes and can be as short as 250 to 500 words.

Expanding authority through Google Authorship (Chapter 4). When approaching other sites about contributing articles and blog posts, put a premium on those sites that have implemented the rel=author tag on their content pages. Also make sure to add the site to your

Google+ profile contributor list. Sites that promise little more than "exposure" can actually boost your authority by making sure that your high-quality content is recognized by search engines.

Higher search engine page rank. Regardless of whether the site you place an article on uses Google Authorship, you can use keywords to tag your subject matter. Keywords make it easier for search engines to determine what this bit of content is about, ranking your web content higher. Writers are now including their keywords at the bottoms of their articles under a heading marked *Keywords* so that they don't have to repeat the keywords artificially and repeatedly in the article.

Multiple exposure. In the same way that advertisers place the name of their company behind home plate during the World Series, you want your audience to gain familiarity with your book and author brand. Some studies show that customers make a purchase decision only after seeing a name seven to eight times.

Our author client Bob LeVitus is a prolific veteran book author and columnist featured in the success story at the end of this chapter. Bob maintains a healthy bank of written articles and advises authors to "Blitz it! Get as many articles out there as you can; write whatever can get you more eyeballs on your name and your book titles. My articles are mostly original pieces, but I also combine writing pieces. For example, I get the rights back to my articles and then post them to my 25,000 followers on my newsletter with added comments and sidebars. I also allow my articles to be reused on campus newsletters like the University of Texas, where I teach courses." Bob has written articles for many years and says, "That's why my books sell so well! My credibility has grown over time as I've shown dedication to my subject matter. Now I have a growing loyal audience following."

Cross-marketing: As readers find, read, and like your article content, they often link to and comment on your articles on their own websites and social networks. When this happens, it's time to cheer! When your article is shared, not only does it give your article an immediate boost to higher search rankings and bring people to your author website, but reposting also pushes your content in the direction of winning you the desirable title of "influencer." In other words, the more your articles are shared, the better. Article directories, discussed later in this chapter, help to get your articles repurposed on other websites, too.

A Brief Guide to Article Rights

When you write a magazine article—print or online—be sure you understand the terms of the transaction. Bob LeVitus mentions "get(ting) the rights back to my articles"; to reuse your articles, you have to have the rights!

Most print magazines buy first North American serial rights: This means they get to be the first print outlet in North America for your article, but you keep all other rights to resell your article in any other region or for a different market (as LeVitus does with his newsletter).

Many outlets buy reprint rights, which acknowledges that the article was first printed elsewhere, but they think the article has value for their readers.

When offering an article or guest blog post to an online market, get an agreement on when you can offer the article elsewhere. Many sites will ask for a period of exclusivity; aim for a fair time period—a month or less.

Unless you're absolutely certain you'll never use that article again, avoid markets that ask for all rights or work-for-hire, especially for a lengthy (or permanent) time period.

Contracts are always negotiable, so try to get the best deal—even if you're agreeing to write an article without getting paid.

Widening opportunities for book reviews. If you get published in a traditional or online publication, you have an opportunity to build a relationship with that venue. If that publication likes your work, the chances of your book getting reviewed there are increased due to being included as "one of their own" writers.

Choosing Topics for Original Articles

For original articles, the challenge is to choose related subject matter to write about instead of exhausting your book's subject matter. Choose topics that enhance your book, along the lines of your blog subject matter, because people don't want to read advertising copy about your book. Remember that the goal of your articles, whether in blogs or in other printed publications, is to lead people to your book and author brand.

For example, from this book alone, we can generate a list of 50 different article titles, which could include anonymity vs. publicity, how to get motivated to begin promoting, inside looks at the traditional publishing industry, industry interviews, common errors made in any of the steps in this book, etc. That is, "anything but" the 14 steps in this book.

To make the article-writing process easy, some authors are using voice recording capability on their mobile devices, dictating talks on topics that can be transcribed and sculpted into articles.

Types of Articles

Back in Chapter 2, we covered various types of blog posts. Because blog posts are articles, the same styles and types apply to writing articles for other publications, too. Here are some ideas:

- **News reporting of current issues in your niche.** One way to show your expertise in an area of interest is to cover the latest developments in your subject area in the same manner as a journalist.
- **Lists.** Ask any editor and many bloggers: Readers love lists! For example, if your subject matter is related to medicine, try something like "What are the seven warning signs of cancer?" The American Cancer Society posts articles you can extract from. If your book involves comedy, name the "10 Best Comedy Writers of the Last Decade." Lists are easy to write and easy for the reader to scan and are often both informative and entertaining.
- **Interviews with prominent personalities.** Unlike the high school music writer in the movie *Almost Famous* (or his real-life counterpart, Cameron Crowe), you may not be able to score time on a tour bus with a major celebrity early in your career, but paying attention to what's happening in your community can pay off in a big way. For example, Mike was just starting out as a technology reporter when a local professor was elected president of the global Internet Society. Larry Landweber readily agreed to an interview, which became a cover story in the local alternative weekly.
- **Anecdotes and other personal experiences.** If you have an important story to tell about your book, and a powerful or entertaining way of telling that story, editors (both for magazine and publishers) will want to print it.

- **Local events.** If you attend conferences or happenings in your town, write an article for your hometown paper or locally focused webzine to get noticed. For example, if your book is related to travel, cover your city's summer music festival or some offbeat celebration.
- **Analysis and opinion concerning your industry or niche.** With some authority in your field, your ideas will be sought out by other reporters and editors who publish journals in your niche. You can also offer your ideas directly as an opinion column, starting with your blog and then reaching out to other publications.
- **Background information.** Long-standing controversies and issues exist in every field of human endeavor. Pulling together histories and other background information can often bring light to an over-heated discussion. The importance of such stories is highlighted by the annual Pulitzer Prize in Explanatory Journalism.
- **Questions and Answers.** The favorite format choice among our author clients. You can present background information as a list of questions you expect readers are asking and answer these questions in a regular column.

Article-Writing Strategy

To become well-known as a subject matter expert, reach out to as wide an audience as possible. The web is an enabling tool to do just that. Start small and build up over time. Publish your articles on your blog, then write guest blog articles, and finally query the largest-circulation publications and publish as many articles as you can in both large and small publications. The smart way to connect all the pieces of your author platform is to remember to cross-reference all of your articles by linking and listing them in your bio and throughout your websites and referring to them on all your social networks.

Using the web writing style and article format presented in this chapter, create and continually add to and save your own "article bank" database. Generate a number of articles in advance, ideally to be released in the six months before your book is published, with a high-quality blitz of articles publishing right before and after your book's release.

Always Include Your Byline

There are no doubt times when you stop in the middle of a really interesting article and ask yourself "Who wrote this?" You look at the top of the piece for a byline, but knowing the name isn't always enough. You look around for some other tidbit about the writer, and sooner or later, you see a small description defining who this writer is, sometimes with a dash of humor or self-deprecation. You might also see a thumbnail photograph and/or a URL. Curiosity sated, for now at least, you return to the article.

Ever wonder who creates those small descriptions? You'll be happy to know that this will be your task!

Your byline/bio is the essential piece that must show up on all your articles. It's your mini-résumé, showing a head shot, author brand name, URL, with a tagline like "I write about business technology," keywords, and personal contact buttons, including Like and Follow. Bylines are tidbits of instant promotion that rise to the top of search rankings. Craft these words carefully, making sure that your byline captures your author brand and that it's 100% consistent across all the articles and short pieces within your author platform.

Best Practices for Web Article Style

The new rules of writing web articles have trended away from traditional article writing, which makes it easier for authors to write short pieces to get promotion in multiple locations. As with speaking, no longer is there a necessity to write a long article stretching over multiple pages. The overload of information on the web has changed ways of thinking to favor information in short, meaningful bursts that we can consume easily. The new rules of online journalism have diverged from the traditional in some significant ways:

Web readers scanning articles. People are inundated with massive information on the web, so online readers tend to scan rather than read every word.

Keywords. Searchability is critical, so online writers must include keywords to be found.

Lists. Online readers tend to gravitate to lists, whether bulleted or top ten–type lists, as they are easy to scan and grab information from.

Fewer words. Online readers skip from site to site, so welcome to the rise of the short-attention-span article. Often it's under-500-word articles that have replaced long articles.

Catchy titles and subheads. In order to entice the reader to scan the article, the title and subheads must pull in the audience.

Casual tone. The long-winded formal authority figure is fading fast, being replaced with a more informed and casual conversational style that invites the reader to comment.

Interactivity. Web 2.0 has allowed interactivity between writer and audience via comments. The engaging dialogue with your readers is a great platform tool. Authors who master the short comment dialogue show that they are in tune with their audience, which attracts even more attention through comment boxes.

Generating Content for Articles

As an author you have a rich built-in content reservoir to reprint and repurpose: your manuscript. There are always the outtakes that didn't make it into the final published book, the capability to excerpt all parts of your own manuscript—that is, up to a specific word limit that might be written in your publishing contract—and the beauty of the spin-off and repurposed article.

Reprinting Original Content

Find publications who express interest in "syndicating." Some publications want to reprint verbatim some portion of your book content, and others are open to short excerpts from your manuscript. A wealth of articles can be generated by reprinting small pieces of content from your blog, excerpts or a chapter of your book, outtakes from your book, or even content from your book proposal.

Repurposing Original Content

There are many creative ways to reuse and repurpose content. Create new documents based on existing writing by changing formats. For example, change prose into a condensed list. Or create a companion workbook based on the table of contents, or a book club readers' list of discussion questions and thought-provoking answers.

Spinning Off Content for Different Audiences

Many authors take their original writing and adapt it for new audiences. As you look through directories of magazines, consider how your book might be used by their specialized audience. For example, this book addresses authors, but everyone needs a platform. We can use existing material showing how to create a platform for a sales force magazine, or for a magazine intended for a student audience joining the workforce.

A perfect example of a spin-off that has been embraced by millions is Jack Canfield's Chicken Soup for the Soul. This series has been adapted from the very first general volume to address 200 unique and different audiences, like teens, parents, couples, and teachers. This approach of adapting to specific audiences is so successful that now we are seeing retail book racks for this series as gift books, right next to greeting cards. The spin-offs are not exact duplicates; they can reuse some material but they focus on new text and can include a different language style, different points, and new quotes.

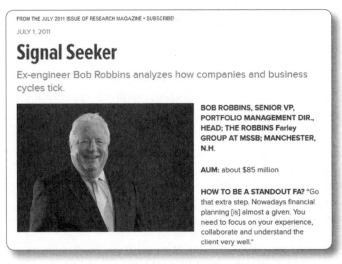

FROM THE JULY 2011 ISSUE OF RESEARCH MAGAZINE • SUBSCRIBE!

JULY 1, 2011

Signal Seeker

Ex-engineer Bob Robbins analyzes how companies and business cycles tick.

BOB ROBBINS, SENIOR VP, PORTFOLIO MANAGEMENT DIR., HEAD; THE ROBBINS Farley GROUP AT MSSB; MANCHESTER, N.H.

AUM: about $85 million

HOW TO BE A STANDOUT FA? "Go that extra step. Nowadays financial planning [is] almost a given. You need to focus on your experience, collaborate and understand the client very well."

Author client Bob Robbins' article "Signal Investing."

First Stop for Publishing Articles: Blogs

The most essential location for your article writing is your own blog. Where else do you exert the powerful influence of being publisher, editor, and author? If you haven't already, be sure to refer to Chapter 2 for instructions on creating your blog, where most of your articles should begin. Always announce your new articles on your social network sites. WordPress can do this for you automatically with the Publicize tool; other blog platforms have similar methods to share your new content.

Guest Blogging

As your audience grows, query other bloggers in your niche to republish your blog posts. LinkedIn and Google+ are great places to make blogger connections. Guest posts on popular blogs increase your visibility as well as the visibility of the blog you post on. As you add to the content presence of others' blogs, you gain friends, widening into others' audiences while enhancing your reputation as a master storyteller or subject matter expert.

Many popular blogs get so many requests for guest posts, they have guest posting policies. As with any other article market, be sure to read these policies before you query, and follow the instructions to the letter. This is not only a courtesy to your host, it shows you know and respect the audience that blogger has.

A Word About Duplication

Don't duplicate your article posting word-for-word as it appears on other blogs or websites. Google and other search engines work to filter out duplicate content in order to give the user a better match to their search. Vary the language of your article; if it appears twice, the search engine may delete a search result for your article, and worse, it may fail to show the result for the article's presence on your own website, the most important location of all. Avoid this problem by writing an alternate version that is a variation, not an exact copy.

Second Stop for Publishing Articles: Publications Seeking Content

While the era of paper journals may be narrowing, we still see plenty of choices on the bookstore and checkout-stand magazine racks. At the same time, online sites like Slate and Salon have demonstrated that there's been a place for magazine-style writing on the web practically since its birth. Even better, each month more new online magazines appear.

Whether you repurpose content or write original short articles, the path to the largest audience is to hop onto others' existing audience and networks to increase your own circulation. Publications seeking articles abound on the web, and the optimum consideration in prioritizing your time spent in placing articles is to find the ones with the highest audience circulation numbers. One article in a key publication with mega-circulation like Huffington Post will gain you maximum exposure, so it's well worth submitting your articles to both the major and minor publications well before your book publishes in order to allow lead time should your article be accepted.

If you're an experienced freelancer, you can probably skip this section, but if you've never seen your byline in print on glossy paper, we can help.

Magazines

Seek out lists of publications that feature your subject via Google or other search engine. Lists are included on Amazon, but the best single source is *Writer's Market*. This annual publication shows magazine names and subject areas of interest along with submission guidelines, what kind of query letter they want, and, most importantly, names of editors and other relevant contact persons, with postal and email address. The WritersMarket .com website offers an updated database because editors can change at any time. The deluxe edition of the book includes an annual subscription to WritersMarket.com, or you can just subscribe online. *The Writer* magazine also offers an online market database at writermag.com. For fiction authors seeking placement of short pieces in literary magazines, try clmp. org/directory/ to find a list of hundreds of magazines that publish short stories and poetry.

If you research the magazines in your niche, you'll become familiar with the style of articles they publish. Ask all the magazines on your list for their writer's guidelines (check their website, too; guidelines are often posted there), follow them to the letter, and write your query letter. Be sure your query includes:

- A clear summary and synopsis of your idea;
- Justification of the topic importance, and why it's of interest to their readers;
- If applicable, a list of experts you plan to interview;
- Your qualifications for writing the article; and
- Your writing credits.

The Simple Short Prose Article Format: For authors new to written articles, here's the simple standard format:

> **Short Headline (Title).** Catch the attention of the reader and relate it well to the topic.
> **Byline.** Your photo, your name, professional title, URL, list of books.
> **Lead.** Dig deep for the first sentence to capture attention. Include subject, focus, and tone.
> **Body.** Generally two or three main points with a short paragraph for each.
> **Conclusion.** Give closure: use a final quote, lead to a future topic, or offer a simple conclusion.

An example of the Simple Short Prose Article Format may be found here: http://finance.yahoo.com/news/heres-first-mention-google-mainstream-144000685.html.

Newspapers

Local newspapers love local authors, so first query the one with the largest circulation if you have multiple local newspapers, and then follow these steps below:

- Contact the submissions editor of your local newspaper or the editor of the section that matches your subject matter. Local publications prefer to cover local residents and tell interesting stories about them.
- Read the information regarding submissions on the individual website of the publication and/or on the editorial page.
- Follow their policy for submissions.

- Create your "pitch" of your idea, similar to how you pitch an idea to a book publisher. All editors are looking for a specific story peg or angle, so if your idea is selected, you may be asked to write to that particular angle—which is why you should pitch your idea *before* writing up the article.

Huffington Post

This publication is in a category all its own. A mega blog and a news aggregator, Huffington Post is the gold standard of online article publication, attracting 26 million visitors per month, more than *USA Today* and close to the readership of the *New York Times*. Check out the Huffington Books segment alone as a significant location for online articles in addition to the breadth of subject matter they publish online. Publication in the Huffington Post is like getting published in *People* magazine; it's far and away the most-read publication on the web. In every case, submit a query using their guidelines to create an article at huffingtonpost.com/contact. Over a cup of coffee, do a search on the more than 30 Huffington Post–type sites that focus on your subject matter.

Helium

Labeling their own site as "citizen journalism" joined to "share knowledge," this site allows you to post short articles about a wide array of subjects in addition to supplying content to other online sources seeking content. Owned by RR Donnelley, a heavyweight in the printing business, Helium is much more than a free article site. It runs writing contests and includes a community aspect. You can even get paid assignments through the Helium Content Source program.

Need to Get Your First Byline? A Few Ideas

ARTICLE DIRECTORIES

Article directories are online web locations comprising collections of articles on many subjects by many different writers. These directories accept articles that are original, not duplications or spin-offs. The articles listed in these directories can help drive traffic to a website or blog through the use of an interesting article link. Most directories will pay you a small amount of money for posting your articles to their site. Following are a few of these directories, and there are many more. Only sign up if you are guaranteed a photo and full byline/bio.

EzineArticles.com. This site allows you to post original articles to the site, which they then market to other online sources. The site claims an audience of more than 30 million monthly visitors, so the barter arrangement of submitting your articles in exchange for exposure and increased traffic to your website is worth it. When you register for a free Basic account, their editorial staff reviews your first ten submissions to ensure they conform to their editorial guidelines. These guidelines are basically designed to weed out spam and other low-quality writing. Once you complete this probationary period, you can submit an unlimited number of articles as a Platinum or Diamond Author. You will get information on publishers who view your articles on the site, but not necessarily who publishes them.

GoArticles.com. They claim to be "the Web's Largest Free Content Article Directory." They target email newsletter editors; for this reason, they ask that you format articles to 65 characters per line. Your articles must be between 400 and 2,500 words. Your author bio, limited to 400 characters, is the only place to include links to your site(s). The front page of the site includes an Author Showcase sidebar and another listing of Top Authors.

ArticlesBase.com. This directory claims over 300,000 registered authors. As with GoArticles, they also require 400-word articles, with a 12,000-character limit. You're permitted three links in each article and three links in your bio. You are also permitted to customize your bio for each article you submit. The site home page includes an Editor's Picks section with six featured articles, along with an Author Spotlight sidebar. Like eZineArticles, this site offers traffic statistics for each article.

ArticleDashboard.com. This site is similar to GoArticles, without the emphasis on authors. Topics (and advertising) dominate the home page, and bylines appear nowhere on the article links.

EHOW AND OTHER DEMAND MEDIA SITES

"Discover the Expert in You" is the tagline for this site, where anyone can write How-To articles for a small payment. This can be a nice start for a first article with a byline, as you get your author name included (without your book title) and are paid about $15 per article. To become a writer for eHow, just fill out an application and submit a writing sample to Demand-Studios.com. When you're approved, eHow allows writers to choose from 20,000 available titles, chosen by eHow by watching how people use terms to search Google.

Author client Mireille Schwartz, author of *The Family Food Allergy Book*, featured in Huffington Post.

Additional Online Tools

Here are a couple more resources for article writing that many of our authors recommend:

- Grammarly.com gives your article a free grammar check.
- PRLeads.com ($99/mo) is the one service we most highly recommend if you are willing to spend the money. This resource helps authors get quoted in others' media using PR Leads. Journalists subscribe to this site looking for subject matter experts to quote. Journalists post queries to this site and authors can respond with credentials and answers. If interested, the journalist or reporter will contact you directly.

Writing articles extends your reach and visibility as a writer. Find as many places as you can to place articles and repurpose your writing as it will pay off in visibility and credibility for you and your author platform.

Checklist, Step 8: Article Bank

- ➤ Create an article bank of 500-word original articles.
- ➤ Include your byline description with your name, photo, and book titles listed.
- ➤ Create articles that repurpose portions of and outtakes from your book.
- ➤ Publish articles on your blog and sites and get permission to publish these on blogs and sites of people in your network.
- ➤ Submit original articles to large and small publications and article directories.
- ➤ Repurpose original material into spin-offs for publications addressing various audiences.
- ➤ Work to get quoted in others' articles and on others' websites.
- ➤ Blitz the web with as many articles as possible with your byline, which should mention your name and book title and URL, especially near the time of your book launch.

Success Spotlight: Waterside Client Bob LeVitus (boblevitus.com)

- 70 books
- 2,000,000+ copies sold
- 12 language translations
- Newspaper and magazine columnist, including 12 magazines

Favorite Quotes:
"Omit needless words."—William Strunk Jr. and E. B. White
"The hardest part of writing is keeping your ass in the chair."
  —Wallace Stegner

Beginnings: A graduate of California State University at Northridge with a B.S. in Marketing, Bob worked in Los Angeles producing television commercials, radio spots, and print ads for agencies including Kresser & Robbins and clients including SelecTV. Bob didn't really like working in advertising, quit his job, and bought a new Macintosh computer. Soon he was asked to become the editor-in-chief of *MACazine*, an early Mac-specific magazine purchased by *Macworld* magazine a few years later. Next an acquisitions editor for Addison-Wesley got in touch with Bob, saying they would love for him to write a book. The book was *Dr. Mac*; the acquisitions editor was Carole Jelen, now representing his work for 20+ years.

Platform: A leading book author and top newspaper and magazine journalist, Bob led a radio show (*Inside Mac Radio*, CNET Radio, 2001–2), hosted a popular television series (*Mac Today*, syndicated, 1992–93), and is working on a new TV show.

Bob is also a speaker, having presented more than 200 seminars, workshops, conferences, and training sessions in the U.S. and abroad, including Macworld Expo keynote addresses in three countries.

Bob's advice to authors: "To build a brand around yourself, you have to put yourself out there. Seek out opportunities to put yourself, your product (book, video, ebook, app, service, or whatever), and your brand in front of receptive audiences. Find relevant trade shows, conferences, and affinity and offer to speak to them. Contact podcasters, broadcasters, and other influencers and send them copies of your work. Make yourself available for interviews and use your social media to promote your appearances. You are the product—sell yourself.

"Now here's the great secret: The more you do it, the less you have to do it in the future. Eventually you will be contacted for events—in my case, that includes international travel on cruises … for the next year the nice folks at Insight Cruises will be promoting my brand and my books in all of their marketing materials!"

Bob LeVitus's final word on author platform building: "Writers don't talk endlessly about what they're writing; they write it and then talk endlessly about it. Giving free copies of your work to those whose opinions matter is an investment, not an expense. Finally, promote your brand and book using your book titles in every email you send."

CHAPTER 9

Finding Your Voice: Radio, Podcasts, and More Audio Adventures

"Words mean more than what is set down on paper. It takes the human voice to infuse them with deeper meaning."

—*Maya Angelou, poet*

T HE YEAR WAS 1938, on the eve of Halloween, when the now famous radio "panic broadcast" happened. Orson Welles read and dramatized H.G. Wells' novel *The War of the Worlds* in the style of newscasts on the Columbia Broadcasting System so realistically that some people actually believed that aliens were invading Earth and panicked in the streets. It's amazing how beliefs and actions can be moved by the power of the spoken word. We remember some of the most dynamic people who have ever lived through their radio broadcasts, like Albert Einstein discussing his relativity theory, Martin Luther King's "I Have a Dream" broadcast, Mahatma Gandhi's "Soldier of Peace" radio broadcast speech, and Sylvia Plath's famous radio reading of her poem "Daddy."

All of these people were book authors, and their broadcasts are fortunately available to listen to on the Internet for all time.

In the publishing world we don't underestimate the power of radio and audio recordings, and we look to the models of those who have used audio well and those who still are using it to reach out to readers.

Audio is a natural medium for authors, from storytelling to news events to personal interviews. Thom Hartmann is a top progressive radio talk-show personality with millions of listeners per week, and also our author client success story in this chapter. Thom advises authors to broadcast on audio, and "Tell stories! We are story machines; that's how we learn; whether you write fiction or nonfiction, tell stories." He stated that "Radio is an intimate medium that reaches out warmly to people, like a phone call."

Authors who understand how to use radio and audio effectively can reach a wide audience to expand their readership because the written word translates so easily into audio without photos or videos. In fact, audiobooks sell so well that Amazon owns the audio book company Audible and keeps up a bestseller list just for audio titles at audible.com.

While large non-Internet radio stations trend away from interviewing noncelebrity authors, the great news is that Web 2.0 tools enable authors more audio choices than ever before. Audio opportunities abound that writers in prior times never dreamed of, from smaller network radio stations to the ability to create your own Internet station, if you're so inclined! In this chapter, you'll learn how to find traditional network radio interview opportunities, plus how to pursue the newly enabled do-it-yourself radio programs—that is, podcasts—and then how to optimize your Internet option of recording your audio segments to permanently place them on websites for ongoing promotion.

Get Used to the Sound of Your Voice

Most people don't like the sound of their own voices; it's normal. In fact, only a small percentage of people even recognize their own voices hearing them for the first time on a recording. Without going into the scientific explanation of why our own voices sound different to us, we advise pushing past this common limitation by recording your voice as radio DJs do in training, at least a few times a day. First yawn to relax your vocal cords, then record, listen, and adjust. Relax and repeat often, and your comfort and good results will follow.

Your First Audio: Record a Sound Clip for Your Author Website

Recording your voice repeatedly before speaking on the radio gets the best results. Audio recordings are a little more behind the scenes than making public speeches, so they also make good practice for appearing in public. With a headset microphone, it's easy to start out by recording a simple reading of some of your text from your book, and then posting the best audio take on your website. We've heard readings of every length, from one minute to an hour, so the choice of length is yours depending on your purpose. In most cases, listeners just "sample" audio clips and only stay tuned for a short time, so it's best to choose a short, memorable portion of your book as an audio clip. As these clips come to a close, they typically trail off in volume to indicate that more is available in the book.

Your computer may have a microphone built in, or you can invest in a headset with a microphone. While you can certainly spend $2,500 on a headset, you can also get an adequate one for less than $50. The cheaper headsets and microphones plug into separately identified jacks on your computer, but there are also USB headsets that offer fine sound. For best sound quality, we advise you purchase the best one you can afford. The headset is basically all the hardware you need. You can get started without spending any more money by following the steps below.

Planning Your First Recording

The choice is yours as to what you should record as your maiden audio voyage. People love stories, so the best option—even for a how-to book—includes the example, or story, behind the action. If your book is about travel, it could be a description of your travels to Provence. You could offer your readers a treat, suggesting they close their eyes and just relax, listen, and imagine they're there. If your book is about meditation, you can demonstrate a special meditation technique, or if it's about music, you can demonstrate some chords. Read one of your stories, poems, or passages aloud and record it. The sky is the limit on material you can excerpt, stories you can tell, and virtually anything else you can teach, show, and inspire via an audio clip.

That said, try to keep your excerpt to no more than 15 minutes. The best storytellers don't overstay their welcome. When making a selection, look for something short that will whet the listener's appetite for more, but not with a cliffhanger ending that will leave them feeling angry and suckered—unless you promise to complete the story in the next episode. Of course, then you have to deliver the next episode.

> Want some ideas and inspiration for your audio reading? Visit the NPR *First Reads* page. Go to npr.org and use the search engine to find *First Reads*. You'll read (and hear) authors read excerpts of their latest work. *First Reads* also has a podcast version that you can subscribe to on iTunes.

Record with Free Software

Audacity is free, open source audio recorder and editor software that runs on Linux, Windows, and Mac computers. You can download it from audacity.sourceforge.net/ and install it on your system. You might be a little intimidated at first by all the buttons and such, but it makes a fine basic recording and the software is not difficult to learn.

Have your headset plugged in before you open Audacity so the software can find your microphone. Once you've selected what you want to read (scroll the text from your book in a separate window in Word or have your script printed out, whatever's more comfortable), and click the **red circle icon** in the middle of the screen to begin recording. When you're done, click the **square button** to stop. Click the **triangle icon** to play your recording.

If you're new to recording your voice, you should repeat the entire process until you're happy with how you sound. While you can use Audacity to edit your recorded reading, you should focus first on developing confidence in your radio voice.

Upload Your File to Your Site

When you're ready to publish your recording, save it as an MP3 file to your computer. You can then upload the file to your author website or elsewhere on your author platform. Add a new post in WordPress. Then enter some introductory text about the recording, with a description of the audio clip. You can give your audio clip a simple title, such as "Excerpt from (book title)" if you like. Alternately, you can write a whole blog post about the importance of this particular audio excerpt and give a compelling reason why it's important to your book. If there is a lesson to be learned from the story recorded in your clip, tell what it is.

When you've completed your introductory text for your audio clip, click the **Add Media** button. The **Upload Files** screen will appear; you can either drag your file to the window from your file manager, or use the **Select Files** button to browse for the right file. Add a title so visitors can see this when they mouse over the audio player. Click **Insert Into Post**. Assign this post to any relevant category and consider adding an Audio category. Apply appropriate tags. When you're done, publish the post. WordPress will display an audio player so your readers can listen right on your site. Now you have your audio sample ready to show off to radio producers and podcast hosts.

Pitching Local Talk Shows

For radio spots, your first job is to let radio stations know that you're available. Local stations help to establish your authority on a topic and grow your presence in the media, so try to get booked on as many of these as possible, especially in the months leading up to the publication of your book. If you are already associated with local organizations, try to get media coverage and offer an interview based on that organization. For example, Mike got his first statewide radio interview by virtue of being the local chair of an organization that was written up in the local news. When you connect with groups and let people know about your profile, you're more likely to be contacted by scouts who want you to do radio interviews.

Check local listings. You may already know which radio stations in your hometown have talk shows. If you don't, a web search for "talk radio <your city>" should yield decent results. Visit each station's website to note how much of their schedule is taken up with syndicated national shows and what time periods are devoted to local hosts. Station websites show the types of topics each show covers, so watch for interviews that somehow relate to your field. Where AM talk radio typically focuses on politics and current issues, public radio can be an excellent venue for authors involved in all types of subject matter since many have book segments. Some talk shows are devoted to literature and fiction, and others to science, health, history, biography, and other types of nonfiction.

> **Side Note:** When looking for a show to pitch, don't just focus on who might be interested in your specific topic, but also consider (a) who covers your field more broadly, and, perhaps more importantly, (b) on which shows you're seen as a person of interest. For example, Barbara Kingsolver is an "environmental" novelist. She's interviewed on NPR and KQED to explore climate change from different perspectives, and on other public radio stations about topics like "What it feels like to see the monarch butterflies" she writes about in her plot. Just search on "Barbara Kingsolver Radio Interviews" for more examples.

The following process for finding radio station interviews was shared with us by friends at Bay Area radio stations KKDV and KKIQ:

Call the station you're interested in. Yes, inquire by phone first as a general rule. Ask to speak to a show's program director. Don't ask for the show's host—that person is not the decision-maker; ask to talk to the program director, who will likely be unavailable. Your first contact point will likely be the office manager, who will screen the call to direct you correctly and then connect you to the program director's phone line.

Leave a voice message for the program director. If you have done your homework to understand their audience and programming, you will leave a very targeted short message in regard to what you have to offer for their listeners. For example, KKDV is a local music station, so they do talk interviews with nonprofits only for "Helping Your Home Town" segments.

Give the program director a reason to call you back. Show why their audience would care, that is, a "benefit statement" from their point of view. Your goal is to get the program director to call you back, so keep it short and enticing. If they don't call you back, go to the station website, which will likely list the program director's email. Then email a short "Just thought I'd follow up in regard to my phone message" reiterating what your message was.

Follow up. Write a single nonfold notecard like a "thank you" in an envelope saying "Just following up. I heard Program XYZ on your radio station and feel like my work is a great fit for your audience. I left you a message on (date). Just asking if you'd be so kind as to call me to hear more." Keep it very professional, and add your business card. Since most people don't send paper notes anymore, you'll generally get more attention than via email.

The Pitch

Try to find book radio programs, and you have a natural fit to pitch; then develop the bullet points of your pitch. List why you would be a great guest, including the fact that you are an author. For example: "I think your listeners would be interested in hearing an interview with me because . . ." As we noted earlier, give the program director a reason why they would consider you, or they will not book you. Like publishers and agents, radio stations are specialized, so you have to find those that fit your book and/ or subject matter in some way. Always check the station website for their programs and time slots and listen to a program or two to become familiar, and keep the bullet points of your pitch handy.

Focus on the relevance of your topic, your expertise in the area, and the audience you already have built from your website, blog, and social media connections. Consider this call both a query and an audition. A confident tone and the ability to think quickly in responding to questions will demonstrate how you'll do on the air. Point the producer to your website and online press kit, as they will ask for all additional information.

Demonstrate your familiarity with the show. Your chances of being booked are better if you show you understand its format and, to the extent possible, its audience. Then explain in detail why you'd make a great guest. If you have previous radio or podcast experience, provide links. If you've followed the steps of building your author platform up until this point, link to your author website to give evidence of your expertise and existing audience.

Close with your short-term availability; if your book or a related article is coming out soon, tell them so that they can book you as part of your launch (Chapter 14). Then follow up with the show periodically to keep yourself on the radar until you get a response.

In a perfect world, the program director will immediately book you for tomorrow's show. More likely, you'll give your contact information and get into their address book for some future date. You may not be booked yet; you may just be in the "maybe" file. Let them know when your publication date is or when you're doing a reading in the local area, and they just may help publicize it. Stay flexible, as station schedules can change; you can get bumped on a week's notice due to rescheduling. Stations like news, so make radio interviews part of your book launch activities.

When You're Booked

When you do get booked to appear on a show, first celebrate and post the news on your websites and social media! Unless you're a celebrity, interviews take place in radio studios because the audio quality is far superior to the inferior sound of a phone call. While you may find the idea of an in-studio interview scary, you'll have the benefit of seeing the host and responding to his or her nonverbal cues. The host is there to help make the show go smoothly and will be on your side throughout.

Before your appearance, try listening to the show to get a sense of how it's organized. It's best to avoid any confrontational-type shows, so you'll want to be prepared. How long are the segments? Is there a discernible structure to the interviews? Does the host ask all the questions? Do listeners call in? If so, be prepared for oddball call-in questions from the listening audience, too.

> **Side Note:** Practice being interviewed before going on the air. You've got to feel comfortable in order to do a great interview, and the only way to feel comfortable is to practice. We cover public speaking in Chapter 7 and offer more practice tips in Chapters 9 and 10 (creating podcasts and videos), so practice your interview as if it were also a speech, and record it a few times to work it to a level you're happy with.

Always keep your goal first and foremost—creating a path for people to find your website, subscribe to your lists, and ultimately buy your book.

Protect against drawing a blank: It helps to hold your business card with your contact information—including your web address and social media handles—when the host asks you where people should go for more information about you, your URLs, and the like.

In Chapter 14 you'll find more information about creating your own book tour, so if you go on the road, research and contact the stations in cities on your route in advance. If you let the program director know when you will be in town, with details of your reading, you may even be able to find a sponsor for your reading.

Pitching Larger Radio Stations

While it's been a while since radio was the dominant mass media, the proliferation of talk shows on the AM band and public radio reach a good number of book buyers. People love something that will take their minds off their captivity in their cars while commuting, or as a background while working on something else. Check your local listings for opportunities in your area. In the San Francisco Bay Area, for example, KGO is the dominant news talk show, which also has a book segment: Book Passage President Elaine Petrocelli appears on the Bay Area's *Ronn Owens Show* and talks about current books with conversation and reading recommendations.

The Top Book Radio Programmer: NPR

A few minutes spent at npr.org/books will help you understand why National Public Radio (NPR) is the prime target for authors looking for national exposure. The page features its own bestseller lists, reviews by the ton (many of which appeared on air), and a whole section of author interviews.

Story-based programs like *A Prairie Home Companion* by Garrison Keillor (heard by 4 million listeners each week on more than 600 public radio stations!) offer readings, voice acting, and music opportunities. Our author client and banjo specialist Bill Evans has the distinction of being asked to play background music for *A Prairie Home Companion*.

NPR is in the business of creating what they call "Driveway Moments"; those stories that are so interesting, listeners stay in their parked cars until the segment is over. For that, they book guests with the right story to tell, a great venue for fiction writers. In *Sound Reporting: The NPR Guide to Audio Journalism and Production* (University of Chicago Press, 2008), Jonathan Kern describes how guest bookers troll the web, their email, and letters to newspaper editors to find the right people to talk to.

Don't hesitate to send news releases about your book and related expertise to NPR (and your local NPR station—many of them do author interviews, too).

Finding Other National Radio Shows

The place to start searching is the list of popular shows at radio.about .com: radio.about.com/od/syndicatedradioshows/Popular_Syndicated _Radio_Shows.htm.

Start with the query process shown earlier in this chapter and remember that shows need talent like yours. Customize the bullet items of your pitch in terms of the value you add to their particular show and then contact via phone, email, and mail. Be sure to list any previous radio interviews; a list of credits with links to your clips is helpful. The more you build up your smaller online podcast and radio interviews, the more likely the larger shows will take interest.

Finding Online Podcast Interview Opportunities

Podcasts are do-it-yourself Internet-based radio shows. Many of these are talk shows that number in the thousands around the world, and they need you!

iTunes Store Podcasts

Podcasts got their name from "broadcasts on iPod," so it's no surprise that Apple's iTunes Store is the largest and most popular directory of these shows.

Pre-Recorded Podcasts

iTunes' Essential Podcasts directory contains 40 categories, from Action Sports to Yoga and Movies to Great Stories and ways to manage your money. There's no accurate measurement of size of the audience of these podcasts, but podcast listeners are usually passionate and are likely to follow up with book purchases. iTunes sells podcasts as portable versions of shows. For example, most NPR shows have podcast versions. Many more podcasts are produced by bloggers and other enthusiasts about their specialty topics, too. Some of these have grown from podcast to major platform, such as "Grammar Girl" by Mignon Fogarty and "The Nerdist" by Chris Hardwick.

iTunes hosts thousands of hours of podcasts on its servers. You can run Apple's free iTunes app on any Windows or Macintosh computer and, of course, on any mobile device running Apple's iOS operating system (iPod, iPhone, or iPad). Many recent car models have a USB port connected to the radio so you can play music and podcasts from your mobile device through the car's sound system with the same cable you use to charge the mobile device. Download the desktop application from apple.com/itunes.

Open iTunes and click the **Podcast** tab at the top. The podcast section of the iTunes Store appears in the window. If you're new to podcasts, just look around a little to see the variety of available shows. Over on the right, you'll see a drop-down menu that says **All Categories**. Click the **arrow** to see a list of broad categories; find yours. At the top of the screen, you'll see the New & Noteworthy list, followed by What's Hot. Click on a logo that looks interesting to see a description of the show and the available episodes. Below the episode list, you'll often see some related shows in the Listeners Also Subscribed To section.

Look for the website link; the site should have contact information for the show. Don't make a pitch until you have listened to at least a few episodes. Podcasts are free to download and you can subscribe to ones that appeal to you; your podcast manager will download every new episode when it's released.

Other Podcast Directories

Of the other podcast directories, Stitcher Radio (stitcher.com) is probably the best organized. Stitcher offers more than 15,000 live podcast radio shows, with topics in every subject area. As with other radio shows, do your research before pitching yourself as a guest. Listen to a few episodes of a show to see what topics they cover and how they work with guests. Try to picture yourself on this show and determine how you fit into the show's format. Besides the website, Stitcher offers mobile apps for iOS and Android.

Check directories such as the one at podcast411.com/page2.html for more podcast lists.

Live Podcast Radio at BlogTalkRadio

BlogTalkRadio.com hosts thousands of live Internet radio shows. Search there for hosts that cover your topic as well. Each show has a profile page with contact information for the show. Later on in this chapter, we also talk about using BlogTalkRadio as a host for your own show.

Linking Up with Podcast Hosts

Use these outlets to make a direct connection with podcast and radio hosts actively seeking guests:

- The BlogTalkRadio support forum has an ongoing topic, *Post your Guest Availability here! "I am available to be a guest on Blog-TalkRadio."* Post your pitch at getsatisfaction.com/blogtalkradio/topics/i_am_available_to_be_a_guest_on_blogtalkradio.
- Help A Reporter Out (HARO) often hears from radio and podcast hosts and producers looking for guests. Sign up at helpareporter.com. Emails with fresh requests come to you three times each weekday. Respond to the items you can.
- RadioGuestList.com puts hosts, guests, and publicists together. Hosts and producers post requests for guests on a particular topic. Each request is emailed to the list of potential guests with information on the show and its audience. You respond where you fit.

Regardless of how you connect with a podcast host, remember these rules for your appearance:

- When you're asked to appear, be professional.
- When you commit to a time for the appearance, be there.
- Follow any technical instructions you're given. That means call in with a landline if they ask you to (to decrease the risk of dropped calls or low-quality sound, as noted earlier) or use Skype if that's the format they prefer. The audio headset you purchased to make your initial recordings can be used for your Skype interviews.

Making Your Own Online Radio Station (Podcast)

Crafting your own podcast means you have complete control over how you present your subject. How best to engage your readers? Review Chapter 7 (which is about personal appearances) and strive to entertain with just enough information each time to leave them wanting more.

Finding Podcast Guests

While many experienced hosts can hold the interest of listeners for 30 minutes a week by themselves—and you can certainly do that on occasion —you will probably want to follow the example of many podcasts (and radio shows throughout history) and have guests on your program. When you're first starting out, tap your own network of friends and associates. Audiences like hearing bantering between friends, and in the process you may just find a cohost you can rely on. If you've already appeared on other podcasts, approach the hosts to return the favor on your show.

Look around the web for people creating interesting content in your niche. You can interview bloggers who cover your beat, or a reporter for a publication (online or print) who broke a hot story. Local academics and businesspeople also may be able to bring a different perspective to important issues in your niche.

Most experts are inclined to respond positively to interview requests, but be mindful when approaching people outside your own circle. Define the time commitment required. Does the interview have to take place at a particular time for a live show? Do listeners call in? Be prepared to answer questions about your audience: How big? What sort of folks listen? Is this group worth the expert's time? If you don't think so, neither will the expert.

Once you've worked out what your show is going to be like and have a few guests lined up to make your show happen, it's time to make a podcast. If you're comfortable with Audacity and producing the show on your own, go ahead. You can also experiment with the following services.

Using BlogTalkRadio

BlogTalkRadio (BTR) is the powerhouse in hosted Internet-based radio and podcasting for the nonprofessional radio host. They claim more than 15,000 active hosts, with some 1,800 shows created every day. BTR shows typically are live, with listeners able to call in and comment or use a chat room to interact with you as the host. Shows are recorded and made available as podcasts, so people can access them through the iTunes Store or any other podcast directory.

You don't even need a headset or microphone to host a BTR show. Everything is run over the telephone. Hosts, guests, and even listeners (the live ones) all call in to BTR (it's not toll-free, so don't view BTR as a completely free service). While BTR notes that landlines offer better sound quality, you have the option to use Skype or another voice-over-Internet (VOIP) system.

BTR offers a lot of hand-holding for the new host, offering a one-on-one training session with a veteran host upon registration (even for a free account). The BTR Learning Center offers video tours of the various pieces of the BTR site and introductions to the Studio recording tool.

After the initial batch of training at the Learning Center, BlogTalkRadio University offers even more extensive video sessions for more advanced tools.

MAKING A BTR TEST SHOW

With your computer and telephone at the ready, you can start practicing to run your show.

- From your account page, click **Schedule Show**.
- Choose a Title and Description for this episode. Add any keywords that apply.

- Pick a date and time for your test. At a minimum, schedule for 15 minutes from now.
- Under **Visibility,** select **Test** to keep your show private. Click **Submit**.

Wait for your scheduled time. Log in to your BTR account about 15 minutes early, and click **My Studio**.

Over in the upper right corner, you'll see the Host Call-In number and your PIN. You'll also see the Listener/Guest Call-In number, which you can share with any cohosts or guests participating in the test.

Run your test. Talk for a while, see how things work. Upload a music file to play as an intro. You have up to 15 minutes (by default, set when you scheduled the test) to play around. Hang up the phone when you're done. Return to your profile page and see what your test sounds like. Repeat as necessary.

GOING LIVE ON BTR

Once your testing is complete, it's time to write a script and prepare to go live on the Internet.

Before scheduling your first episode, be sure to connect your Facebook page and Twitter accounts to BlogTalkRadio. BTR will automatically notify your fans and followers when you have a new podcast to share on the system.

Schedule your first appearance as described in the last section. Work harder on defining a title (keep it short and simple; six words maximum) and description of the episode. This material will appear in the directories and help potential listeners decide whether they want to hear you.

When it's time to roll, have your script ready and log in 15 minutes before your scheduled time. Open the Studio application. Relax, take a deep breath, and start the podcast!

BlogTalkRadio lets you have a daily 30-minute show with five live callers (counting you and any guests) for free. Other plans offer more time, more callers, and more promotion.

Using Spreaker.com to Create and Broadcast Your Show

While Spreaker.com is more oriented toward music-DJ types, it produces talk shows, too. You can sign up with your Facebook account or set up your own login credentials. When you log in for the first time, you are taken to a Dashboard page to fill in your profile and get a look at your current statistics. We'll show you how to post your Spreaker show to iTunes later in the chapter.

On the right side of the dashboard, you're asked to Complete Your Profile. By now, you know the profile drill: Spreaker wants to know where you live and when you were born. Change your public URL from spreaker .com/user/<random user number> to spreaker.com/user/<yourname>. Submit a biography and upload a photo.

Through your profile page, Spreaker posts links to each episode of your show to your Facebook, Twitter, YouTube, and Tumblr accounts as well as the audio sharing site Soundcloud.

MAKING A SPREAKER TEST BROADCAST

Click the **Broadcast** button to get started. You'll be given the option to upload a recording you've already made, but in this case you want to run a live test and broadcast with Spreaker's recording console. Type in a title for your episode; you'll see an open lock icon labeled **Public** below this. Click the icon to change this setting to **Private**. Click **Next** to open the DeeJay recording console, which looks similar to the Audacity recorder.

Make sure your headset is connected to the computer; the microphone icon should appear in the left side of the screen. Click **Record a New Podcast** to test your recording options. At the top, you should see the Recorder area. Click the **red button** on the left to start recording. You may have to wait a little bit while the console finds a server to store your audio on, but the Recorder will tell you when you're ON AIR. Record yourself speaking for at least a few seconds to ensure that your microphone is working and to check your audio levels. Click the **black square icon** to stop the recording. You'll then get to hear the results automatically.

You can make any number of test recordings for up to 30 minutes each. Each replay offers you the choice to publish the recording, making it available to your listeners.

GOING LIVE ON SPREAKER

When you publish your episode, Spreaker takes you to a page where you can add information (also known as "metadata") about the episode.

Adding this information is critical in finding an audience for your podcast. Select the right category and add the appropriate tags for this episode. Then write an interesting (but not too lengthy) description of the episode for the casual visitor who found your podcast while surfing through the iTunes directory.

All this material is included in your RSS feed, and iTunes picks it up and displays it with your podcast. Make the most of it!

The Spreaker "Free Speech" plan gives you 10 hours of audio storage, with a 30-minute maximum length for each podcast episode. Various premium plans offer more storage, no mandatory ads, and additional features.

Posting Your Podcast Episodes to Your Website

Linking your podcast episode to your site is the first step in getting your audio into the ears of your core audience. Fortunately, WordPress makes this pretty easy, whether you use Spreaker or BlogTalkRadio.

Before you add your first podcast to your site, you should add a Podcasts (or Audio Posts) category.

On a technical level, you want to remember that a podcast is really just an audio (or video) blog post. Spreaker (find **Embed**, and look for **Share on WordPress**) and BlogTalkRadio will both create automatic links to your saved audio file. All you have to do is copy that link at the audio site, go to your blog page, and add a new post.

Include some introductory text on your blog post, in the same manner as suggested earlier when you made your Audacity recording. When you've completed the introductory text, click the **Insert Media** button. A big screen will appear; click **Insert from URL** on the left side. Paste the URL in the box that says "http://" (make sure you delete that when you paste). Add a title for the episode so visitors can see this when they mouse over the audio player. Click **Insert Into Post**. Don't forget to assign this post to the Podcasts category and any other relevant category, and then apply appropriate tags so people can find this episode. Add **Subscribe From iTunes** links and any other directory you've listed in the post text. When you're done, publish the post. WordPress will display an audio player so your readers can listen from your site.

Getting Your Podcast in the Directories

So you've made your first podcast! How do you get people to hear it? The first step is to add your podcast's RSS feed to the main podcast directories.

iTunes

The single most important location for you to offer your podcast is the iTunes Store. When you have an RSS feed dedicated to your podcast, submitting the feed address to iTunes is done directly through your copy of iTunes.

Where do you get that dedicated RSS feed? If you use Spreaker, go to your show's page.

1. Find the **RSS feed icon** above your episode list (to the right of the Statistics tab)
2. Right-click on the **little orange RSS feed icon**. Select **Copy Link Location** (in Firefox), **Copy Shortcut** (in Internet Explorer), **Copy Link Address** (in Chrome), or **Copy Link** (Safari).
3. Open iTunes.
4. Click the **iTunes Store** box.
5. When at the iTunes Store, click **Podcasts**.
6. Under **Podcast Quick Links**, click **Submit a Podcast**.
7. Paste the link to your feed URL in the box. It should be in the form of: spreaker.com/show/<Your show's feed ID number>/episodes/feed. Click **Continue**.
8. Select a Category and Subcategory to make your podcast more findable.
9. Click **Submit**.

You'll get a confirmation email noting that iTunes has received your request. The powers that be at Apple will review the content of your feed to make sure it's original (not someone else's copyrighted material), not obscene or hateful, and isn't just an infomercial for whatever product you're selling. If it passes muster, you'll get another email from Apple with your iTunes link. Within 24 hours, everyone should be able to find your podcast on iTunes.

Stitcher SmartRadio

Stitcher collects an assortment of radio shows and podcasts for distribution on its mobile apps for Apple iOS and Android. Once you become a Partner at Stitcher, they handle the upload. Stitcher also pays you for each new listener you bring to their app.

Apply at stitcher.com/content-providers. You'll be asked for your contact information and the following material for your show:

1. Show name
2. RSS feed URL
3. Show format (live stream or podcast)
4. Genre (pick from a list of 15 broad categories)
5. Language
6. Optional: current number of listeners, Twitter handle and Facebook Page, keywords (140-character limit)

Rockument audio channel, created by author client Tony Bove, musician and author.

How to Use Your Book Cover as Your Podcast Logo

Along with your podcast, the iTunes Store wants you to submit a graphic 1,400 pixels square, the size of an 8½ × 11 sheet of paper. The graphics wizards at Apple take it from there. We suggest that you use your book cover for your podcast logo (since you are promoting your book) by doing the following:

- Download and install the open-source Inkscape image editor from inkscape.org.
- Go to openclipart.org.
- Use the search box to locate an image compatible with your podcast, like the blank book cover in the figure (openclipart.org/people/dniezby/dniezby_Generic_Book.svg).
- The OpenClipArt collection allows you to edit the image online, including the text.
- When you have the image the way you want it, click the **Save** button to download the edited image to your computer.
- Open the image in Inkscape.
- Go to Edit > Select All.

A sample podcast icon, created with free tools.

- In the upper right corner, you'll see some boxes with numbers in them. Change both the W (width) and H (height) boxes to 1,400 px.
- Go to File > Export Bitmap.
- Under Bitmap Size, make sure the width and height are both 1,400. Check the file name so that you know what this file is. It should also have a .png extension.
- Click **Export**.

Whether you create audio clips, radio or podcast interviews, or create your own radio station, find creative ways to use audio to enhance your author platform.

Checklist, Step 9: Audio

➤ Practice recording yourself with a headset.
➤ Post the best audio clip on your author website.
➤ Pitch local and national radio shows for interviews.
➤ Find podcasters in your niche for interviews.
➤ Create your own podcast.

Success Spotlight: Waterside Client Thom Hartmann
(thomhartmann.com)

- 20 titles published
- 500,000+ copies sold
- 8 language translations

Favorite saying: "Luck is where opportunity meets preparation."

Beginnings: Thom Hartman says he's a "hyperactive kid that grew up, with an entrepreneur's temperament." Born in Michigan and raised in a conservative Republican home, Thom started his early life with ADD. He attended Michigan State University, majoring in electrical engineering. That's when he became a part-time DJ at a local country music station. Thom loved radio, so he continued moving upward in radio in a variety of roles for different stations for many years.

Radio. *The Thom Hartmann Program*, 2.75 million listeners a week, rated the most popular liberal talk-show host in America.

Publishing credits. The most acclaimed title he has written is *The Last Hours of Ancient Sunlight*, for which he was invited by the Dalai Lama to spend a week in Dharamsala. As a result of a book on spirituality, *The Prophet's Way*, he was invited in 1998 to meet Pope John Paul II. His book on the JFK assassination (written with Lamar Waldron), titled *Ultimate Sacrifice*, is cited in Gore Vidal's autobiography as having "finally solved" that case. Thom Hartmann also contributed to *Air America, the Playbook*, covering writings and interviews of liberal radio personalities, reaching the *New York Times* bestseller list in 2006.

Cinema. Leonardo DiCaprio's web movie *Global Warning* was inspired by Thom's book *The Last Hours of Ancient Sunlight*. Hartmann appears in DiCaprio's 2007 documentary *The 11th Hour*, as well as the feature documentary film *Dalai Lama Renaissance* (with Harrison Ford) and *Crude Impact*. In 2010, Warner Bros. and Leonard DiCaprio announced they are making a major motion picture based on the book *Legacy of Secrecy*, authored by Lamar Waldron and Thom Hartmann. Hartmann also narrated the 2011 documentary film *Heist: Who Stole the American Dream?*

Thom's advice to authors: In our interview for this book, Thom says we all are story machines, and whether you are a nonfiction or fiction writer, "start with a story because that's how we learn. The more real, the more personal, the better." According to Thom, the audio route in talk radio is the most intimate medium, like a telephone in your ear.

"The key to communications is connecting—one on one. Each person needs the sense that you are talking only to that one person."

Thom has done everything in his career knowing that "audiences don't read … people do. If you speak or write to an audience, you are 'speechified.' If you write and speak every time to a specific person, you're talking with individual care and concern."

On the radio Thom envisions only one person on the other side, and that someone has three criteria. It's someone who 1) knows him, 2) likes him, and 3) is interested in him. Thom recommends that you put a picture of a person who fits these criteria right up on the wall in front of you while you're writing and speaking, and communicate with that person, as a conversation.

Tom Hartmann's final word on author platform building: When you write about what you have passion about, it will carry over to your audience. Passion is infectious.

CHAPTER 10

Video: Book Trailers, YouTube, Linking, and More

"We want to entertain, inform, and empower people with video. What our users want is to watch themselves. They don't want professionally produced content."

—Chad Hurley and Steven Chen, the creators of YouTube

I$^{T's}$ UNIVERSAL; we all love watching videos. Before delving into just how effective videos are for promoting books online with Web 2.0 tools, let's glimpse into the future through the statistical lens and then look back to the present.

First, according to a 2013 Cisco survey, by the year 2017, Internet video traffic will comprise *69% of all global consumer Internet traffic.* Second, the Cisco survey finds that *shoppers prefer to research products online prior to making in-store purchases* and so recommends making video available in-store by kiosk, touchscreen, and smartphone integration.

Imagine yourself someday talking about your book on video right at the point of purchase in a physical bookstore.

Now back to the present, we hope to bowl you over with the rate of consumers' preferences to view web videos. Some numbers:

- Visitors who view product videos are *85% more likely to buy* than visitors who do not, according to Internet Retailer in 2010.
- According to Comscore in 2010, *96% of online shoppers* watch online video.

- In the United States, *187 million* people watched *48 billion* online content videos in July 2013. That means the average American watched around *22* online videos in a single month!
- Approximately *half* of marketers who use video in email campaigns see increased click-through rates, increased time spent reading the email, and increased sharing and forwarding, according to eMarketer in 2013.

These hard-driving statistics are the reason that sites like Amazon and networks like LinkedIn have enabled you to upload video onto these sites. At first, it may not seem the natural thing for authors to use this visual medium to represent the written words of their book, but think again. Consider the countless numbers of fiction books that have been translated into screenplays and consumed visually, and even nonfiction works like *Fast Food Nation, Under the Tuscan Sun, Gorillas in the Mist, The Perfect Storm, The Men Who Stare at Goats,* and *My Life in France.* Then consider how web tools enable you to fill a video screen with words played to music or the fact that you can overlay words on a photograph or the other nearly limitless ways you can use video as your vehicle for promoting your writing. The new rules of web promotion involve finding ways to apply video to your creation, and we help you get started right here.

The Rise of YouTube

You're likely one among 120 million people in the United States who visit YouTube every month. With 25 million hits in a single day, YouTube has become a household word; 100 million videos are watched every day. Network TV news programs show and report on the latest viral YouTube videos. Depending on your topic, your presentation, and the whims of the ever-puzzling zeitgeist, you might even become a YouTube superstar.

Welcome to the new world of do-it-yourself TV, enabled by Web 2.0 and an inexpensive video camera. There's not much of a barrier for any author to reach out to the huge and ever-growing YouTube audience. Videos send powerful communications when kept short, simple, and entertaining.

> **Side Note:** The top YouTube videos of all time are naturally music and dance-craze videos like Psy's "Gangnam Style," but smack in the middle of these professional entertainment productions sits the most home-grown, simple, and touching video of two little boys in "Charlie Bit My Finger," well worth taking a look if you haven't seen it. If you can figure out how to appeal to people as universally as this video did, you'll hit a gold mine of viewers!

As with every element of your author platform, think through your video creation first and keep to the master plan that binds your platform together. Then take a few minutes to learn the hows and whys of making videos. In this chapter, we'll help you get up to speed on making your own book trailer and other promotional videos, and we'll show you how to create links to your videos from all parts of your author platform.

More Reasons to Make Video Part of Your Platform

Video is memorable. Whether you are a visual, auditory, or tactile learner, people generally remember 10% of what they read, 20% of what they hear, 30% of what they see (pictures), and 50% of what they see and hear (pictures + sound = video)!

We live in a "sound bite" society. People's time is precious. The average reader has a limited number of books he or she can read in a month or year. A quick video presentation about your book can help them quickly judge the value of your book in a minute or two.

Novelty is still there—for now. You'll see some statistics in this chapter about the number of book trailers now being made. It's a substantial number, but considering the number of books published every year—and with the explosion of self-publishing, even more titles will be released—a video trailer for a book is still a standout in terms of promotion. While writers have been giving media interviews for more than a century, most writers have never had the unfiltered opportunity to explain themselves and their work on camera directly to an audience. Publishers are quick to catch on: The marketing department at Penguin Press and others have endorsed video as a promotion vehicle for authors and in fact have created

YouTube channels, with many more publisher-sponsored YouTube channels likely to come.

Tools for making quality video are inexpensive and easy to use. You don't need expensive studio time, gigantic cameras, and a team of producers to create quality moving images aimed at marketing you and your book. You're probably carrying in your pocket a better video camera than Neil Armstrong had photographing his first step on the moon. (It makes phone calls, too!) You can also use the video capabilities of inexpensive point-and-shoot digital cameras (most of which should have handy tripod mounts) and basic software to edit your video may already come with your computer. And the distribution network is easy to access here in the developed world.

Google owns YouTube. Thus your YouTube videos automatically become part of the Google-based search system. In this chapter, we show you how to use your Google+ author page to create your very own branded YouTube channel. That channel, combined with your Authorship tags, will make you and all of your high-quality content writing more accessible to those who belong in your audience.

Shows you information about your viewers faster than from your readers. At the largest video distribution sites—YouTube, Facebook, and Vimeo—commenting and circulating are part of the culture. Your marketing department, whether solo or with a publishing team, also gets instant feedback from these channels about how many views your videos get, knowledge that will help you grow your audience.

Personal connection with your audience. As with a live bookstore appearance, a well-made video can let readers see you, hear your voice, and make a connection with you and your work. Videotaping your personal appearances multiplies your audience.

Deliver information to visual learners. Some people, especially an increasing number of young people, learn best from visuals, and video is the natural medium of choice for them.

Author Video Strategy

The first part of author platform video strategy includes creating a short one-minute book trailer, a bank of short interview video clips, plus video clips of all teaching, instruction, talks, or other speaking, and then uploading videos to as many video sharing locations as possible with the right tagging information for searchability. The second part of the video strategy is to create links to all of your web locations. And finally, you want to take the opportunity to create your own YouTube channel so that it can grow. Start with uploading your own trailer, interviews, and clips and add related videos over time as you collect them. This will bring other people's networks over to your channel. The more times your channel is viewed and made a favorite, the better exposure for you and your book and author brand. Check out a variety of types of author videos by typing "best selling author videos" into the search box.

Making a Book Trailer

Here's your chance to make your own book trailer, similar to a movie trailer for a feature film. Authors can hire a professional videographer if they like (authors with a budget might even go so far as to hire actors and special-effects masters, as in the trailer for the 2009 parody novel *Sense and Sensibility and Sea Monsters*) or you can make a solid book trailer for next to nothing with just the software included with your computer and some royalty-free background music.

Find Models

Visit YouTube and type "book trailer" into the search box. You'll find tens of thousands of trailers, ranging from fiction to nonfiction; short ones with still photos, all-type screens, and a musical background to professionally produced trailers. For a smile, search on "best book trailer." Thanks to the power of self-marketing, you'll find an even higher number of results. Watch as many as you can, taking note of their strengths, and find a model similar to what you feel works for your budget and style.

The Simple Interview Book Trailer Format

Publishing marketing departments know about the power of video promotion, and some will even pay for book trailers for their published authors. Bill Gladstone, founder of Waterside Productions, has a book

> ### Video Book Trailer Repositories
>
> - Moby Awards—Best and Worst Book Trailers (mhpbooks.com/2012-moby-awards)
> - American Library Association Book Trailer Awards (ala.org/awardsgrants/book-trailer-contest)
> - Covey Book Trailer Awards (thenewcoveyawards.blogspot.com)
> - Tumblr for Book Trailers (bestbooktrailers.tumblr.com)
> - List of Top Book Trailers (therumpus.net/2013/06/fantastic-book-trailers-and-the-reasons-theyre-so-good)
> - One more: A very good "What inspired you to write this book" trailer (reallygoodmom.com/authors/video)

trailer created and professionally produced by his publisher, Vanguard, a division of Perseus, for his novel *The Twelve*.

The Twelve trailer is a great model for a very effective and preferred trailer format. In Bill's trailer, he uses an interview-type format to answer questions and then the video cuts to his book cover and other images related to his book. In his case, this involved a discussion of the Mayan calendar and other relevant themes to his plot. Bill's best advice for authors is to work with a professional videographer, then be relaxed for the interview portion and enjoy the process. The reward? You can keep costs down, and the trailer will still pay for itself by expanding viewership and audience. Bill placed the publisher's trailer on his own websites and attached it to emails during the launch email campaign.

Bill also has an additional professional trailer for *The Twelve*, created by videographer Richard Greninger, that ran on Hungarian television when *The Twelve* was published in translation. This trailer was quite effective as a selling tool for international rights, as international agents and book publishers use video trailers as information sources to select which American books they will translate for their markets.

Make a Simple "Storyboard" on Paper

Plan out what each screen will look like. You might want to storyboard your video, as Tim Ferriss, author of the *New York Times* best-selling book *The 4-Hour Chef*, recommends. Ferriss compares the storyboard to "a comic book for your trailer." Brainstorm ideas for their visual impact and coherence, with an eye toward quickly and elegantly communicating your book's message. Make a set of drawings that outline what you want in your video: type of graphics, animation (this can include simple transitions between scenes), and whether you want real people on camera, just words on the screen accompanied by music, or a blend of these elements.

Professional feature film trailers run a little over two minutes, so we recommend the short book trailer of one minute with multiple changes of scene, including your book cover and perhaps some bullet-point screens, spoken message, graphics, a compelling background, and some sound to hold it all together.

Prepare the Media Types That Fit Your Book

Collect the right graphics. Start with the most important visual of all: your book cover, which should be repeated throughout your video. You can also display drawings and photographs (including your author photo) and can find royalty-free images at sites like iStockPhoto, MorgueFile .com, and OpenClipArt. BurningWell.org is also a great site for public domain photographs.

Of course, you can also shoot still images specifically for your video. Likewise, a webcam will take still photos of you, and some webcams even take screen shots of your computer desktop if you want to use those shots in your video.

Select your music. Red alert: Don't use copyrighted material unless you're prepared to pay a fee—sometimes a hefty fee—to license it. YouTube will also block download of a video if it contains any suspicious music tracks, so pay special attention to music permissions. As casual a process as this seems, remember you are making a product for commercial purposes.

Here is a list of royalty-free music available under Creative Commons (CC) and other sources:

- Most of the music at Incompetech (incompetech.com/music) is licensed under a Creative Commons attribution-only license, where

What is a Creative Commons license?

For copyright holders, CC offers the opportunity to share work with other people. Where the standard copyright notice reads "All Rights Reserved," CC offers the notice "Some Rights Reserved." What rights are we talking about? CC basically affects four different types of sharing:

- Attribution: Anyone can copy, display, distribute, or perform your creative product, but they have to give you credit for creating it.
- Share Alike: Essentially "Do what you like with this collection of words, notes, beats, and vocalisms, but the work has to be shared in the same way you got it."
- No Derivative Works: Anyone can copy, display, distribute, or perform the content, but don't remix it or change it substantially.
- Noncommercial: "Do anything creative you like with this content, but if you try to sell your performance or there are ads attached to the web page my content sits on, we'll need to talk about that."

A combination of any of these four pieces of the Creative Commons puzzle constitutes a CC license. When you're looking for free CC-licensed material for your book trailer, look for the Attribution license. If you're willing to spend some money for music or other creative products, contact the creator (especially if the Noncommercial tag is applied) and see what you can work out.

you need only credit the composer to include the piece of music in your content. It's nicely searchable.

- Freesound.org has thousands of Creative Commons–licensed tracks.
- ccMixter.org is oriented toward people looking for remixes and samples, but is popular for YouTube and podcast audio tracks, too.
- More than a million tracks on SoundCloud.com have Creative Commons licenses. Not all of them support commercial use, so check the license before using.
- AudioMicro.com sells licenses to use in web videos for thousands of songs in assorted genres for $40. Jamendo Pro has a similar program for a little bit less.

Choose Your Software

If you have Windows running on your computer, you may already have Movie Maker installed on your system; if not, you can easily download it from Microsoft. With a Mac, you already have an installation of iMovie. These tools are more than adequate for your basic trailer-creation needs. They may even surprise you with the number of features they have.

IMPORTING SOUND AND IMAGES TO MOVIE MAKER

Open Movie Maker and drag the pictures into the big window (or use the Browse function to locate them in your file manager). Drag the pictures around until you've got them in the right order. You can add visual effects to each picture (or all of them).

Select a picture and add a caption (some words on the screen). You can choose the font, how long it appears on the screen, and how it appears (and disappears) from the screen. By default, each image displays for seven seconds, but this is adjustable, too—and for the layperson, adjusting the frame length is relatively easy, handy if you're looking to time frames specifically to your audio track. If each image is on the screen for the default, roughly ten images will cover your trailer.

Now you can add the sound. From the Home menu, choose **Add Music** to locate the music you selected. If you prefer, you can also add voice narration or webcam video.

When you've gotten everything in order, add a title screen at the beginning and a credits page at the end to round out this little production. Click **Save Movie**.

The running time of your trailer is posted in the lower right corner of the play window. Play your trailer a few times to make sure it's good to go.

Movie Maker even facilitates automatic uploads to the most popular video-sharing sites: YouTube, Facebook, Vimeo, and Flickr. Click the **logo** to upload to your Facebook author Page—but hold off on YouTube for the moment.

Want to see what kind of trailer you can make with a bit more budget than we outline here? See "How to Create a Viral Book Trailer (or Get 1,000,000 Views for Almost Anything)" at fourhourworkweek.com/blog/2013/04/10 /how-to-create-a-viral-book-trailer-or-get-1000000-views-for-almost-anything.

IMPORTING SOUND AND IMAGES TO IMOVIE

To create your trailer with iMovie on your Mac, open iMovie and go to File > New Project. Name your trailer. Keep the other default settings.

Your toolbars are in the middle of the screen; the Media Tools are over on the right. Click the **camera icon**. All of your still pictures appear in the window. Select the pictures for your trailer and drag them into the project window. Drag the pictures into the order you want them.

Use the Title tool (the T next to the camera on the Media Tools toolbar) to add a caption. Select from the many available styles and drag it over the photo it will accompany. Double-click to write the caption and set the font.

Double-click each photo to set the Duration each item appears on screen.

To vary things a little bit, add some Transitions in between the images. Transitions are next to Titles on the Media Tools toolbar. Again, you have many options.

Finally, add some sound. Click the **musical note icon** to locate the soundtrack for your trailer. Drag the clip under the images.

When your trailer is ready to go, press **Play** in the lower left corner of the iMovie screen to see how it looks.

As with Movie Maker, you can share your trailer automatically with an assortment of video sites directly in iMovie. Go to the Share menu at the top of the window and select from YouTube, Vimeo, CNN iReport, iTunes, or Facebook.

Record Video Clips of Yourself with Your (Web) Camera

It's not necessary to appear in your own trailer. In fact, plenty of authors simply use music and written screens to show what their book is about; for an example of this, look at Kimberly Jackson's book trailer on YouTube: https://www.youtube.com/watch?v=sz3zkh8CRkE.

If you decide you want to be included in your own book trailer, try a practice run. Using the webcam that's likely built into your laptop or monitor, just open a document on your computer and start reading. The advantage of reading off that very same monitor is you nearly always have to maintain eye contact with the monitor to read the words off the screen.

Keep practicing until you get the results you're looking for—remember, it takes time and repetition to get the impact you're seeking.

While you're practicing (and this will take more than one try if you're new to this), always remember: Don't panic! Don't let your nerves get the better of you, and relax. Follow some simple rules:

- Pretend that the monitor is a close friend; you're just talking.
- Remember that you know what you're talking about; confidence is everything!
- Slow down. When you're nervous, you'll talk fast. Slow it down, and more people will understand you.
- Watch your hands. This is less important for the trailer, but make sure your hands move to emphasize the points you're making, not just making random gestures.
- Don't be boring! Present in an entertaining way, and deliver just enough information so that your readers are left wanting more. Try to create a question mark at the end of your video, or trail off with a clear call to action—"For more information, visit my website at . . ." or "Read my book (title)."

For more tips, check out the Vimeo Video School (vimeo.com /videoschool), which we'll discuss later.

Combining All the Parts: Edit Your Video

Your webcam probably came with some type of software that allows you to do some editing of your video, so it's time to get familiar with how it works. You won't be adding any funny hats to your display, but you may find some of the effects useful. You also want to know what format(s) the software saves your video in. On Windows machines, chances are the default is Windows Media Video (WMV), and Macs use the MOV format, but there may be other options.

Uploading Your Videos

Video sites like YouTube and Vimeo were created to allow people to share videos with each other. It's easy to do, and nearly as easy to associate videos you make with the rest of your platform. In fact, since you already have a Google account, most of the work has been done for you. In this section, we'll describe how to upload videos, organize your contributions, and link them to your author website and other parts of your author platform.

Tagging Your Videos

It's critical for searchability to make descriptive tags to accompany your video before you upload it. Add metadata, including your book title, description, and category, as is directed on the YouTube upload site.

Be sure to email your whole network asking them to visit your video and leave a comment, even if it's one word. Then put your video link on all of your groups and forums. Additionally, some sites offer you a place to add your video link, such as eBaum's World forums, Fark, and Digg.

Creating Your Own Connected YouTube Channel

In some ways, it's incorrect to say you create a YouTube channel. With a Google (or pre-buyout YouTube) account, simply liking or subscribing to someone else's videos creates the channel. What you do with it is up to you, however.

In 2013, YouTube introduced the One Channel design, which incorporated a number of changes, the most significant of which allowed channel owners to create landing pages, which are eye-catching and help persuade viewers to subscribe to your channel.

Before uploading your trailer or some other video in support of your writing career, let's get it connected to the other outlets of your platform. Start by going back to your Google+ profile page. Ideally, your YouTube channel will appear in the Links section. If it's not, edit the page to define the link.

More importantly, you've made an author page on Google+. This page can have its own YouTube channel—a wonderful thing if your personal YouTube channel is filled with stupid cat trick videos you like. Not only can your fans easily access your book trailer and other video material related to your career on Google+, but you can also organize Hangouts.

You can even host Hangouts on Air, which are then stored on your page's YouTube channel!

The YouTube Subscribe Widget plugin for WordPress lets you connect your author website to your YouTube channel.

Uploading Your Videos to YouTube

We showed you how to upload your book trailer to YouTube directly from Windows Movie Maker and iMovie earlier, but what if you want to share another video, like a webcam reading or some other video you made previously? Well, the old-fashioned way is nearly as straightforward as the YouTube button in Movie Maker.

From the YouTube home page (youtube.com), you'll see the **Upload button** at the top, between the search box and your name (if you're logged in to your Google account, which you should be). Click the **Upload button**, and you have the option to either drag and drop your videos directly from your file manager or click the **big arrow** pointing up to open a file window.

You also have options to make a fresh video using the Webcam Capture option, create a photo slideshow (not unlike what you made in Movie Maker), or start a Google+ Hangout (discussed in Chapter 4). All Google+ Hangouts are stored on YouTube forever. You also have the option to edit an existing video in YouTube, which has a plentiful, free, and easy-to-use set of editing tools.

The amount of time it takes to upload your video depends on your Internet upload speed (nearly always slower than its download capacity) and the amount of traffic Google's servers are experiencing. You should be able to view your video on YouTube in minutes.

When you post a video, be sure to announce this throughout your author platform as well as Twitter, your Facebook author Page, LinkedIn, and Google+.

EMBEDDING YOUR SITE INFORMATION ON YOUR UPLOADED VIDEOS

You can embed links to your author website or Google+ profile in your videos, but some preparatory work is required before you do this the first time.

1. Make sure you're signed up with Google Analytics. (See Chapter 1 for details.)
2. Go to google.com/webmasters/tools/associates.
3. Click the **name of your site** to associate with YouTube (your author website).
4. Click **Configuration** on the left. Choose **Associates**.
5. Click **Add New User**.
6. Add the email address associated with your YouTube channel.

Your author website is now associated with YouTube. But Google wants to make sure that you are who you say you are, so you have to verify this fact. With a phone nearby, go to youtube.com/verify and enter the phone number. Google will call you back immediately and give you a number to enter on this screen. When you type in the verification code, you'll get some bonuses on YouTube: the ability to upload videos longer than 15 minutes, and the option to embed annotations to your clips.

Visit your channel and open an uploaded video for editing. Click **Annotations**. If all has gone well with the setup, you'll see a banner at the top of the screen asking you to enable your account for external annotation links. Click **Enable**.

Click **Add Annotation**. Choose from Note, Speech Bubble, Label, or Spotlight (it doesn't really matter which). Check the **Link box**, and you'll get choices, including Google+ Profile/Page, Video, Channel, Subscribe, Playlist, Associated Website, and Fundraising Project. Add a message in the text box ("Visit me at my website"). Click **Publish**.

Uploading Your Videos to Vimeo

Vimeo offers an alternate location for your video presentations. With a free account, you get to upload 500MB per week and up to 10 uploads per day. You also have the opportunity to join (and form) groups.

To get a feel for the site, click the **Watch tab** at the top and choose **Couch Mode**. Vimeo will play a set of random videos from the site. Hover your mouse over the screen to get the running time of the film you're watching. If you like a video, you can declare that here by clicking the heart.

Adding videos is as straightforward as on YouTube. Click **Upload** from the main screen, select the video to upload, and Vimeo does the rest. You can further classify your video with categories and tags. Categories range from Everyday Life and Education/DIY to Experimental and Animation, with further subcategories.

Be aware that Vimeo prohibits "video intended for commercial use," but grants an explicit exemption to authors and other creative types "who want to promote the work they have created." Thus, there are thousands of videos with the "booktrailer" tag sitting on Vimeo for your perusal.

Vimeo also has mobile apps for Apple, Android, and Windows Phone. You can upload from these apps, too.

Setting Up Your Vimeo Account

Once you've registered, look at the Me tab at the top of any Vimeo screen. On your profile page, you can upload your standard photo, add some biographical information, and define your location and gender.

Your Vimeo URL is your user number by default. Change it to something more human-friendly, preferably your real name.

Add a link to your author website in Your Websites. Vimeo users who visit your profile page will then be able to connect with you.

Click the Videos tab in the settings dialogue to define how people can view and use your uploaded videos. You can restrict access in the Privacy settings, restrict comments and downloads, and choose whether to allow others to embed your videos on other sites.

This tab also makes it easy to assign a Creative Commons license to your videos. Just click the button next to the appropriate license for your content, and it's done!

The Advanced Settings tab gives you control over Vimeo notification emails and other site preferences.

Vimeo Helps Make Your Video

The Create tab at the top of the Vimeo screen offers beginners and experts help in making your videos great.

The Vimeo Video School (vimeo.com/videoschool) is geared for the novice video maker and consists of short videos (around five minutes per lesson) on tools and techniques for shooting your masterpiece. If you're completely new to the process, start with Video 101.

Click Music Store to find tracks to play under your video, many of them free of charge. The tracks that are not free go for $1.99 for a personal license. The Enhancer will not only add the soundtrack, but will give you a background theme for your video, too.

Finding Community: Vimeo Groups

Groups are folks who come together to discuss and learn from each other about the art of making video, and who are fans of particular kinds of video. Thousands of groups are listed in the Vimeo groups directory. Many of those have thousands of members. Groups can choose a category to help people find them, matching the categories that Vimeo uses to organize its clips.

Typically, a group member points the group to a relevant video for Likes and comments. Groups can create forums for more structured discussion.

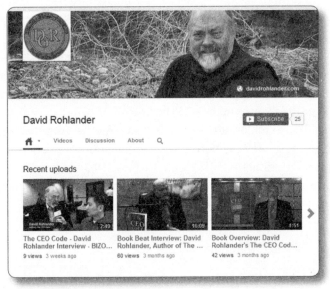

Author client David Rohlander, author of *The CEO Code*, on YouTube.

Post your trailers to the Book Trailers and Author Interviews group (vimeo.com/groups/booktrailers), a fairly active place.

Linking Your Vimeo Videos

Be sure to repurpose all videos that you collect, from interviews to instruction to speaking, even small clips. By placing your videos in various locations, your audience will find multiple ways to connect with you in this powerful medium. Vimeo lets you connect your account to Facebook, Twitter, LinkedIn, and Google+. From your Settings page, just click the **Apps tab**.

Connect your Vimeo account to your Facebook author Page instead of your personal account. Click the **Connect button** under Facebook. In the drop-down **Publishing To** menu, select your author Page, and define what you want to share there. Do the same with your Google+ link.

---

30 Places to Upload Your Book Trailer for Free

Thirty video-sharing sites for book trailers are posted here at savvybookwriters.com: savvybookwriters.wordpress.com/2012/07/16/30 -video-sharing-sites-to-upload-your-book-trailer.

Video Blogging

As a blogger, you don't have to restrict your posting to print and audio. You can run a video blog, too. Use this method occasionally to spice up your blog fare, or commit wholeheartedly to video blogging (sometimes called vlogging). If you hope to be a television personality as well as a well-known writer, video blogging is a good training tool.

Some of the best video blogs are created by the technology bloggers at *This Week in Tech* (TwiT, for short). This cast of technology experts and journalists produces 30+ hours of video programming a week, ranging from the daily *Tech News Today* to *iPad Today* to *Ham Nation*, about amateur radio. Learn more about technology, and how to create great Internet TV, at twit.tv.

Video blogging is pretty much like audio blogging (that is, podcasting) but with pictures. So before embarking on this path, review the podcasting section of Chapter 9. The big difference, of course, is the pictures. You will need a video camcorder and video editing software, like CyberLink PowerDirector, Adobe Premiere Elements, or Corel VideoStudio Pro X6.

Video Interviews

The video interview is a powerful way to get known by your audience, and publishing marketing departments recommend their authors do as many of these interviews as possible.

When we watch authors from a wide range of fiction to nonfiction in the book segments on *The Daily Show with Jon Stewart* or *The Colbert Report*, we're instantly drawn into the central message of the book in a fun way that makes us feel like the authors are very approachable. The Q&A video interview is the easiest visual format with the most punch and reusability. At Book Expo America, the real Steven Colbert interviewed his own character featured on *The Colbert Report* to announce the publication of his own book.

In Chapter 9, we talked about the process of getting interviews on local radio shows. There are likewise multiple opportunities for video-based interviews on the web and television.

Local TV show interviews. While the television landscape isn't quite as fertile on the local level as radio, there is an outlet that you as an author and expert can pursue. Nearly every local television station has a morning news program that helps viewers start their day.

Besides traffic and weather reports in urban areas, these morning shows take after their network counterparts by scheduling interviews with authors and other experts on items in the news. Local authors are prime candidates for these interview slots.

Check your local stations' websites for contact information for the morning show producers and email them a pitch, as outlined in "The Pitch" in Chapter 9; if you have a news release for your book, include that in your pitch. If you're fortunate enough to have your topic become newsworthy, make that connection as well. If you have clips of other TV interviews on your site, include those links with your pitch.

Book TV on C-SPAN2 is a special programming block dedicated to interviews with published authors; check their site for contact and demo submission guidelines.

Your self-made video interviews. Create a channel with a collection of short interviews under your subject matter heading; if you post to your social networking groups, professional groups, and clubs, you'll find a large group of people who want to be a part of a video channel that connects to their brand. Start small with your own interview to frame the others to come, then set up the channel so that others can post to it. One suggestion is to ask your audience to upload short video reviews of your book and how they found it helpful, which in turn helps them to promote their own brands; it's a win/win.

Side Note: Post your videos everywhere: your author page on Amazon, interview sites, your agent's website, publisher's video page, and others' websites.

Creating a video trailer for your book is an option that we highly recommend, but beyond this one video, you should create videos as often as possible and link to them throughout your author platform.

Video Sharing Sites for Authors

Barnes & Noble video page (barnesandnoble.com/bn-studio/videos-podcasts /index.asp)

Huffington Post Book Videos (huffingtonpost.com/2010/12/06/book-videos -best-and-worst_n_791645.html)

Oprah's Book Club Videos (oprah.com/oprahsbookclub/Oprah-Author -Interviews-The-Best-of-Oprahs-Book-Club-Videos)

Scholastic Video Page (scholastic.com/teachers/collection/book-videos -author-interviews-author-read-alouds-book-trailers-booktalks)

Reading Rockets video page (readingrockets.org/podcasts/authors)

Penguin video page (us.penguingroup.com/static/pages/multimedia/index .html)

Berrett-Koehler Author Videos (bkconnection.com/authvids.asp)

Workman Author Videos (workman.com/authors/videos)

Checklist, Step 10: Video

➤ Practice and videotape a short author interview about your book.

➤ Videotape all talks and instruction.

➤ Tag videos carefully with keywords for searchability. Include your book title and URLs.

➤ Create a short book trailer video.

➤ Upload your book trailer to YouTube, Vimeo, and other video sharing sites.

➤ Create a YouTube channel and upload all your author/book videos and grow over time to include related videos of others for cross-promotion.

➤ Connect YouTube and Vimeo to your book and author websites, social networks, and author platform locations.

Success Spotlight: Waterside Client Dr. Brian Alman (drbrianalman.com)

- 11 books published
- 14 global language translations
- 300,000+ books in print

Beginnings: Dr. Brian Alman studied at Suffolk University in Boston and then went on to receive his clinical psychology Ph.D. at the California School of Professional Psychology in San Diego. He complemented his degree work by studying with international masters in the mind/body field, including Dr. Milton Erickson, the definer of mind/body healing and medicine. Early on, he found his calling in helping people find effective and permanent health and wellness solutions and has worked with celebrities and sports figures.

Platform: Dr. Alman has become a world-renowned expert on stress, behavior change, and medical weight loss and is the author of the best-selling book *Keep It Off*, which was positively reviewed by Deepak Chopra. Dr. Alman's book *The Voice* (2011) details revolutionary methods for helping people overcome physical and emotional challenges. Dr. Alman's health and wellness techniques (live and on mobile apps) have been a key part of Kaiser Permanente San Diego's Department of Preventive Medicine.

Through his company, TruSage, Dr. Alman has been delivering stress management, wellness, and weight loss mobile support for 15 years to tens of thousands of people globally. He has appeared on national talk shows and authored books, tapes, and videos in the areas of self-discovery, relaxation, and self-change, including *Self-Hypnosis: The Complete Manual for Health and Self-Change*. He works with the world's largest health-care organization, Kaiser Permanente, using his Keep It Off Program to bring proven weight loss solutions to health-care providers around the world.

Dr. Alman's Advice to Authors: "Here's the main thing I've learned: Relationships are the most important thing. Plus, continual content sharing for free helps build your community and network."

CHAPTER 11

Publish a Book Website to Attract More Audience

"The great thing about the Internet is you can launch a product, and within just a few hours, people will tell you what they think about it."

—Susan Wojcicki, head of product development, Google

PRIOR TO THE WORLD WIDE WEB, in traditional publishing there were fewer ways to promote news of a book's publication to audiences. Print advertising in newspapers and magazines had astronomical price tags generally too steep to pay for. As a result, publishers developed "co-op" advertising for new books. By splitting the huge cost with bookstores, both the publishers and bookstores won publicity, but paid dearly. At Addison-Wesley we also courted the "flyer in the box," which meant a full-sheet ad for our books included right in the box a product was shipped in. A flyer about our book right in the box the product was shipped in was a sweet plum. This offered benefits for all: a major ad for our book right at the point of sale, and a way for the company to instruct their buyers with an otherwise "missing manual." And the most important promotion took place via the ace salespeople at publishers who were and still are key promoters, securing bookshelf space and big buy-ins at the chain bookstores and shelf space at independent bookstores.

These were long routes to get to the same destination that authors using Web 2.0 can now quickly reach at a very low cost. When you compare pre-digital advertising methods to the new rules and capabilities on the web for authors, the web wins. Authors who couple their author platform efforts with successful traditional publishers' efforts are in a position to supercharge promotion and distribution that beats do-it-yourself self-publishing, hands down.

Authors who are not using free online tools to promote their books on the web are shooting themselves in the foot. It's baffling to talk to authors who resist creating book pages on the web and on free social network sites like Facebook and LinkedIn. As an essential promotion tool, it's easy to create a website just for your book and your book alone. There's no good reason any author would not invest the small amount of time necessary to create a professional-looking book website, given all the good reasons to have one.

As an author, you sacrifice to create your manuscript; you work amazingly long and hard to pour your heart and soul into your publication. Now, think of the creation of your book's online web presence as the final piece of your manuscript; it's like you are creating that last chapter or index to your book's contents. Don't delay or resist: Start now. Give your book its own identity online and spur the resulting conversation from your audience via your book website.

Think Like a Publisher

On the web you are your own publisher, so authors need to begin to think like publishers, as our author client David Meerman Scott suggests at the end of Chapter 1. Publishers of nonfiction and fiction generally won't move forward to contract without a proposal in hand that contains a road map to the book, where several things need to be clear. First, the defined market for the book. Next must come a well-defined audience description and table of contents or summary of what the book is about geared to that audience. Finally, the proposal should include a list of the top three competing titles and a clear author bio showing why you are the perfect author for this book along with a summary of your author platform. The book proposal, with this information, is the ticket to have in hand before a publisher will make an offer on your book; from there the details in your proposal are used over and over as a reference point for every decision on how that book will be promoted and sold. Whether you self-publish or traditionally publish, craft your book proposal (use the format at waterside.

com) carefully and with depth, and then use it to guide how and what you publish on your author platform.

Most importantly, publishers already understand the new mind-set online: It isn't about pushing an advertising message; it's about delivering quality content to a well-defined audience. Only by understanding what your audience is interested in can you use the Web 2.0 tools covered in these chapters and master that flow of audience interactivity to your advantage. The built-in avenue for conversation with your audience via comments delivers rich information from your audience for you to respond to, and when you deliver what your audience needs, in their own terms, they will end up buying more.

Create a Website for Each Book

Once your book is written, it takes on a presence of its own, like any creative work of art. Your book is a catalyst, creating its own following that can become distinct from your following as an author. In fact, many readers can't remember an author's name but will more readily remember and recommend a book title.

When you create a website for each book you publish, you permit the book to draw in audience. Then each site connects back to your author site via links, like spokes back to the hub. It might seem excessive to dedicate a separate website to each book—versus the quick route of presenting all your books on one site—but there are strategic reasons for creating separate sites.

Reason # 1: Multiple Sites Enable Readers to Find Your Book by Its Title and by Keywords

Authors often overlook this simple fact: Online shoppers must be able to find your book before they can buy it. In a brick-and-mortar store, face-out book covers in displays and circular racks and books prominently displayed by the register are competing to catch the customer's eye, and a book website serves the same purpose. With increasing numbers of book titles being promoted online, you and your associates, publisher, or team need to do whatever it takes for your customers to find your book.

When your potential buyers search by keyword or title on Google and other search engines, you want your book to pop up in every case. Therefore your book site must use all of the possible keywords they may search on, including your book's title. The keywords lead your audience right to your book's website, including your fantastic book cover, compelling copy that convinces your customer why they need to buy your book, and endorsements of your work.

Reason #2: Your Book Website Doubles as an Online Bookstore

Your book's website is an easy vehicle for your customer to use to make a purchase using a credit card number. Sell your book directly from your site by including a very prominent Buy Now link that takes your reader to Amazon or another online retailer to make the purchase. Or better yet, join the Amazon Affiliate program and Amazon will give you a tiny portion of your book's sale price when you place their Buy button on your site—more on this later.

Reason #3: Your Book Website Is an Information Kiosk for Booksellers

Your book website not only connects your book with your audience, but it also connects your book to the publishing world, including booksellers.

Before the web, bookseller buyers—those who made the choices of what to stock on the shelves at chain bookstores—were generally approachable only by publisher sales reps in closed-door meetings. These nationwide buyers for the bookstore chains were powerful, as they ordered books for all of their national brick-and-mortar stores. It was gut-wrenching to watch books being pitched in one-minute increments to these buyers in far-too-short meetings, and often by the catalog-sized load. As an editor, I sat in on some of these meetings, trying to add value and substance to presenting book titles that flew quickly by the buyer. We worked long and hard to make these books great, and we had about two minutes to present each one. Now, via the book website, book retailers can take as long as they like to peruse your site, so be sure to make your book site compelling for this audience.

Previously, booksellers heard sales promotion copy read to them by salespeople twice removed from the author and once removed from the publishers' marketing department that wrote this descriptive copy. Your book site is your chance to be heard in your own authentic author's voice; use it as a springboard for in-store book sales.

If you're publishing through a traditional publisher, your efforts are more than doubled via the publishers' own glossy catalogs handed out to booksellers by the sales team and at industry shows like Book Expo America. Traditional publishers live and breathe via the bookseller relationship; they understand and cater to this relationship, so by all means research publisher book catalogs for models of copy that appeal to book retailers.

> **Side Note:** Online book sales have dramatically changed the bookselling landscape in the same way that pretty much all areas of online retailing have changed the sales landscape. The resulting change for authors in Amazon's rise as a mega-digital bookseller is that it has enabled the rise of do-it-yourself publishing, shelving self-published books side by side with traditionally published books. What a lot of authors don't realize is that traditional publishers are also in the ebook business and sell both electronic and print versions of the same book.

Book Clubs, Booksellers, and Your Book Site

Booksellers who come across your book site are usually in the process of searching the Internet for product information. They want to find out more about the titles they are considering selling and want to anticipate which titles are a good fit for book clubs that may be organized by the store. Many of these are independent bookstores in smaller settings, so the booksellers tend to research and choose their titles carefully. Design your book site anticipating the information booksellers need most:

Provide a book summary booksellers can use. In bookstores, book summaries often appear on notecards, handwritten as a "Staff Recommends" paragraph. If you provide that paragraph on your book website, you'll save booksellers time and increase the likelihood of having your book placed on in-store promotional tables.

Categorize the reader's experience. Buyers categorize and shelve titles explicitly in their stores, so with your book summary, make it easy for your buyers to place your book in the category where you and your publisher think it belongs; indicate clearly on your book site whether your book is fiction, self-help, informational, inspirational, or some other category. Paper books always carry a back-cover description of where to shelve the book, so be sure your site description is consistent with that.

Highlight your book's book club potential. Describe for the benefit of all the book clubs out there why your book is noteworthy and provocative. You can help these groups by giving some suggested discussion points for your book. Research typical book club discussion points, which might include such questions as "Is the book believable?" "How is the story told?" or something as simple as "What is the book about?" Keep in mind that book club sales are viral and many books have remained on the *New York Times* bestseller lists because of ongoing group sales to these discussion groups. Some groups even hold "Bookies," award ceremonies where clubs vote for their favorite annual read. Award ceremonies also create excellent speaking opportunities for authors. It's obviously a treat for a book club to host an author anytime. Call your local bookstore manager to volunteer to speak at any upcoming book club events.

Include Amazon page copy. Work with your publishing team to make the product description on Amazon as effective as possible. If you're self-published, use Amazon's Author Central to edit this description. Go to the Books tab of your Author Central page. Align your book with other top-selling books, mentioning those books in manner of "you'll like this book if you liked titles x, y, and z." We'll cover Author Central more thoroughly in our Amazon chapter, Chapter 12.

Indicate speaking availability. Let the world know that you are available for speaking engagements at local bookstores, at book club meetings, and other events to increase your opportunities for promotion. An active author-appearance calendar is one of the main strategies independent bookstores have used to survive in the current bookselling climate. When you contact bookstore owners, include existing video links to your past speaking appearances, which you would have started recording according to the guidelines set out about video in Chapter

10. Also broadcast that you're happy to contribute to in-bookstore newsletters. Many book club selections are made because authors are willing to visit the clubs and speak about their books. Readers buy more books directly at live talks because of the effectiveness of hearing and meeting the author in person.

Choose a Model Book Site

Research websites of books similar to yours for ideas on how to model your own site. Study how Amazon showcases and markets books to attract readers, engages them with interactive reviews, and provides samples with their Look Inside and Buy Now buttons; you can emulate these techniques

Book website for Timothy Keiningham and Lerzan Aksoy, authors of *Why Loyalty Matters.*

on your book site, especially if you're planning to sell books from your site directly. Also review the book sites associated with BenBella, our publisher, who we chose based on their strong list of unique and eclectic titles and their ability as an independent publisher to create multiple *New York Times* bestsellers. You can find model book sites from titles listed from BenBella at benbellabooks.com.

Our publisher, BenBella, created the book website for *Why Loyalty Matters*, which effectively draws in the reader because it's not overloaded with advertising and glossy promotion. Instead, the copy appeals directly to the audience, starting with a question that acknowledges the problems that need solving and then showing how the book addresses these issues. The ideal book site strategy is based on the buying cycle of attracting your audience, then quickly engaging them further, leading them into your free sample writing excerpt and then converting readers into buyers so that they click Buy.

Solve Needs to Attract Audience

How can you use web interactivity to grow your audience? Some authors use the direct method—asking their audiences what they need. Some ask directly via Q&A feedback, where the readers ask the questions and post their problems. People are becoming accustomed to expressing themselves on the web; if you're tuned into soliciting feedback often, and noting their needs as you listen, you'll be able to respond to their comments and questions in a helpful way that will build your audience. The effectiveness of your book site depends on knowing and addressing these needs.

A Simple Format for Your Book Website

What makes a great author book site? First, all eyes must be drawn to your book cover. Keep an open look and feel surrounding your book cover. Yes, it's tempting to choose from all the cool bells and whistles available to dress up your site, but minimal design, simple graphics, and easy navigation ought to draw your audience to the main attraction: your book. As brick-and-mortar bookstore managers know, it's important to avoid too many visual elements that distract people from buying. A minimalist website design using open space creates ease of use and enables easy purchasing on both desktop and mobile devices.

Getting your audience to your book site and keeping them there means their user experience needs to be easy and pleasurable. Here are the essential pages you'll want to have in place.

1. **Landing page.** This is the page your readers see when they click over to your book site, so make it shine with your high-resolution book cover photo. Before you post a cover photo to your book site, compare your graphic to the quality of the images on Amazon or on publisher sites to make sure yours looks equally professional. This means no blurring, cropping, tilting, or distortion. On this page include:

   - Back-cover book copy: Use models from publisher websites, preferably in an easily digestible list; consider the top three reasons why your readers want to read your book and find the fewest words to express that in bullet form. You can find more models of enticing, descriptive back-cover copy on the back of published books. Include a Read More button that connects to your book's About page.
   - Praise quote: A positive quote from a notable person or someone who found your book helpful.
   - Author photo: Professional, consistent with your author platform look.
   - Contact information: Invite your audience to reach out to you directly about your book. Provide a direct link to your author website, and also list on your book site all the contact information you provide on your author site: your email, phone number—which can be through Google Voice—your social media handles, as well as a link to a Contact Me form. Many authors include basic contact information in the footer of every page of their book websites.
   - Bio showing your expertise: A short list of your qualifications, also linking to your About page.
   - Freebie: A link to a free downloadable excerpt from your book.
   - Book trailer or video: See Chapter 10.
   - Navigation Tabs: Clear places to click on to link to the other pages on your book site.

2. **About page.** Accessible from the Read More button on your landing page, this page offers behind-the-scenes information with an easily scannable bulleted list of what readers will learn from your book. Add a longer version of your author bio related to your expertise or just more personal, humanizing facts and stories—but no embellishing the truth here.

3. **Reviews page.** Use this page for author testimonials, media reviews, and other favorable comments, many of which can be harvested from your associates, your social media channels, clients, fans, and students you're connected to.

4. **Press Room page.** This page includes the press release announcement for your book that you or your publisher create at book release. This is also the place to promote media placements that pertain to you and your book, including any outlets that have published excerpts from your book. Add links to audio and video clips (media interviews and past appearances) as they become available. This list is fluid, so continue to add to it as you expand your author platform.

5. **Coming Soon page.** A place to list all upcoming events, including what your next book will be about. Your audience will want to know about your next book and publication date, virtual and live book tours, availability to speak, upcoming newsletters, webinars, webcasts, videos, speaking engagements, and all other events.

Book Website Content Strategy

Your book site is created for your readers to find your book, so it helps to know how to write the copy that will make it as easy as possible for search engines to find your book site. As a search engine, Google puts an emphasis on having the best content rise to the top of searches. We've emphasized throughout this book that you want links to your author platform as close to the top of search results as possible. Ideally your author website, book site, your publisher's site, and the Amazon page for your book will all appear prominently in all searches related to you and your niche.

Google's role in raising the bar for quality web content is a variation on the traditional publisher's "gatekeeper" role. A publisher can simply choose not to publish a book, but Google cannot choose not to include all information in search results. Instead of preventing poor-quality information from showing up on the web at all, the Google search engine will just rank low-quality entries so low that nobody will be able to find them.

Best Practices in Creating Book Website Content

Our key message to you is focus on what you do best as an author: write well and cover topics and stories that your audience wants to hear about. To guide authors in creating web content, we advise them to pay attention to the criteria that Google has created showing "what counts as a high-quality site":

- Give trustworthy information, always.
- Present high-quality, well-edited writing.
- Publish content written by an expert who knows the topic well.
- Avoid duplicate or overlapping articles.
- Avoid errors in spelling or errors that are stylistic or factual.
- Have topics driven by the genuine interests of readers.
- Show originality in your information, reporting, research, and analysis.
- Provide substantial value compared to similar websites.
- Give even treatment to both sides of a story.
- Include complete, comprehensive descriptions.
- Provide insightful analysis, interesting information beyond the obvious.
- Give readers motivation to share, recommend, or bookmark your content.
- Don't display ads that distract from or interfere with your content.
- Have writing good enough to be in a book or magazine.
- Show great care and attention to detail.

Adapted from "More Guidance on Building High-Quality Sites," Amit Singhal, Google Fellow.

Improving Your Search Results with Incoming Links

Keep in mind that each link to a page on your book website from another site adds to your site's page rank. As you build your platform and make more connections, don't hesitate to ask your fans to link to their favorite content on your site. Those connections won't come overnight, so ask well in advance of your book's publication date.

Also, thanks to Google+ Authorship, discussed in Chapter 4, now your online authorship profile lets you establish your authority in your niche. As you put more reliable, high-quality content online, everything you write should rank higher in the relevant Google search results.

Create Your Book Site in WordPress

Just as with your author website, you can create all the elements of your book site in WordPress. In this part of the chapter, we'll show you how. In Chapter 2, we showed you how to choose a theme. In this chapter, we will walk you through adding pages to your book site beyond your landing page and show you how to create a custom navigation menu.

We'll assume you have installed WordPress on your host's server, separately from your author website. You can have more than one site working from a single WordPress installation, but with sufficient disk space, it's easier to work with separate installations. Work with your hosting company for guidance about how to set up your book site separately from your author site.

How to Create Your Press Room and Other Pages

Because WordPress has its roots in blogging, a WordPress landing page naturally shows individual posts scrolling in reverse chronological order. For your book site, nearly all of your content will appear on what Word-Press calls Pages. These are the parts of a site where the content changes infrequently, if at all.

The Press Room page will have links to all your publicity material. This includes high-resolution photos of you and your book cover, a news release, and perhaps links to audio and video content stored on your author site or elsewhere.

From your WordPress admin page, click **Pages** to see the default page. Click **Add New**. Type "Press Room" for a title at the top of the page. In the editor, type "Author Website," select the text, and click the **hyperlink icon** (looks like a chain link). Type the address of your author site in the URL box and choose an alternate title (something like Home Base for Author <name>). This alternate title serves a double function. It appears as a tool tip if a visitor's mouse hovers over the link, and if an audio screen reader is being used to browse the site for a visually impaired visitor, it will report the alternate title instead of spelling out the URL.

To include a PDF version of your news release, click **Add Media**. Drag the PDF from your file manager into the window (or just choose **Select Files**). WordPress automatically puts the file name into the Title box; you can edit this if the file name isn't that attention grabbing. If this were a picture, you could add a caption, and a description is always nice, if not required. When you're done, click **Insert Into Page**. WordPress automatically turns that into a link to the title you selected.

If you make an ebook excerpt of your book available for download, you can use the Add Media window to create the link to it, along with any other PDF content you want to share.

Use the Add Media window to include those high-resolution photos. If your audio and video clips are stored on your site—as opposed to a dedicated video-hosting site like Vimeo or YouTube, discussed in Chapter 10—use this process. You can also use **Insert from URL** in the **Add Media** window to link to YouTube or whatever external site your multimedia content is located.

When you're finished making your page, click **Preview** to see how the page will look on your site, then click **Publish** to add the page.

Repeat this process for the Why This Book, About the Author, and Reviews pages.

As you receive media coverage for your book, consider adding a separate Posts page with a chronological listing of links to news stories. Add links to audio and video clips (media interviews and past appearances) as they become available. Link this to the Press Room page.

Adding a Navigation Menu

Now that you have some pages pulled together, help your readers more easily navigate your site. The best way to do this is through a custom menu, supported in all WordPress themes (though some themes support more than one menu on a site).

Go to Appearance > Menus on your admin page. Type in a Menu Name (for example, Navigation) in the appropriate box, and then click **Create Menu**.

You'll see a list of all the pages you have created. If you want all of them on the menu, click **Select All**, otherwise just check the box next to the ones

---

Book Websites We Like

- Carol Roth, *The Entrepreneur Equation* (theentrepreneurequation.com)
- Haruki Murakami Books (murakamibooks.co.uk)
- Trevor Blake, *Three Simple Steps* (trevorgblake.com)
- Lauren Oliver Books (laurenoliverbooks.com)
- Christopher Kennedy Lawford, *Recover to Live* (christopherkennedylawford.com/recovertolive)
- Lindsay Nixon, The Happy Herbivore series (happyherbivore.com)
- Christy Whitman & Rebecca Grado, *Taming Your Alpha Bitch* (tamingyouralphabitch.com)
- William Gladstone (12thebook.com)
- T. Colin Campbell, *Whole* (thechinastudy.com)
- Sophia A. Nelson, *Black Woman Redefined* (blackwomanredefined.com/about-the-book)
- Joe Sweeney, *Networking Is a Contact Sport* (joesweeney.com/networking-is-a-contact-sport)
- Gino Wickman, *Traction: Get a Grip on Your Business* (eosworldwide.com/traction/eos-traction-book)
- Napoleon Gomez, *Collapse of Dignity* (collapseofdignity.com)
- Shama Kabani, *Zen of Social Media* (shamakabani.com/books)
- Craig Brandon, *The Five Year Party* (thefiveyearparty.com)
- Sean O'Neil and John Kulisek, *Bare Knuckle People Management* (bareknucklepeoplemanagement.com)

you want (Press Room, Why This Book, About the Author, and Reviews). Click **Add to Menu**. They will appear in the Menu window on the right.

Don't like the default order? Just drag and drop until it's set the way you like it. Want to set up a hierarchical structure for the menus? Drag a subordinate page to the right of the item you want as the main menu.

When you're done determining the size and scope of the menu, click **Save Menu**. Select this menu as your primary menu in the Theme Locations area. Go to the black bar at the top to view the site. You can return to the Menus page to make any more changes you like. Remember to click **Save Menu** before leaving the admin page.

Your book site should now look dazzling and be useful for your audience, too.

Linking to Booksellers

To keep things simple, always have your graphic Buy Now button (however many times it appears on your book site) go to the same bookseller, whether it's Amazon or your publisher, and in Chapter 12, we'll tell you how to maximize the resources at Amazon.

Wherever your Buy Now button leads to, you'll still want to consider linking to other booksellers—a sale *is* a sale, after all!—and it's fine to list those under a heading that says something like "Buy This Book from the Following Booksellers."

Beyond Amazon, consider listing the following:

- Your publisher's site: In the case of this book, that's BenBella (benbellabooks.com).
- BarnesandNoble.com: The largest brick-and-mortar chain, and home of the Nook family of tablets and e-readers. BarnesandNoble.com offers an affiliate program through Rakuten LinkShare that gives you a small slice of every sale you send their way.
- IndieBound.org: This site from the American Booksellers Association (the trade group of independent booksellers) allows readers to buy your book online or find a local outlet to buy from. There's an affiliate program here, too.

What's an Affiliate Program?

Some authors finance their website expenses by selling things available through other sites. Most online booksellers will give you a sales button with a code attached. When someone visits your site and clicks the Buy at <vendorA> button, when the purchase is complete, VendorA will credit you a referral bonus. The individual bonus usually amounts to a few cents on each purchase, but they can add up. Also, if a buyer clicks from your page to another page and purchases a much larger item, you receive a small percentage of that sale, too. Amazon, for example, sends out affiliate bonus checks monthly and emails you a sales report, even if "You did not earn any advertising fees during the last payment period."

The good thing about affiliate programs is that there's no cost to set them up, so it could effectively become a source of "free money." Whether you want to take the time to jump through the registration hoops in hopes of a few dollars is up to you.

Your book site is the central location where your readers and book-sellers can find your book by searching by its title. The book website is a showcase where your book takes on a life of its own. The site also serves as an online kiosk for selling as well as a repository for information specifically for bookstore owners and buyers and book clubs. The rewards far outweigh the time and effort spent in creating this site.

Checklist, Step 11: Book Website

➤ Create a book website in addition to your author website built during Step 1.
➤ Use your book title as your URL.
➤ Showcase a large photo of your book cover on the landing page.
➤ List your book's back-cover copy in short succinct points on the landing page.
➤ Place a **Buy Now** button next to the book, linked to Amazon.
➤ Create pages beyond your landing page.
➤ Include a link back to your author site.

Success Spotlight: Waterside Client Tee Morris
(teemorris.com)

- 12 books
- 4 translations
- 3 podcast novels
- 5 podcasts
- 7 awards

Genre: Epic fantasy, detective fiction, steampunk, nonfiction

Beginnings: Tee Morris began writing adventure stories in the fifth grade but "never took it seriously enough to think I would be a writer." He graduated from James Madison University, majoring in theater and mass communications.

Morris advised in our interview for this book, "Always write for fun and keep your day job." Interspersed with his fiction writing, he has written books on social media and video editing, and has worked as a columnist. In 2011 his novel *Phoenix Rising: A Ministry of Peculiar Occurrences*, cowritten with his wife, Philippa Ballantine, won an Airship Award for best written work.

In 2005 Tee Morris became the first author to podcast a whole novel, *Morevi: The Chronicles of Rafe and Askana*. Morris is also one of the founders of Podiobooks.com.

Morris decided that even though he had great ideas and knew he had an audience out there, he also knew he needed to build up the business aspect of his work. He learned more about getting a book published and how to market it, and then created his strategy to carry him through the process.

Tee's advice to authors: Know that you need a business aspect to your work as a writer. Read all you can about it, choose the team and elements that work for you, craft your strategy, and then go out there and implement your whole plan.

CHAPTER 12

Amazon.com—Your Author Toolbox and World's Largest Online Bookstore

"If you build a great experience, customers tell each other about that. Word of mouth is very powerful."

—*Jeff Bezos, CEO & President of Amazon.com*

- The marketing department at Berett-Koehler Publishing rallies authors to regard Amazon as "Your billboard to the world."
- McGraw-Hill marketing tells authors to use Amazon's Author Central as "a free service provided by Amazon to allow you to reach more readers, promote your title, and help build a better Amazon bookstore."
- The Penguin marketing department tells authors to use Amazon as "an online marketing tool."

JEFF BEZOS CREATED AMAZON.COM as an online bookstore, disrupting both paper-based publishing and brick-and-mortar bookstores. Yet at the same time, he opened virtual doors to a substantial place for readers to find and share books, for self-published books to stand side by side with traditionally published books, and for authors to build author platform and audience. The customer experience at Amazon shaped the era of the electronic bookstore and the electronic book. The whole Amazon retail experience grew out of selling books online.

Amazon's ability to digitally warehouse books gave Amazon substantial advantage over brick-and-mortar stores. The costs of doing business online were significantly lower, and the exposure of all book titles online was larger than shelf space at any physical bookstore.

Amazon's online retail book presence grew, and the development and sale of their ebook hardware soon followed. The slim, portable Amazon Kindle became an instant success, followed by the equally successful Kindle Fire. Soon Bezos' innovative approach to the online book business led to Amazon's growth into the world's largest online retailer, now selling every conceivable product, from clothing and housewares to appliances and more. Along the way, Amazon also pioneered tools that make it possible for readers to encounter new books in ways they wouldn't have otherwise.

Reasons Readers Flock to Amazon

Book readers love Amazon; we can easily find the books we want at great prices, get recommendations and sample book text, and find used and rare books as well as ebooks on topics that longer books may not cover in depth. But Amazon is more than a fantastic place for book lovers to search for book and author information; it's also a fantastic place for readers to talk directly to authors and for authors to grow audience.

Reasons to Use Amazon Author Central

As an author, your power spot at Amazon is Author Central. The second your book is published and your book has an ISBN, Amazon allows you to create your free author account. Once set up, your account prompts you to create an Author Page. The beauty of this page is that you are the only one who creates and controls it. You decide how to present your author biographical information and book synopsis, not an intermediary. This means your readers have a point-of-sale location that you control, to explore further information about you and your work. This is point-of-purchase magic in the digital age. Here are even more reasons to set up Author Central:

Purchases of your book made through browsing. The latest studies show that only about half of book purchases are made by people looking for a specific title. The other half? People browsing, discovering titles they previously had never heard of. The discoverability of your title by avid readers looking to find a book that interests them boosts your book sales significantly.

Searchability. Once your Amazon page is done, your readers can find you and your book outside of Amazon, too. When people use Google or other search engines, they'll see your Author Page since it is indexed by Google. When you add a link to your Author Page to your author platform, including your author website and social networks, you'll increase your discoverability factor, which in turn leads to a boost in your book sales.

Retail book presence at the world's largest online bookstore. Book buyers at physical stores simply cannot stock all book titles due to limited physical shelf space. Unfortunately, if your book doesn't show up on the shelf at a physical bookstore, readers generally purchase some other title. It's a better situation for authors at Amazon since every book gets on the shelf, and with author information and a book synopsis right next to the virtual cash register. When you create your Author Page well with compelling information about your background, your photo, and links to your author platform, you inspire and enable your readers to look deeper into your table of contents, leading to the purchase of your book.

Connecting and engaging directly with your potential buyers. Readers visiting Amazon are generally giving thought to making their book purchases, and some buyers never explore other online book retailers. Think of Amazon as a place to meet and greet qualified buyers of your book and to put forth your best impression for the customer to experience you and your book. The bottom of your Author Page offers a Customer Discussions area, with a forum where you and your fans can post questions and opinions about your work. Depending on how active your fan base is, and your ability to manage the interactivity, the forum could become like a Facebook page where you can interact, very much like interacting at the point of purchase. See the author page discussion later in the chapter for more information.

Free advertising built into Amazon carrying your book for sale. Consider that Amazon could charge authors a signup fee for Author Central if they wanted and that most authors would gladly pay it for the exposure. Also consider the high price of a Bestseller Campaign (covered later in this chapter) and you'll begin to appreciate the fantastic opportunity you are handed with your free Author Central account.

Access to sales figures through Nielsen BookScan. Amazon Author Central partners with Nielsen BookScan to give authors free access to weekly sales updates. Formerly, the BookScan information was a very expensive way that publishers gained inside information about sales in the industry. Now authors have the same ability at Amazon, *knowing* instead of just wondering how well your book is selling in relation to others. You will also get additional information to help you further; by knowing exactly where, geographically, your book is selling, you can target your media events to places where your book sells most. If your book is selling well locally, you could positively impact sales by scheduling additional local events and book club appearances.

> **Side Note:** BookScan's main limitation is that its sales figures reflect only approximately 75% of U.S. sales.

Create Your Author Central Page

Before creating your page, it's best to look at others' Author Pages to get a flavor for what you feel will be most interesting to your audience. It's always good to take a look at books that you feel are similar to yours so that you can position your work in its own unique category. In the publishing industry, editors work to make a statement to the sales department about why your book will sell instead of or in addition to another book of its kind, so it's best to think through your unique proposition before writing your page.

In this section, we walk you through creating the basics of your Author Central account. We also show you how to keep control of the pieces of your author platform. As with all the steps in this book, you'll want to create your Author Page so that it's connected to your author website and consistent with the other elements of your author platform.

First, sign up for Author Central at authorcentral.amazon.com. Click **Join Now**. You can use your email address if you already make purchases on Amazon or click **No, I am a new customer**. Next, click **Agree to Author Central's Terms and Conditions**. Enter your author name consistent with the way it appears on your author platform (and, we hope, on your published book). Next, choose from the list of possible book matches that appear, which creates your account.

Amazon will contact your publisher to confirm that you are the author of the book you're claiming, and three to five days later your Author Page will show up on the Amazon site. You can, however, begin adding content to your Author Page as soon as you sign up.

In Author Central, click the **Profile tab**. You'll see sections for adding or changing your biography, photos, videos, speaking or other events, and blog feeds. Stay consistent but fresh by rewording instead of exactly duplicating your information for your audience, and add tidbits that are relevant. Most importantly, focus on what elements will be of most interest to your readers, as you've heard in comments and other feedback.

Later on in the chapter, we'll show you how to add cool Amazon widgets that link your author and book sites directly to Amazon.

Click **Add** or **Edit** next to any section you choose. Instructions appear, along with space to add information. If you do not add information to any particular section, this section will not appear on your Author Page, so be sure to add all information you can or remind yourself to add it later.

Adding Site Updates and Twitter Feeds to Your Author Page

Keeping your readers (and potential readers) informed about what you're writing and thinking about is a pretty easy task, as Amazon allows your Author Page to link to your Twitter feed and blog.

As Amazon considers any site with an RSS feed to be a "blog," one advantage to using WordPress for your author website is that your site will have an RSS feed by default.

On your Author Central profile page, click **Add Blog**. In the box that appears, just type "http://<your site URL>/feed/" and click **Add**. If you prefer, visit your site first. Look for a link called **Entries RSS**. Right-click and select **Copy Link Address**. Go back to Author Central and paste that URL into the **Add Blog** box.

Amazon checks that feed once a day for new content. Anything you post to your site will appear on your Amazon Author Page within 24 hours, but content posted before your Author Page "subscribed" to your site will not appear.

Your Author Page will also post your most recent tweet. Click **Add** (or **Edit**) **Account** in the **Twitter section** of your profile and type your Twitter user name into the box. Note that Amazon will only link to one Twitter feed, so if you have separate Twitter accounts for your books or characters, you will have to choose one account at a time. In nearly all cases, you should use your primary author account.

Maintaining Your Author Page

Once you have your Author Page set up, you'll want to monitor its progress with your audience so that you can adjust it to better meet its needs. Check it periodically to see:

- How your book is being reviewed.
- How your book is selling.

Aside from the automatic updates that your Author Page will pull from your website and Twitter feed, you'll want to keep your Author Page current with:

- **New books and biographical information:** As new titles appear in the bookstore, make sure Amazon associates your name with your next project. We will cover how to do this later in the chapter. Update your biographical information as new and wonderful things happen in your life: honors, new jobs, sales records, and new projects.
- **New photos:** Only in JPEG format, 300 to 2,500 pixels width and height, no larger than 4MB.

- **Fresh videos:** Under 10 minutes and 500MB. Must be uploaded from your computer (YouTube links not permitted).
- **Upcoming events:** Live or online. Post the date, time, venue, and a brief description of your event.

You'll also want to periodically update your Reading List and correct any product details, amend book pages, update your book cover image if needed, and add any Book Extras.

EDITING BOOK DETAILS AND ADDING NEW BOOKS

People aren't perfect. Perhaps someday you'll look at your Amazon book page and realize the page count is wrong or you'll identify a misspelling. While Amazon retains full control of everything on the book page, registered authors can propose changes to correct errors from Author Central.

Log into Author Central and go to the **Books tab**. Under **Book Details**, you'll see the general information for your book; at the bottom click **Suggest Product Information Updates**. A form will appear that allows you to make corrections for Title, Contributors, Binding (paperback, hardcover), Publisher, Publication Date, Number of Pages, Edition, Format, and Language.

When you've made your changes, you must identify where Amazon can verify the changes. They won't just take your word for it, but if, for example, you can take a picture of the "real" last page, along with the book's ISBN or barcode, you can upload the image to confirm.

Similarly, if Amazon hasn't automatically added your next title to your Author Page, you can update this information from Author Central as well. From the **Books tab**, click **Add More Books**. You'll be asked to identify the book by title, author, or ISBN. Click **This is my book** from the search results to confirm. Amazon will add this title to Author Central within five days.

Link Your Author Website to Author Central

Remember that an essential part of author platform building is to maintain a clear and consistent central location, which is your author website. Everything, including this Amazon page, links back to your author site.

To do this, look at the top of your profile page, where you will see the **Author Page URL widget**. As with LinkedIn and other sites where your profile page is normally represented in the site's organization by a number, the Author Page URL allows you to define a more human-readable link to your Amazon Author Page. Click **Add Link** to create this URL.

Amazon will suggest a URL, such as amazon.com/author/<yourname>. For consistency's sake, it is always best to use some form of your name, but you can choose anything up to 30 characters. The box will determine if your selection is available, before you make it final by clicking **Save**. Among the options, you can add a dash (your-name), a period (your.name) or an underscore (your_name) to differentiate yourself from any other authors who may share your name.

Amazon pledges that any links to your new Author Page URL will be live in 30 minutes, so feel free to add the URL to your author and book websites, email signature, and anywhere else you can think of to promote the page. You'll even find handy links on your profile page to post your Author Page URL to your Facebook author Page and Twitter and to add to your email signature. See the **Author Page URL** heading in the right sidebar, and click the respective logos next to **Share this URL**.

While we do not recommend that you connect Amazon to your personal Facebook page, as it allows Amazon to use information from your Facebook profile, you can safely post the Amazon Author Page URL to your author or book Pages on Facebook. Click the **Facebook icon** on your profile. When your Facebook share page appears, you'll see an option to share on your timeline. Click the drop-down menu to select **On a Page You Manage**, then select your author or book Page. Click **Share** to post.

Amazon Book Reviews

In 2010, Amazon was reported as being the largest single source of Internet consumer reviews. Since most book buyers read posted reviews before they buy, they can be very strongly influenced by what others have said about your book. We explain book reviews in detail in Chapter 13 and focus on the intricacies of Amazon's reviewer process in particular.

Here are the rules of the game:

Third-party reviews are posted directly. Amazon allows readers to write book reviews and then post these reviews to your book page, along with a rating from one to five stars.

Reviews are permanent once they are posted. As an author, you cannot change or delete book reviews posted to your Amazon book page.

Reviewers can remain anonymous. At Amazon it's not required to leave a real name. Reviewers can use their badging option to reveal their real name if they wish. Use of a real name cannot be faked, as Amazon authenticates real names based on confirming credit card numbers.

Amazon has designated Top Reviewers. These Top Reviewers have more clout than average reviewers because they have proven to be reliable, fair, and prolific in creating many reviews. As an option, you can send an email query to any of these Top Reviewers directly to ask for them to review your book. For the list of Amazon Top Reviewers, go to amazon .com/review/top-reviewers and search for reviewers who review similar titles. One of Amazon's Top Ten Reviewers tells authors how to ask for the review here: badredheadmedia.com/2013/02/26/suggestions -for-writers-when-contacting-amazon-reviewers-by-guest-tunguz.

Customers can comment or vote on the reviews. Reviews accumulate comments that indicate whether or not a customer found a particular review helpful to them. If a review is given enough "helpful" hits, it always appears on the front page of the product. It's important that your first reviews are positive, because they will likely get enough Helpful votes to remain on the first page.

> **Side Note:** The sad side of Amazon reviews: Amazon checks names with the credit card name of the reviewer, but even so, we've seen many cases of fake reviews being written, posted, and later discovered by Amazon and discredited. We've heard of both extremes: instances where competitors have used separate email accounts with pseudonyms to write negative reviews and cases of authors writing fake rave reviews for themselves.

Managing Amazon Reviews

You've come to the stage when building your author platform pays off. If you've worked to build up an audience that trusts you, they will generally champion your work. Conversely, if you have not worked to build up an audience following and only blasted advertising to people who really don't care, you're unlikely to be capable of the next step, which is to influence people to write and post book reviews. Here are some ways to motivate people to write reviews and to manage them effectively:

Simply ask people for reviews. This includes everyone who supports you: friends, associates, connections, and members of your early audience. It helps to have a tribe or community of writers, clients, and associates. If you belong to a literary agency like Waterside, with a very large database of authors who can review each other's books, so much the better. It never hurts to ask all these people. Mike has friends who have occasionally alerted him to unfavorable reviews, the response to which usually is to ask a friend or colleague to counter with a positive review. The point of soliciting any praise, however, is not to accumulate all 5-star reviews—otherwise the write-ups will seem fake. You're going for sincerity. For nonfiction, it's better to have your reviewers explain what they liked about your book and how it helped them, which will read as more sincere to customers just discovering your book. For fiction, it's better to ask your reviewers to focus on a single aspect of your book that they liked best that touched, moved, or entertained them.

Don't stop at one or two. Get as many reviews as possible, as it shows lots of people are interested in your book. If there are authentic negative reviews, try to accumulate as many positive reviews as possible, since people generally read the first few reviews before moving on; if there is a long list of reviews, Amazon will only show the first few, and you'll need to click Additional Reviews to see more. If the reviews are overwhelmingly positive, it doesn't matter if a couple of them are negative.

Read all of your reviews. Keep an eye out for trolls, nasty personalities, or competitors who attack by writing nasty reviews of your book to make their own work "seem" better. There's a difference between a negative review (which can help you find the gaps and other weaknesses in your work) and an all-out malicious attack on an author or book. Amazon's Community Help Department sometimes helps delete messages that are malicious and that do not review the book itself. Our author clients have had this happen to them, and although devastated, they sometimes have been able to get help. To challenge a malicious review, you need the help of your publisher, or you can make your case directly by writing community-help@amazon.com. Include the reasons why you perceive the review as an attack and why it should be removed. Be sure to name author, title, ISBN, reviewer's stated name, date of review, and first sentence of the review for referencing.

Spotlight Reviews. These are the two special reviews that Amazon chooses to keep posted at the top permanently. How does Amazon select these two? Spotlight Reviews are chosen by Amazon based on how well the review was written and how helpful it was to customers.

Editorial Reviews at Trade Publications. You can also add reviews of up to 600 characters from trade publications. From your Author Central page, click **Books**. Click the book you have a review for, then click **Add**. Enter the name of the person who wrote the review and the name of the publication, website, or forum in which the review appeared. Paste the review into the window, and click **Save Changes**. Use this same process to add a comment "From the Author" or paste material "From the Inside Flap" or "From the Back Cover." For each of these sections, you can enter up to 8,000 characters.

Connecting Your Site to Amazon

Amazon wants to help you sell your books—through Amazon, of course. To that end, they will provide all sorts of graphical connections to your Amazon pages. We discussed the links from your author website to Amazon pages earlier. Through the Amazon Associates program (also known as Amazon Affiliates), Amazon will even pay you a small percentage of the sales you generate from your site. Note that Blogger and WordPress. com do not allow associate programs like Amazon's on their sites. If you're blogging on these sites, but believe you can generate significant income (whatever "significant income" means in your situation) through associate programs, you should move your blog to a self-hosted site.

Signing Up with Amazon Associates

1. Go to Associates Central at affiliate-program.amazon.com (or click the **Become an Amazon Affiliate** link on your Author Central page).
2. Click **Join Now for Free**.

3. Sign in with your Amazon account.
4. Confirm your address (where they send the checks!).
5. Tell them a little bit about your website, both for technical and marketing purposes. You'll be asked for the name and URL of your site, and then there is some space to tell them "what is your site about?" This can be a simple sentence: "Main website for <your name>, author of <book title or genre you work in>."
6. Verify your identity.
7. Amazon will send you a link to your new Associates account at Associates Central.

Now that you're an Amazon Associate, you can start generating income by including the special Associate links on your site.

Adding Associate Links on Your Site

At Amazon, where Author Central is the hub for your writing identity, Associates Central site is a hub for your merchant activity as an Associate. In practical terms, you have the ability to sell almost anything in Amazon's catalog on your site, but you'll want to focus on your own material. You can now search for your book title from the Associates Central site that you just joined above. Click **Get Link** to add a text link that, when clicked from your website, will generate a small chunk of change for you.

How big is that chunk of change? In practical terms, the first six sales you make in any calendar month generate an "advertising fee" of 4% of the retail price for each sale. This rate increases to 6% for sales between 7 and 30 in that same month, and escalates up to 8.5% if you sell more than 101 items per day in that same 31-day month.

A simple way for your readers to connect with your titles is the My Favorites widget. From Associates Central, click the **Widgets tab**. You'll see the available widgets listed. Under **My Favorites**, click **Add to Your Web Page**.

Use the search box to locate your title(s). Search by title or your name to get the whole list. When you find the right book, click **Add Product**. The title appears in your widget list on the right of this screen. You can add a comment to briefly describe the book. Save this item to your widget. Add others as you get them, then click **Next Step**.

Next, name the widget. By default, Amazon chooses "I recommend." You may want to choose something else ("<Your Name> on Amazon.com," for example). Customize the widget further, if you wish. You can choose from several colors, designs, and sizes. When it's ready, click **Add to My Web Page** to generate your widget.

Some really ugly text will appear in a window. Click **Copy** to put it all on your computer's clipboard. Go straight to your author or book website, and log into WordPress.

From the admin page, under **Appearance**, click **Widgets**. Depending on your theme, you will see at least one place to store widgets on the right side of the screen (go back to Chapter 1 for a refresher on adding widgets to your WordPress site). Drag a Text Widget somewhere into the sidebar, then paste the ugly-looking text into the big window. Choose a title if you like. View the site to see how it looks. Tweak the widget settings back at Amazon and generate a new widget if you need to. You may need to adjust the size of the widget to make it appear properly in the sidebar.

When someone buys one of your titles after clicking this widget (which appears in the sidebar of all pages on your author site) you will get Associates credit for referring the customer.

Take advantage of the many more options at the Amazon Associates site.

Amazon Strategy #1: Connect with Your Readers on Your Author Page

Amazon was one of the pioneers of using the capability of Web 2.0 social interaction, and those connections keep getting deeper. In this section, we'll show you how to organize discussions on your Author Page and how to contribute to Customer Communities.

Author Page Discussions

Scroll down to the bottom of your Amazon Author Page and you'll see you've got your own reader forum! With a little bit of thought, you can come up with some discussion starters for the folks who visit your Author Page.

Some possibilities might include "How did you find this page?" or "What's your toughest problem <in my niche>?" Check regularly for answers and be sure to respond to them all. Every interaction with a reader is a chance to engage with them . . . so be engaging to build audience! There are few things more exciting for a reader than to find evidence that one of their favorite writers is an actual presence in an online forum.

Join Amazon Customer Communities

Among the millions of Amazon customers, you can find groups who have a wide range of interests. It doesn't take a lot of time to join Customer Communities to broaden your audience because that is where you can share thoughts, experiences, and passion for your subject with other readers.

Find Amazon Customer Communities by going to the Amazon tag cloud page; also, each product page shows the Customer Communities associated with that product. Scroll down below the Customer Reviews section to find them. Or search Amazon for communities by using a keyword followed by the word "community." For example: author platform community. If there is a community on this topic, you'll see the link to the forum for discussion.

Any visitor on Amazon's site can read the discussions in any given community, so it's a highly visible platform for you to use to great advantage. When you find a community, it's easy to jump right in—all you have to do is reply to a thread on a given topic or begin a new topic with a comment, question, or suggestion. Use keywords to "name" the topic so everyone in the community can see it.

Find the customer discussions on individual Amazon book product pages. If you have a book that's already been published, you can visit your product page and see what discussions are already taking place, and then join in.

Amazon Strategy #2: Create Listmania Lists

Amazon's Listmania is an amazing tool that puts your book next to others in your category, right at the book display. By placing your book right next to a competing book, you're giving your readers a choice: They found another book but suddenly they see yours. Instead of just purchasing the book they found, they can look at yours, too. It may become a choice between buying your book and the one they were looking at . . . or possibly, they'll buy both. Amazon allows you to create a Listmania list of up to 40 books (including yours) that have a common theme.

How to Create a Listmania List

You can create your Listmania list by adding your book title first, then adding up to 39·more books. Just search for and identify the top-selling books in the same category as your book. When any single one of these other books is searched on, your book may appear next to the other title. When adding books to your list, start by including the books your primary audience needs, and then consider the needs of your secondary audiences to fill out the list.

Follow these steps when constructing your list:

Name. Your list must have a catchy name that entices readers to find out more. Think of your audience when you create your Listmania title, and filter it through their eyes. The best suggestions we've seen use the audience perspective with the word "you" in the title, such as "14 Steps You Need to Create Your Author Platform."

Qualifications. Indicate what qualifies you to make your list, which in this case is that you're the author of a book with expertise in certain areas; borrow language from your author website to complete this field.

Introduction. Show through a statement why you are creating this list, at the same time demonstrating a need for your book. Many authors use a question in this section, such as "Do you know how to create your author platform quickly and easily?" after which you'd list the best books that show you how to do this.

Add a product. List your book first, at the top of the list. Choose competing or related books, which helps you because this increases your chances of showing up in search results among people who know of a competing book but didn't know about yours. When they click on a competitor's book, readers will see a Listmania of similar books.

> Make more than one Listmania list that includes your book. This will boost the appearance of your book on Amazon; the more books on your list, the more often that list will appear throughout Amazon.

Once it's set up, Amazon will display your Listmania list on your book detail page. Amazon uses the subject matter on your list to determine in which categories it should place your book, then places your Listmania on the other book pages so your audience can view your list on competing book pages. Use the best-selling books in your category so that your associations are strong.

Look Into Your Sales

Amazon Sales Rank

When your book comes out, you'll be forgiven if you spend the first week or so constantly refreshing your book's Amazon product page. From here you can see how your book is selling, at least compared to everything else Amazon sells. About halfway down the page, after the Editorial Reviews, is the Product Details section. At the bottom of that is the current Amazon Bestsellers Rank for your book. The overall ranking might be disappointing, since your competition here includes the latest celebrity memoir, heavy hitters like John Grisham, J.K. Rowling, and David Sedaris, and Oprah's latest book club selection.

With a little bit of luck, you may crack the bestseller list in one or more genres or nonfiction categories. Amazon categories can get pretty narrow; as an example, *WordPress in Depth* made these bestseller lists all at once:

Books > Computers & Internet > Home Computing > **Blogging & Blogs**
Books > Computers & Internet > Home Computing > **Internet**
Books > Computers & Internet > Web Development > **Web Services**

This will tell you how you're doing—this hour—against your real competition. You can look at these lists as a genuine barometer of the strength of your author platform. The longer you stay on those lists, the more likely it is you'll reach more of your targeted audience.

If you go back to your Author Central page, click the Rank tab. Here you can see how your books are selling at Amazon over time. Until 2012, you needed third-party help to see these statistics. No longer. With the Author Rank tab, you can see how all your books sold over the last two weeks, month, six-month period, and all time, via "all available data." You can also see a separate graph for Kindle ebook sales. Point your mouse at one of the dots on the graph to get your rank for a specific date.

BookScan data represents real sales, which eventually translates into earning out your publisher's advance to you, followed by royalty checks you can take to the bank. Because Amazon doesn't tell you directly how many sales you make on their site, you may not be able to take your Author Rank to the bank, but you will get a strong sense of how effective your promotional efforts are.

Join Search Inside the Book

Amazon's Search Inside the Book lets customers search Amazon's full book catalog by typing in keywords. Almost 200 publishers have agreed to let users search tables of contents, sample chapters, and more via this feature.

You don't have to worry that users can download the pages of your book and reuse them without buying your book. The search pages only show nontransferable, nonprintable images, and there's also a limit to how many pages can be accessed.

One benefit of having the Search Inside feature activated for your book is that all of the words contained in your book sample will be searchable, increasing the chances of your book showing up in Amazon search results—well beyond if a user had just typed your name or the title of your book into a search engine. This is why you will see many books listed with a short and a long version of the table of contents: a short one for a quick overview, the long one to yield keywords that will show up in searches. And of course, the more search results that contain your book, the more easily readers will find it.

Amazon Bestseller Campaign

How would you like to be at or near the top of the Amazon bestseller list, with your name and book title on Amazon's home page? Some publishers and book marketing firms offer a service called the Amazon Bestseller Campaign. Some people love the temporary spike in sales so that they can truthfully boast a #1 title. Technically if your book reaches #1 even for a day, you have the right to call the book a bestseller, even if it never sells another copy beyond that day.

How does this campaign work? Just pay for the service and select your target date. The service will identify existing email lists in your niche (or just book buyers in general), craft an email for the lists to send out to their subscribers, and get agreements from those list managers to include your message. On the appointed day, emails go out to your list, plus the contracted lists. This email offers readers a "free bonus gift" (ebooks, seminars, or other products) if they buy your book that day. If a user buys more than one copy, he gets more rewards.

If you have more time than money, you can try to organize both your free gifts and your network of lists on your own.

Of course, there are drawbacks to this service. Just as "Rome wasn't built in a day," an audience isn't built overnight. Aside from the high cost of this campaign, this type of email does not directly target people in your specific audience who are likely to buy your book. Informing 1,000 interested buyers is more effective than telling 10,000 uninterested people. This kind of email is also one that many people are likely to delete or ignore, as it's being blasted out to an audience of buyers who may or may not care about your book. Also, some ISPs funnel this kind of email into spam or into a Promotions folder. That said, if you have thousands of dollars to spare, the excitement of either a quick sales spike or having your book appear briefly on the bestseller list may be worth the cost to you. If so, go for it!

More Tools

Kindle Singles. These relatively brief ebooks (think of them as long magazine pieces) typically sell for $1.99, and never more than $5. The writer or publisher keeps 70% of the sale price. Kindle Singles have proven to be a lucrative market, especially for short fiction writers. Big names like Stephen King, Chuck Palahniuk, and Lee Child (of Jack Reacher mystery fame) do well, of course, but so does Mishka Shubaly, who "writes true stories about drink, drugs, disasters, desire, deception, and their aftermath. His work has been praised for its grit, humor, fearlessness, and heart." A 2012 report by paidContent.com indicated that some writers had generated six-figure incomes from the sales of Kindle Singles.

Marketing departments at publishing houses ask all authors to make full use of the many Amazon tools specifically for authors and made available on Amazon.com. With the rise of the total number of books published spiked by self-publishing, all authors need to build a very visible, engaging presence at the retailer, and Amazon delivers this opportunity as a high-traffic online bookstore and book community site.

Checklist, Step 12: Amazon's Author Toolbox

➤ Join Amazon's Author Central.
➤ Create your Author Central page and keep it updated.
➤ Upload photos and videos to your Author Central page.
➤ Cross-link to all your online locations.
➤ Solicit as many book reviews as possible from colleagues and Top Reviewers.
➤ Join and participate regularly in Amazon Customer Communities.
➤ Create Listmania lists to link your book to similar titles.

Success Spotlight: Waterside Client
John C. Havens (johnchavens.com)

- Author, *Hacking H(app)iness*, next title already in progress
- Articles: Mashable, The Guardian, and The Huffington Post plus a series for CSRWire, Fast Company, Good Men Project, and iMedia
- Twitter, Facebook, LinkedIn
- Founder, The H(app)athon Project
- *H(app)y Newsletter*
- TEDx video: https://www.youtube.com/watch?v=2obu9YY-0hI

John's best advice for authors looking to build their audience through social media:

"I think what's key with social media is to understand the time you'll need to dedicate to build genuine relationships with people on Twitter, Facebook, or other social outlets as you promote your book. While you may be able to create a video that could get a lot of hits or do a one-off campaign to build followers, they may not last if you don't reach out and connect with people about their shared interests in the topics you've written about as a way for them to stay connected with you on a long-term basis."

John became a storyteller in grade school because he was always a big ham. He was in a theatrical version of "Stone Soup" when he was a kid, got a big laugh, and was hooked. This led to a professional acting career where he fell into writing because he was good at improvisation. On certain jobs people essentially asked him to rewrite scripts, which he agreed to do after they agreed to pay him. From that point on he ghostwrote four books, wrote two ebooks, and then became About.com's first Guide to Podcasting, where he learned how to write for the "how-to" and business genres. In 2008 he published his first "traditionally published" book for Wiley Publishers.

Final word of advice: "ABC—Always Be Curious. In my case, for my first book I realized that companies were missing huge opportunities to make connections with customers by trying to protect their message to such a degree that they alienated their audiences. That's where the notion of 'Tactical Transparency' came into play. For my current work, when my Dad died I had a serious time of self-reflection that made me realize I didn't want to spend so much time trying to boost my numbers on social networks and instead wanted to help people optimize their well-being/happiness by helping them learn their worth beyond financial wealth."

CHAPTER 13

Motivate Your Audience to Talk About You: Book Reviews

"What I really like is an intelligent review. It doesn't have to be positive. A review that has some kind of insight, and sometimes people say something that's startling or is so poignant."

—*Patti Smith, singer, poet, author of* Just Kids

THE PUBLISHING INDUSTRY PUTS MUSCLE behind rock-star authors who promote their books, including Barbara Kingsolver and Dean Koontz. At the 2012 Book Expo America I attended a conversation starring two rock music stars who had crossed the line to become authors, Neil Young (*Waging Heavy Peace*) and Patti Smith (*Just Kids*). In fact, *Just Kids* won the National Book Award for Nonfiction in 2010. These two mega-musicians both clearly understood the power of promoting their books to their book audience. Here they were without guitars, sitting on a well-lit stage in two armchairs at a civilized Book Expo America book talk.

These rock stars also clearly understood the viral importance of the resulting book reviews to growing their reading audience.

It doesn't matter what kind of writing you do as an author. From nonfiction to memoir to fiction, if your audience doesn't know your author brand and book via your author platform, it will be tough to reach the next critical stage of your author platform: securing multiple positive book reviews.

Roger Stewart, a veteran in the publishing industry and Editorial Director at TAB/McGraw-Hill, calls book reviews "golden." Roger asserts, "Now as publishers, we must turn to authors to promote their books as a reaction to the dramatically changed landscapes of both bookselling and media. The Internet has changed everything. Fewer people walk into brick-and-mortar bookstores to see in-store displays." We chatted over lunch in San Francisco recently about the new rules inherent in the rise of the Internet that now apply. Roger notes "as browsing in the brick-and-mortar bookstores declines, readers learning about books online increases. Now the mega book review sites have grown, such as Goodreads and online versions of the *New York Times*, the *Guardian*. But that's not all: Dozens, if not hundreds, of popular blogs and podcasts, with local and national radio shows live on the Internet, keeping podcasts online long after the broadcast is over. These reach thousands of potential customers, and the more they appeal to the specific niche the author's book fits into, the better."

Roger's most important point: "There's no review more important than the customer reviews next to the Buy button." This means that an author's pursuit of reviews on bookseller sites such as Amazon.com and Barnesandnoble.com can and does launch books into the limelight for purchase. In the view of publishers, these are more valuable than a review in a newspaper or magazine. Why? Location. What could be more powerful than an excellent review right at the point of sale?

The editors at the major publishing houses ask authors for contact information for bloggers, podcasters, magazine and newspaper reviewers, and even colleagues of theirs who would be willing to write a customer review on Amazon in order to get review copies into their hands. "Bloggers and podcasters who speak to a specialized or niche audience can reach more motivated customers than a review in a general-interest newspaper or magazine," Stewart says. "A smart author who really knows his or her customer base can do far more than a busy publicist can to target the right reviewers and interviewers."

Formerly, the print newspaper and magazine book reviews had a finite circulation number. Today book reviews are digitally available for the whole world to read, and they stay posted; reviews likely will stay with a book and author brand throughout the life of the Internet.

In keeping with the overall strategy of this book, this chapter shows ways to build up great, honest reviews at the right time and in the right place. Remember, no marketing post-publication of your book will substitute for the positive interactions with your audience and your colleagues in the months leading up to the publication of your book.

Why Reviews Are Critical

There is no doubt that good reviews strengthen sales of a book, or any other product, for that matter. In a nutshell, positive online and in-print reviews are springboards to the success of your books. The new rules in publishing success involve interacting with as large an audience as possible on an ongoing basis. As you follow the 14-step program outlined in this book, you're already linked to your audience in multiple ways and engaging in a communication system that flows both ways. Think of reader reviews as an extension of your ongoing conversation with your audience. As your audience reviews your work favorably with thought and insight, their reviews spread through word of mouth to enlarge your community of readers even further. Encourage all review comments, from single one-line comments to full written paragraphs; you want to enable as many reviews and review comments as possible for a number of reasons:

People need to hear good things being said about your book. Consumer reviews and recommendations of friends drive most purchases.

People need to see a lot of people are paying attention to your book. Even if negative reviews turn up, and likely they will, lots of buzz that's mostly positive with a few negative reviews mixed in outweighs no buzz at all.

Strong reviews propel search results for your book to the top of search engines, no matter which genre. As a reader, you're going to look quite favorably on any title described as "a must-read" or "the definitive work on XYZ; you don't need any other book on this subject." Search engines behave in the same way.

How to Ensure Reviews: Build Your Audience in Advance

By creating a broad audience for your book before you publish it, with an ongoing conversation about it by the time your book comes out, reviews naturally follow. The more people who collaborate in the creation of your book and the buzz around it, the larger that conversation will be. Because building an audience takes time, it helps to already have an audience based on groups you interact with regularly, such as a customer base, client list, memberships in societies and clubs, and presence on social networks and forums. By now, we hope you're already in direct dialogue with the audience that seeks what you're offering, and that audience will help launch your book by discussing it virally. The wider the interested audience, the larger your book sales.

For decades the textbook publishing industry has understood and used the technique of audience collaboration. Textbook publishers ask teachers to review materials in textbooks as they are being written so that the material will fit better into their classroom. When instructional materials are well tailored to teachers' curriculum, it is natural that they will adopt this title for their own classroom use and then recommend it to other teachers. Additionally, publishers like Cengage Learning have created a new opportunity for teachers to custom publish a textbook directly for the course they are teaching. In this case the publisher, author, and teacher collaborate to ensure the creation of a book product that fits audience needs. The teacher specifies the subject matter needed in the book that they will use as the textbook for their course, and then the publisher meets that need in the table of contents, and voilà, the teacher requires all students to buy it. The teacher's name then appears on the title page of the custom print run. Talk about an ideal built-in book audience at your fingertips! Build your own audience by listening to and addressing their needs.

My first publishing job was as an on-campus sales representative for Prentice-Hall—that paved the way for their textbook sales. To this day, the Prentice-Hall training motto holds true: "First find the need—then do the presentation tailored to the need."

As publishing reps we were trained next to let the audience know the book was coming and show how it met their needs so that they looked for it, bought it, and hopefully reviewed it favorably to influence others. You want an audience to be primed and asking, "When will your book be out?" Once built, your author platform becomes your tool. Use it to reach out to your audience for reviews by asking them what about your book helped them the most.

About Reciprocal Reviews

Using the strategies in this book, you already have connected with other authors and have written good book reviews for them. Take time to read, think about, and write intelligent reviews about others' books. Reviews are like guiding lights that lead the rest of us to what is worth reading, forming the matches and compass left behind for us to find our way through the wilderness of traditionally published and self-published books.

Too often people are either careless or perfunctory in reviewing a book, which often hurts authors and book sales needlessly. If you write reviews, it's far better to say something short and meaningful about a book rather than write a long essay that is not well thought out.

Motivating Readers to Talk About Your Book

Authors become the pivot point in motivating people to talk about their books, whether it's a professional media reviewer or a single consumer of your book. Reviews are the "Consumer Reports" people use to determine what's worth buying. Your positive book reviews form critical "social proof" or "informational social influence." People depend on the opinions of others, assuming that the people surrounding them in numbers have knowledge and information beyond theirs. The need for social proof has been the genesis of suggestion websites like Yelp that "pre-digest" all of the choices so that we can find our best option.

For the months leading up to the publication of your book, your blog will be key to motivating conversation about you and your book. As your book's publication date draws nearer, step up your blog, post thought-provoking questions, provide a teaser to your book, or give your blog readers a free chapter to download. Give a countdown to your book's publication date, answer all comments, and also step up your activity on all your social networks. In Chapter 14, you'll find a number of ways to increase your visibility in an Internet and media blitz during the month your book is published.

Strategy for Managing Negative Reviews

Once you release your book for the public to read, you're inviting unsolicited online reviews, and with a good book that is well written and meaningful, you'll hopefully receive a load of good reviews. However, brace yourself: Most authors receive some negative reviews. Following are optimum ways that our author clients deal with bad reviews:

Expect them. Grow a thick skin in advance because there are readers who love to blast authors and books. And there may be some people who genuinely do not like your book.

Prevent them. Use the techniques in this chapter to point out to reviewers that you would very much appreciate hearing from them in a direct message to you if there is a typo, error, or an unclear area so that you can fix it, and instead, ask that a public review only cover what you thought of the book as a whole.

Ask for ongoing thoughtful reviews. This has the effect of burying a negative review by relegating it to the back pages.

Remove the review. If a negative review is unfair or unreasonably scathing, say, on Amazon, you can ask to have the review removed by contacting the Amazon Community Help Department: community-help@amazon.com.

Best Practices for Getting Reviews

You will want to solicit honest, thoughtful reviews, written by people who have read and show familiarity with your book. One way to ensure familiarity is to publish excerpts from your book early and send out free chapters of your book prior to publication. Here we show you the successful strategy of our top-selling author client David Busch to modify for your own use. This does not mean you want to solicit loads of empty

5-star reviews. Anyone can spot empty, suspiciously over-the-top reviews as bought or fake, which undermines the quality and reliability of your bank of reviews.

Your solicited positive reviews come in all shapes and sizes, from lengthy online book reviews to short endorsements left by fans in your social media channels, all of which can be repurposed in your book, on your author website, and in your publicity documents.

Avoid Fake Reviews

Just as you shouldn't encourage friends and family to write the empty 5-star reviews noted above, don't pay reviewers to write them either! Fake reviews do get exposed and will ruin your reputation and credibility and erode the trust your audience places in you.

You might be tempted by these review-for-money outfits who promise to sell you "honest" reviews, meaning there's no guarantee that the reviews will be positive or negative. That's a gamble just not worth taking and not necessary if you follow the steps in this book. Amazon works to detect and delete these reviews anyway (See "Giving Mom's Book Five Stars? Amazon May Cull Your Review," *New York Times*, December 22, 2012: nytimes.com/2012/12/23/technology/amazon-book-reviews-deleted-in -a-purge-aimed-at-manipulation.html). As suggested, readers have developed a healthy mistrust of reviews as they seek authentic ones, and they openly comment on reviews that look fake. Instead, keep true to your own author voice and share sincerely. Stay true to your passion—whatever it may be—and share it with the world, grow it, nurture it, and over time your audience will find you.

Send Out Free Copies

Publishers send out free copies of books as they come hot off the press to magazines, newspapers, websites, and other media for inclusion in their publications, along with asking for feedback, whether it's an article-sized review or a short comment. Most media outlets receive too many books and requests to read all of them. Face it, most reviewers at major publications like the *New York Times Book Review* simply don't have time to open your book, much less read it cover to cover.

> Some of our author clients send out audio readings of their books instead of printed copies so that reviewers can listen to them during their commutes.

CONTACT EVERYONE WHO IS A POTENTIAL REVIEWER FOR YOUR BOOK

To find reviewers for your book, expand your contacts list to include reviewers. The time to start looking for potential comments and reviews about your book is right when you've finished your manuscript, as Jack Canfield did. In the Foreword to this book, Jack tells how he never ended his day without contacting multiple reviewers and buyers for his book, which ultimately led to the mega success of his series. Once your manuscript is done and on its way to publication, the fun begins: That's your time to list every group and association you belong to and start a new list of those you can join. Make the long list and include these:

Your Interactive Author Platform Audience. This audience is built up through your author website, blog, social network, teachings, and speaking engagements as outlined in the 14 steps of this book. At this point, you are able to contact the people interested in your work and reach out to them for feedback. Be sure to document the help of these many people in your book's Acknowledgments section. This appreciation not only encourages reciprocal acknowledgments down the road; your inclusion of their names in your book increases awareness about your book. When your audience is a part of the creation, it's a point of pride for them to share the news with their friends and associates. When Mike commented on an early online version of Dan Gillmor's 2006 book on citizen journalism, *We the Media*, he was acknowledged along with dozens of others. And yes, he shared that page with more than a few people.

Groups, Professional Organizations, and Schools. Try to contact students, clubs, and alumni groups from schools you've attended: all potential members of your buying/reviewing audience. Tap your social networks, especially LinkedIn, asking these groups if they'd like a free copy of your book in exchange for comments about your book.

When you ask for reviews, make it easy for your potential reviewers to target their comments by posing easy-to-answer, specific questions, such as for nonfiction, "How did this book help you?" or for fiction, "What did you enjoy most about this book?" Include a link to your book page on Amazon so that your reviewers have click-through information at their fingertips.

Customers, Staff, Clients. If you're already represented by a literary agency like ours, then you are already in the company of authors who are likely to exchange reciprocal reviews with you, since all authors seek reviews. If you offer reviews to other authors, they will review your book, too. You can ask your agent to connect you with other authors he/she represents to make the initial connections. If you have a client base, you already have a personal relationship with people you can reach out to for reviews.

Forums/Colleagues/Subject Matter Experts. As you build your audience in advance of your publication, your memberships will be very important in developing your future audience for reviews and sales. Go to Meetup.com (noted in Chapter 7) to seek and join relevant groups of people. You can reach out to and exchange messages with other members on this site, and they are always looking for speakers, too. You can also search your subject matter area online to find other knowledgeable, interested people who share your passion for your subject matter and who might be willing to review your book online. Reach out to people who may want to review you and who may be in need of coauthors, chapter or article writers, or guest bloggers.

David Busch doesn't rely on his publisher to send out all the review copies needed; instead, he increases his number of free titles to 50 so he can send out his own as well. David speaks at local photography forums of about 300 members each, which are his audience. He announces his next book and then asks his audience to sign up for a free copy. When the book is out, he sends a stock letter with his own personalized note and signature saying, "Here is your free copy, no strings attached. If you find a typo or mistake, please notify me privately so that I can correct that in the next edition. If you're inclined to post a public review, here is the URL." These are some of his successful techniques for soliciting reviews that keep his titles at the top of Amazon's ranking system. David has an excellent response rate on accelerated rate of reviews once the book is posted as published and for sale on Amazon.

Amazon Top Reviewers. As an optional plus, you can contact some of the Amazon Top Reviewers. These are unpaid volunteers who review books because they love to do it. The more books they review, and the more that customers indicate that they find their reviews helpful, the higher their ranking at Amazon and the more credibility their reviews have with people looking to buy books. For an added boost, search for these Amazon's Top Reviewers at amazon.com/review /top-reviewers. Search for Top Reviewers who review books in your subject area. Click on a reviewer's name; from there you can look at their Amazon profile to find their website or blog. Amazon Top Reviewers denoted by a prestige badge are ranked higher on Amazon. Reach out and send a concise inquiry to see if one of these reviewers will agree to receive your book for free with no obligation, and you may be selected by one of these prestigious Amazon Top Reviewers.

Pre-publication reviews. If you receive a pre-publication book review from any of the major trade publications, Amazon will allow you or your publisher to post up to ten editorial reviews on your book detail page.

1. Check with your publisher on who will post Editorial Reviews. Whoever posts to this section first owns the section. If you later find a review that hasn't been posted, you have to ask Amazon to update the listing.
2. If you're going to be responsible for updating this section, go to your Author Central page (see Chapter 12).
3. Click the **Books tab**.
4. Click the **title of your book**.
5. Go to the Editorial Review section and click **Add** (if there is no previous review on the site) or **Edit**.
6. Fill out the form. You can post up to 600 words of the review on your page. Include the name of the reviewer and the publication or website the review appeared in.
7. Click **Preview** to see what the review looks like.
8. Click **Save Changes** when you're done.

Timing Your First Amazon Reviews

Your first book reviews count the most by far, as Amazon selects three from the very first reviews that will stay on the site as beacon reviews. The timing is critical to ask for reviews from your associates and audience, as people can't post reviews before the book is listed on the site for sale. Authors post on their blogs when the book is out to let motivated reviewers know when to post.

Other Online Book Review Sites

People have always gathered in various venues to explore the question "Read any good books lately?" so it's no surprise that one of the most popular ways to spend time online in the digital era is to hang out with other people to have conversations about books. As an author, you owe it to yourself to spend some time hanging out in some of these places.

Beyond Amazon, here are some of the other top online book review sites, along with some strategies for how to use these sites to build your audience.

Goodreads

Several sites have tried to be *the* place for sharing book reviews and recommendations with friends and strangers. Goodreads, a site that essentially helps friends talk about books, has won that battle. Launched in 2007, Goodreads was acquired by Amazon in 2013, but it's critical that you have a presence on both. Be sure to update your author page on Amazon and solicit reviews on the Amazon as well as the Goodreads site.

Goodreads users share what they are reading with others on the site and post progress reports as they read. When you add a new book, you can put the book on a "shelf." Everyone has shelves based on whether they've read a book in the past, are currently reading the book, or want to read the book in the future. In addition, you can tag books based on their genre, subject, or anything else that helps you organize your collection.

Users can apply a star-rating to any book and write longer reviews as well. These reviews appear on the book's Goodreads page. This is a place where your community of supporters is essential.

SIGNING UP FOR THE GOODREADS AUTHOR PROGRAM

Signing up as a reader on Goodreads is simple, and you can log into it via social media channels or set up a separate login.

If you haven't published a book yet, you can post your original writing in the Stories section of the site for others to read and comment on. From your profile page, click **My Writing**. Goodreads encourages you to "add just about anything—short stories, poetry, chapters of a book, or even whole books!" This opportunity to share works in progress and the like can attract an audience. Readers, in turn, will visit your profile, driving traffic to your author site as well as getting to know you through Goodreads.

Click **Add New Writing** to start the posting process. Fiction is clearly the star here in terms of readership, but posting any original material where you hold the copyright and all other rights is permitted. Read over the guidelines in the right sidebar to confirm the rules regarding copyright, fan fiction posts, and general etiquette. Fan fiction includes stories based on other writers' characters and settings (think Star Trek, Hogwarts, Middle Earth, and *Twilight*).

Fill out the form so readers can find your work on the site, then copy the text into the edit box provided. Readers can add reviews, so make sure your material is high quality.

If you have published a book, first search for your name on the site. Your title(s) should appear in the results. Click on **your name** to open the Author Profile page. Scroll down to the bottom of the page. Click **"Is this you?"** to send a request to join the Author Program. Within a couple of days, Goodreads will update the database, and you'll see the phrase "Goodreads Author" next to your name.

YOUR AUTHOR DASHBOARD

Once Goodreads has confirmed your author status, you'll see your book cover on your home page every time you log into Goodreads. You'll also see a few statistics about how Goodreads members have been reacting to your book. Click **Visit your dashboard** to manage your Goodreads presence.

Begin by editing your author profile. Every author with a book in the database gets a profile page, but most of them are prepared by site staff.

As a member of the Goodreads Author Program, you can control what appears on your profile.

Your profile page form begins by asking the basic stuff: date and place of birth, and gender. You can safely ignore the date of death field. Share as much of this information as you feel comfortable with; none of it is mandatory. You can also define up to three genres that you write in. Also provide links to your website, Twitter page, and other social media platforms so people who discover you on Goodreads can find you elsewhere.

Most importantly, you can write your biography section in the text field of the form. This is where you can further define your niche and humanize yourself by sharing a little bit about yourself. If you've included an About page on your site, you can simply copy and paste some or all of that material here. Whether you repurpose your bio or write something new, just take care to keep your message consistent.

ADDING IMAGES AND VIDEOS

As with everything related to your online presence in social media, adding at least one professional photo of yourself serves to prove that you really exist in real life. In the new web environment, it's important that your audience feels welcome to reach out and talk to you. Your first "profile photo" will appear on your book pages and whenever you are active on the site (posting in a group, updating your reading list, and the like). Ideally, this is a small version of your consistent author brand headshot. You can also add other photos of you or your books that will appear on your profile page, so if you post more, be sure that they have a consistent look and feel.

We strongly urge you to create a book trailer or at least a 60-second video of a simple reading from your book or excerpt from a verbal presentation. A video recording posted to one of the major video sites is powerful, and you can link to the video and display it here, too. The upload page has a good description of how to get the appropriate embed code pasted into this form. Be sure to use tags to aid findability for your videos; see Chapter 10 for more on tagging and Chapter 14 for additional information on creating promotional videos.

CONNECTING WITH YOUR WEBSITE AND BLOG

As with Amazon Author Central (see Chapter 12), Goodreads offers authors blog space on the site. You can also link to your existing blog's RSS feed. The formatting can be a little strange, but linking saves you enormous amounts of time by displaying the complete content of your posts on Goodreads. Readers can Like and comment on your posts in Goodreads and share the Goodreads link on both Facebook and Twitter.

Goodreads also provides you with three different types of widgets to place on your website. These are configured on your author profile page (no, you don't have to write the HTML text); copy the code, then paste it on your book site (or wherever you discuss the book on your author site). The widgets include:

- **Reviews.** This allows your website visitors to see reviews of your book from other Goodreads users, and then contribute their own review back to Goodreads.
- **Add to My Books.** Also for your book page, lets your visitors add the book to their shelf, see the overall ratings of your book on Goodreads, and (optionally) see which of their Goodreads friends have your book on their shelves.
- **Show My Books.** This widget just displays basic information about all of your books on the site. It includes the cover of each book with a link to its Goodreads page. The widget also displays the number of reviews the book has received and its rating. Great for a sidebar on all your site's pages.

CONNECTING WITH FACEBOOK

Goodreads started on the road to popularity as a Facebook app. It continues to promote the Facebook connection by including a Goodreads tab for your Facebook author Page, which you should enable. First, connect your Goodreads and Facebook accounts by installing the Goodreads Facebook app. Go to the Goodreads Facebook page (you'll probably want to Like it while you're there). Click the **gear icon** and select **Add App to Page**, at which point you'll add the tab to your author Page.

PARTICIPATING IN GROUPS

Where the Goodreads social network really becomes social is in the large number and varied membership of Goodreads groups. Anyone, including you, can set up a group, but as an author, you first want to find existing groups containing your likely audience members. Joining public groups is easy: Find the group and click **Join This Group**. You'll be asked to decide how often you want to get notified of group activity, and then you're in!

The well-organized Groups page offers several ways to locate the right groups for you: Tags are selected by group owners to describe specific areas that their group discusses (such as paranormal romance, nonfiction, and music). Goodreads places groups in one of nine very general categories (Books & Literature being by far the largest), almost to the point of being useless. At the top of the Groups page, you can use the Find Groups search engine to locate pockets of audience members.

After finding kindred spirits in the genre/topic areas, check out the Goodreads Authors/Readers group, "dedicated to connecting readers with Goodreads authors," per the group introduction. This large and active group is divided into genres and different areas to make it easier to find what's of interest to you.

Don't just join groups to lurk—participate! Your goal is to demonstrate your expertise (if you're writing nonfiction) and your style (whatever you write). Don't just promote yourself and your projects; contribute to the success of the group. Answer questions, and ask them, too. Be funny if you can. As you participate, other group members will become your fans and others may become your friends (online, and a few perhaps in real life).

As a Goodreads author, you're encouraged to set up a Q&A group when you have a book to release and promote. With your active participation in other groups leading up to your Q&A, you should have quite an audience to discuss your project with—and you may come away with fans for life!

GIVEAWAYS

Work with your publisher to build word-of-mouth about your book, and set up a First Reads giveaway of a set number of physical books ahead of your book's launch date. Go to goodreads.com/giveaway/new to define the terms of the giveaway: start and end dates, the ISBN, number of copies, and what countries the giveaway will ship to are the required fields. A description of the book, while not mandatory, is clearly an advantage in encouraging readers to enter the giveaway.

Goodreads promotes the giveaway and selects the winners. It's your (or your publisher's) job to ship the books to the winners.

Shelfari

Shelfari is mostly important because Amazon owns it. While it was once designed as a social network like Goodreads, Amazon now positions it as sort of a Wikipedia for books and literature. Nonetheless, the Community area with thousands of registered groups remains.

As with Goodreads (though using just one "shelf"), Shelfari users add books to a Reading Timeline, labeled Reading Now, I Plan to Read, and I've Read. It has the star-ranking system and also allows lengthier reviews. Shelfari doesn't let you report your reading progress, but it encourages you to enter descriptions of characters, settings, favorite quotes, and other interesting material contained inside the book's covers.

CONNECTING SHELFARI TO AMAZON

In Chapter 12, you learned how to sign up with Amazon Author Central. Becoming an Amazon Author on Shelfari involves connecting your Author Central account to your Shelfari account.

1. In Author Central, click on the **Books tab** on your page.
2. Pick one book.
3. Click the **Book Extras tab** on the book page.
4. Click **Visit Shelfari.com**.
5. Log into Shelfari.
6. A banner will appear, identifying you as an Amazon Author, and your profile photo will get a badge, too.

YOUR SHELFARI AUTHOR PAGE

Anyone can edit your author page, but once you've been verified as an author, you have a little more credibility making changes to your own page. Amazon and its group of librarians post the material that already exists on your Amazon profile to identify your bibliography, so if you find any errors on your Shelfari page, check the Amazon page first to verify that the information there is correct. Return to Shelfari to fix the error(s) later.

You can create an Overview of your life and career if you choose. As with the other networks, feel free to paste your existing "about me" information in this section. In the Personal section of your author page, you can (optionally) enter your birthdate and place, nationality, gender, "official website," and the genres in which you write. The latter is a simple edit field, so you can place as many tags there as you like to help readers find you in this field. If your area of expertise is pet adoption, use such tags as nonfiction, pets, pet adoption, dogs, and the like.

When looking at your author profile, visitors click the Books tab to see all of your books, with thumbnails of the covers and a brief summary of each. Both you and your visitors to the author page can initiate discussions about your work using the Discussions tab.

CONNECTING WITH YOUR WEBSITE AND OTHER NETWORKS

Shelfari doesn't have any built-in integration with other social networks. Because Amazon allows authors to link to both blogs and general sites, having Shelfari links to these same venues is less important. As a reader, you can install a widget with the books on your Reading Timeline on your WordPress, Blogger, or TypePad blog.

PARTICIPATING IN GROUPS AND OTHER COMMUNITY ACTIVITIES

When you click on the Community tab in Shelfari, you'll see several ways to find and connect with other Shelfari members. As an author, your best bet to find potential readers is in the Groups section. As with Goodreads, a multitude of groups exist, but finding really active groups in your area may be difficult.

Begin by reviewing the Most Active Groups tab. Here you can see the groups that added the most members, most books, and most posts in the last day, week, month, or "all time." Click the Group Categories tab to see how Shelfari groups their groups. From the Browse Categories pages, the search bar will also help you find relevant groups.

As with Goodreads' Author/Readers group, Shelfari has a Writing Readers group, not surprisingly the most popular in the Authors & Writing category.

LibraryThing

LibraryThing started out as a place for people to catalog their own personal libraries. Later on, the site developed relationships with public libraries, so you can add books you got at the library, too. It's still the most noncommercial of the sites we're discussing. As a reader, you can catalog up to 200 books for free. For $25, you can catalog everything you've ever read. It's a simply designed website that may look a little dated and awfully text-heavy, but there are no ads in sight.

For users, the experience of adding books is a little clunkier than it is on the other sites we've discussed. Click the Add Books tab to get a search engine; type a title, author, ISBN, or Library of Congress catalog number to find a book. By default, LibraryThing will search one of a variety of online library catalogs. Instead of "shelves," LibraryThing lets you organize your books into "Collections." The default Collections include the standard Read, Currently Reading, and To Read. You can add other collections. You can also use tags to further organize your books.

BECOMING A LIBRARYTHING AUTHOR

When you arrive at LibraryThing, search for your name. A list of books will come up. Click on **your name**, and your author page appears. At the top of the right sidebar column, you'll see a box asking "Is this you? Become a LibraryThing Author." Click the link, and you'll be asked to select your title, and "add a message if you want."

Once LibraryThing confirms your identity, you get a LibraryThing Author icon on your profile page.

CONNECTING WITH YOUR WEBSITE AND OTHER NETWORKS

You can add many types of links to your author page sidebar. Link to your website and Twitter account to start. Continue linking to any or all of these pages (called link types):

- Publisher author page
- Wikipedia author page

- Interviews with you
- Press items about you
- An academic site (once they start creating courses on your work)
- Fan site
- The "Other" category, where you can link to your other social sites

You must supply the URL for each site you link to and you can also provide a title, which is what will appear as the link title.

LibraryThing offers a Friend Finder tool to connect you with your Twitter followers and Facebook friends, but not much else in the way of direct integration with other social networks.

GROUPS ON LIBRARYTHING

The default method of finding kindred spirits and potential fans on LibraryThing is perhaps less intuitive, but more fun than the other sites we've discussed so far. We'll suggest that the groups here are also more lively than other sites as well, with the possible exception of Goodreads.

When you arrive at the **Groups tab**, you get a tag cloud indicating what's hot in the groupsphere. Click on a **tag link** to see all the groups related to that area, sorted by activity level. The Groups home page also highlights groups that are Active This Week, new groups, official and standing committees, groups with the most members, and community projects (like "Name That Book," a project where members can recall a book's plot, but no longer remember the title). LibraryThing also will point you to Local Groups, based on the reasonable distance from your location (as you report it to the site).

As you build your collections on the site, a Group Suggestions area will try to connect you with other readers with similar book collections. One final aid is that some groups are identified as "dormant," which gives you the opportunity to ignore or attempt to revive the group, depending on your level of interest.

GIVEAWAYS

Every month, the LibraryThing Early Reviewers program offers users a chance to pick up a free book with the voluntary condition that they provide a review on LibraryThing in the early days of publication. Publishers (including self-publishers) can offer some combination of physical copies, ebooks, or audiobooks for distribution. Usually, there are more than 100 titles offered each month.

Red Room

"Where the writers are" is the tagline for this site, and many big names are displayed on the home page. This is a place for more established writers to deepen their relationships with their audience. The key difference between Red Room and the other networks discussed in this chapter is that Red Room offers some of its registered authors the ability to sell books directly through its own online retail outlet, the Red Room Bookstore. You must invest in a premium membership to sell books through the Red Room Royalties program, but you can earn the money back through a higher royalty rate on books sold through this channel. Red Room gives you 15% of the retail price of your book for every book sold on the site. When someone buys your book on Red Room, you will connect with the buyer on the site. This way you can build a list of buyers and communicate with them on a regular basis if you so choose.

Premium membership also relieves you of many of the decisions involved in creating a standalone website. They maintain the consistent design across the website, and you can just focus on creating content. You can also contribute content on Red Room without a premium membership —you just won't be able to sell books.

BECOMING A RED ROOM AUTHOR

When you join Red Room as a community member (for free), you get your blog space and a biographical area. You can contribute content in the form of essays, poems, and the like. When your book is published, you can link to it here, but Red Room does not consider you a "Red Room Author" until you've become a premium member and then filled out your application.

COMPLETING YOUR RED ROOM PROFILE

All members, paid or not, get access to a dashboard that allows them to add content and update their profiles. The dashboard also tells you how many visits you got on your pages on a daily basis. On the right side of the dashboard, you can update your account settings and build your profile.

Click **About Me** to display the My Profile page, where you can enter and edit your profile information. There's up to five pages of information you can enter, but the only required material is your name and biographical information. You cannot add other content to the site without this. This is also the page to upload your profile picture to.

As you edit each page in your profile, be sure to click **Save** at the bottom.

In More About Me, you can identify your hometown, where you live now, date of birth, and similar information. There are big edit boxes where you can discuss your marriage, family, interests, and hobbies. You may also list up to five nonprofit organizations in the "Causes I Support" box.

Under Reading Interests, you can name your favorite books and authors, then tell people what you're reading now. In Work and Education, you can tell readers where you work and went to school.

The last page, Custom Contact Message, gives you the opportunity to say something to readers who use the site's contact form to reach you. You could use this message to refer visitors to your author site or invite them to subscribe to your newsletter or otherwise connect to your platform.

CONNECT WITH YOUR WEBSITE AND BLOG

When you fill out your profile, be sure to link to your author website in the Web Links at the bottom of the More About Me page.

CONNECT WITH FACEBOOK AND TWITTER

From your dashboard, click **Connect to my Twitter account**. Click **Add account**. Red Room will post your tweets on your public profile page.

While you're there, click **Facebook** from the menu at the top. When you **Enable Facebook**, Red Room will also include your status updates on your public profile page.

CREATE AND MANAGE CONTENT ON RED ROOM

As noted earlier, when you have added your name and biographical information to your profile, you can include a variety of original material to your section of Red Room. You'll see the Add Content pod on your dashboard. Original writing, including blog posts, articles, and book reviews, can help you gain page views and attract fans.

More promotional material, like press releases, book trailers, and interview transcripts, are also permitted on the site. Take advantage of these opportunities.

Review Others' Books

As you read books that you find genuinely helpful, be sure to make it a practice to review them favorably in public and, if possible, send your comments directly to the authors of the books you like. In this way, you build up an author network that will take the time to read and comment on your work, too. Often we forget to make a positive comment when we like something or someone's work because we don't have enough time, and this works both ways when you need others to comment on your work. It's critical that as an author you constantly and publicly express your appreciation—through your writing, social media, and other interactions with your audience, as what goes around comes around.

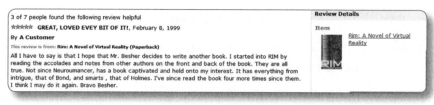

5-star reviews for author client Alexander Besher's novel *Rim*.

Incorporate Reviews Into Your Author Platform

Always put the pieces together by repurposing content to form your author platform. Include all reviews on your book and author site. Ask reviewers to link back to your website, and add a PDF of reviews for easy download on your press page.

Checklist, Step 13: Reviews

➤ Ramp up your outreach to potential reviewers the minute you deliver your final manuscript to your publisher.

➤ Three months prior to publication, send out galley proofs to reviewers.

➤ Send out free copies to potential reviewers as soon as your book is published.

➤ Review others' books positively and let the authors know you did.

➤ Join or use all of your group memberships as support systems for reviews.

➤ Ask audience and colleagues to post positive comments citing a specific way the book touched, moved, inspired, or helped.

➤ Join review sites. Find book review blogs.

➤ Connect all information together on your author website.

Success Spotlight: Waterside Client David Busch
(facebook.com/DavidBuschGuides)

- 200 books
- 12 language translations, including Czech, Arabic, German, Italian, Spanish, French, Portuguese, Japanese, Chinese, Korean, Russian, and Bulgarian
- 2,000,000 copies sold
- 72 hugely successful guidebooks for various digital camera models, including all-time #1 bestsellers for many of them

Beginnings: After graduating from Kent State University, Busch worked for more than 20 years in the public relations industry. He operated his own photo studio and was a principal in CCS/PR, Inc., one of the largest public relations firms based in San Diego, working on press conferences, press kits, media tours, and sponsored photo trade magazine articles. In addition to Kodak, CCS's photography clients included Hewlett-Packard. He sold his interest in CCS in 1992 to become a full-time author, photographer, and reporter. Since then, Busch has become one of the leading photojournalist/authors in the United States.

As a writer, Busch has managed to stumble into a specific niche on five different occasions, moving on to the "next big thing" when each was just a *thing*, and not yet *big*. He says, "Each 'career' change took me into areas where I had a special love or expertise, a desire to learn more, and an eagerness to share what I learned with others."

His underlying premise was that "I didn't need to know *everything* about a topic. I just needed to know more than my readers and have the ability to explain it to them better than anyone else writing about that topic. The more deeply I explored any particular niche, the more I learned and the more I had to offer to a broader audience."

Fan base: I worked to build a fan base that always asks for the David Busch guide because they know the style and kind of information in my books, so I asked my publisher to put a large photograph of me on the back cover. Readers see me as a friend to help them explore their cameras. I do sometimes work with coauthors selected for their particular expertise in a topic, but I write a great deal of the words that appear in each book with my name on it.

Radio: 21 different radio shows nationally and in major markets.

TV: He's been a call-in guest for one Canadian television show, and appeared live on *Breakfast Television* in Toronto, the *Today Show* of the Great White North.

Facebook page, blog, speaker at forums: Per David, "I know my books and audience best, and my past life in public relations/advertising gives me the skills I need to promote my books. Tim O'Reilly once said, 'Obscurity is a far greater threat to authors and creative artists than piracy,' and that's never been more important than in our modern age of ebooks. So I distribute as many as 50 copies of each of my books to readers with a personal note asking them to post a favorable review if they like the book and to contact me directly with their concerns if they do not like it. I spend time each and every day answering their questions. Some percentage of content for each new book comes from direct contact with readers."

David's advice to authors: Yes, perhaps I have stumbled into a niche, but recognize that even a niche can be a moving target. Only by expanding and adapting an author platform is it possible to follow and grow along with them.

CHAPTER 14

The Celebration Announcement: Launch Parties and Virtual Tours

"There are two motives for reading a book; one, that you enjoy it; the other, that you can boast about it."

—*Bertrand Russell, philosopher, logician, mathematician*

W INE CORKS POPPED in the middle of the days that we held company-wide parties for every single hot-off-the-press book at Sybex, before it became a Wiley imprint. Rodnay Zaks, owner and publisher, knew how to do this right. These festivities included unusual treats from the creative San Francisco Bay Area "foodies" growing the category of California Cuisine, and glorious short speeches with much applause made by our editor-in-chief, my mentor, the late Dr. Rudolph "Rudy" Langer. We told quirky stories about how things evolved with projects; we commemorated publications as a team effort; we had that sense of occasion that celebrated great ideas transformed into books.

Grand book parties had a fame and glory of their own during a time resembling a golden era in publishing, when entertainment budgets were breathtaking and contract signings were made with swizzle sticks at the Four Seasons in Manhattan. At Book Expo America in Chicago, Wiley once held an amazing and legendary Blues Brothers publication party, we enjoyed into the wee hours, renting out the top of the Sears Tower at sunset, with live bands, gourmet appetizers, and open bar, complete with black hats and sunglasses for guests. Microsoft Press rented the entire

Chicago Aquarium on Lake Michigan, where we feasted on fresh seafood buffets and enjoyed live bands to celebrate Microsoft Press book releases. Addison-Wesley rented a Boston nightclub for a notable publication party; when Bill Gates arrived, I danced with him to celebrate books. We held lobster races through the halls at Apple headquarters (with critters flown in from Boston) before steaming them and then feasting in honor of Apple's library suite of books. All these parties and countless more were created for the sole purpose of celebrating books.

Don't let your own big moment slip away! This is your chance for the best celebration and marketing event in the life of your book. Here we give you simple strategies and models for you to use in customizing the launch of your own baby, your new publication.

Times have changed since popping champagne corks was the only option; with Web 2.0 tools, authors are now empowered to reach far more than a single group of guests in a physical location—you are enabled to reach thousands globally.

Your book launch party celebrates your inspiration as an author, plus your ideas and hard work writing, for which you've likely given up your social life, sleep, and leisure time for many months! We share your sweat and tears involved in the significant effort involved in writing your book, and its publication justifies appreciation for your loved ones, who suffered through losing you to your manuscript during the writing, rewriting, and editing process.

Use your book party as a time to honor your associates, friends, and family who supported you and missed you during the process—and enlist them as part of your team. You can also ask a friend to host your party and make the toast to your book. This joyful event fills your batteries, drained from writing, to carry you through to the next and last phase of the book publishing process: the celebration and launch.

Advantages to Holding Your Book Launch Party

Book launch party invitations are book announcements: People love to attend a party, so when people talk about the upcoming party, they also announce your book. First and foremost, your book launch party invitations should blast out to as many people as possible in the living world. No matter if they do not all attend; the point is that everyone loves an invitation. Like the opening of a new store in town, there is no better way to tell people the news than by inviting them to a fun live event.

Your launch party offers another opportunity for media coverage. For local newspapers and radio, an event gives journalists justification to mention it and may even attract reporters who want to enjoy and cover the event. Any media is good media, as write-ups beget more write-ups to reach more potential reviewers, booksellers, and readers. If you stream the event live or photo-stream individual shots, any journalist who was not able to attend is still able to watch and report on a live happening.

Show your fun side. People love to tell others about events, entertainment, and the inside scoop: A book launch party is a great chance to go viral by showing sides of your personality that are not otherwise seen. You can use it as a chance to tell something interesting about you that nobody knows, and that kind of tidbit in itself can go viral. Any party gives even more motivation for water cooler talk by commenting on what happened, what was said, what people wore, how others behaved, etc.

Excitement is not only contagious, but also a driving force. Your book launch party galvanizes your excitement and the excitement of your surrounding team that spreads to others. If you're not showing excitement, nobody else will. A party is the perfect vehicle for contagious enthusiasm.

You're in the limelight as a celebrity. Book authors carry a special panache; you as author with your book in hand as the center of attention gives you the limelight to capture while your book is still new. To make it a unique event, wear all white like the author Tom Wolfe if you have to, just try to create a novel experience in your own style.

Jump-start your book sales. With your book available for sale and a roomful of guests you've just entertained with wine and appetizers, you're likely to get a good percentage of sales of your book.

Involve a global community through videoconferencing the event and/or live streaming photographs taken at the event.

Live Book Launch Party Strategy

Plan the party as a business event: Consider this as your grand opening to attract customers, and include ideas in your plan to maximize the business aspect of this event:

Build in appreciation. This is also a thank-you party, so include planning on how you will appreciate and celebrate those who helped you. When you graciously honor your supporters, they will honor you in return.

Involve media. Send your press kit and invitation to all media, including social networks, local papers, and radio stations.

Give reasons to tell friends. When it's entertaining, fun, and interesting, and/or if there is something free like food, wine, and prizes or costumes, people have good reason to tell others about it.

Duplicate aspects of your party for your virtual "tour." As described later in the chapter, you can position your virtual tour to gather momentum right after the party to keep the celebration announcement going.

Link all of your book launch activities. Use every web location possible, such as your own networks and the networks of friends. One added posting option is to pay a fee to announce your book launch in newsletters like "Bookselling this Week," run by American Booksellers Association (bookweb.org).

Using Splash

Some authors recommend using Splash (Splashthat.com) to manage their online and live events. Sign up with your name, email, and a password. Set up your launch party as an "RSVP Event." Splash asks you to give the event a title and identify the type of event from a list (Celebration, Concert, Conference, Fashion Show, Flyer, and Fundraiser), and it allows you to define the date, time, and location (giving you the option to mark these TBD). Splash then creates a website for the event at <youreventtitle>.splashthat.com and suggests a Twitter event hashtag.

Splash lets you send up to 300 emails to your guest list for free. Use one of their templates or design your own. Splash offers you analytics of how many people visit your event site and respond to your invitation.

Splash seems to have thought about the details of party planning. That should help you focus on other things.

Steps to Prepare Your Live Book Launch Party

1. **Define your goals.** Figure out what you want to achieve—for example, how many guests you want, how many books you'll sell, how you'll leverage the event on your networks and sites—and define exact steps to get there.

2. **Make your support team list and your guest list.** Use your entire Rolodex and all social networks to list friends and associates.

3. **Get sponsors.** Ask local restaurants and shops if they will contribute food, drink, or a raffle item in exchange for advertising their name at your event. Talk to local businesses you frequent and ask for a door-prize contribution in exchange for advertising their name at your party.

4. **Secure a location.** A bookstore is a natural location, since this is the ideal bookselling venue. Approach the owner of the store in person to introduce yourself in advance, and bring a leave-behind press kit. When approaching anyone for support, remember to talk about how you benefit their customers. A library, your home, or any location that fits your theme is ideal, so it's fine to think creatively. If you can coincide your book event with a local conference, all the better, as you will likely find a large and interested attendee list.

5. **Select food and drink.** Wine, cheese, and fruit are standard and classy choices, or you can connect food and drink with your theme. We've seen launches with open bars and a special clever name invented for a drink that fits your subject. Budgets can be slim, so ask for help in bringing bottles of wine from your closest supporters if needed.

6. **Plan a theme** for your party that links to your book—fun and optional.

7. **Do invitations.** Send out two months in advance. Create mail-out invitations as postcards with your book cover on one side and a party invitation on the other side. Create online invitations using your book cover as the main visual at a website like Splashthat.com, mentioned earlier in this chapter. It's important to give contact information and ask for RSVPs. Follow up to make sure that everyone did get an invitation and count the RSVPS to make sure you have enough food, wine, and books.

8. **Post announcements** in the form of flyers in your town in every possible location.

9. **Create capability for visuals of the event** to be posted live, while it is happening. Everyone has a camera phone, and people love to take photos and view others' photos at events. Encourage guests to post photos live! You can create a photo station where a friend photographs your guests in a setting backdrop and then posts online; you can later feature these photos on your website. Also ask guests to send you their own photos for you to post later. Some authors use videoconferencing tools to connect to others during the party and will even take live questions from viewers.

10. **Do giveaways.** Have paper and pen ready to gather guests' email addresses. Hold one or more drawings during the party, and give discounts on your book if possible. The grand prize is a signed copy of your book. Depending on budget, check online for shops that will use your book cover image to create T-shirts, magnets, bookmarks, mugs, etc.

11. **Create take-home "goodie bags."** These can be a gift of any kind, including food, a toy or game, buttons, or a coupon from a sponsor —or anything that aligns with your party theme, if you have one. Include your business card, postcard book announcement card, and a reminder to post an Amazon review.

12. **Sell books.** A must at the end of your party. A bookstore will manage book sales at the end of your talk, of course, but elsewhere you need to have a bookstore employee bring books to sell or delegate a friend to do the work of selling your books.

13. **Remember thank-yous.** In your talk, show appreciation for as many people as you can, and follow up with thank-you cards or emails. An online service like Blue Mountain Cards (bluemountain.com) will allow you to set up thank-you e-cards in advance to send out to your specified list you type in, on the exact day you specify.

A Simple One-Hour Book Launch Party Format

We've attended many book signing parties using the following simple format. With too many choices, many authors don't want to take the time to figure out how to go about creating a launch party, and so often they skip this essential part of creating an author platform. The format here saves time, so either use or customize further for your book launch party. The approximate schedule here assumes an hour-long book launch party with a 7:30 start time specified in your invitation and involves delegating to a few friends who will act in specified support roles.

7:15 p.m.	Doors open for early arrivals, cheese/crackers/sweet bites on tables, a friend delegated to pour wine. Background atmospheric music is an option. As the author and host, simply greet every single guest personally, and thank them for coming. Nothing more is needed at this point. Optional: Give each a name tag or a note card and small pencil and ask them to write down one question to ask you later if they wish.
7:35 p.m.	Making sure everyone has visited food and wine, move to the spot you'll speak from casually; your spot can be near the food or in the center of the room.
7:40 p.m.	Appoint a close friend in advance who will play the part of master of ceremonies. This person will clink spoon to glass, then thank all for coming for this grand occasion and deliver a short prepared introduction for you. All is casual, with a warm sense of welcome and humor to keep the party atmosphere.
7:45 p.m.	You're on! Start with a fun anecdote, maybe about someone who helped you or supported you on this book. People love stories about other people. It's a celebration, so keep the fun-and-celebration mood in it. A visual is effective—a show-and-tell item surrounding the book if possible, even a large photo that links somehow to your book. Describe it with a sense of humor. Offer brief thanks by name to those who helped you, and maybe something that people didn't know about you or that you learned about yourself while writing the book. Introduce something that pertains to your book's topic, then hold up your book (never try to sell) and give a short, memorable reading. Then read some questions from the guests' cards (with a few of your own thrown in) and answer in an entertaining way. Finally, thank all for coming to celebrate, tell them to enjoy, that you will be at the back of the room for book signings, and applause should follow.
8:10 p.m.	Music starts for background. Circulate, chat, pose for photos, then sign books near the exit point. Appoint a friend or employee to handle all book transactions; yours is a separate role to just enjoy your party, relate to your audience, and sign books. Ask something about each person who wants an autograph and then personalize your signature with a note or a drawing.
8:30 p.m.	Wind down until last guest has left, doors closing.

The Virtual Book Launch Tour

Now that we have both feet firmly planted in the digital era, most authors are first cultivating local audiences live and then also creating powerful virtual book tours online. These online "tours" are the alternative to multi-city live, in-person book tours, with in-store book signings at multiple locations, speaking at conferences, media interviews, etc. The virtual book tour connects authors with a much larger audience than a store-to-store circuit would allow.

Side Note: Many of our successful author clients target their travel efforts to speak at large user groups or meet-ups that comprise special interest groups. We've found that when our authors speak to very targeted audiences in multiple cities, that does have the effect of creating a spike in book sales of new titles specifically created for these audiences; this is a good strategy if there are groups that are tuned in to your specialty.

A virtual book launch tour is a planned combination of appearances, including social network capabilities for online events, articles and blogs, guest contributions to websites, online radio shows, chats, videoconferences, and appearances on other places on the web where the readers of your book might meet for discussions. This blitz of appearances is effective if it's timed for 7 to 14 days before and another 7 to 14 days after your book is published. Like your book launch party, your virtual tour is a time to talk about your book, the inspiration for writing it, what you learned along the way, and to tell the stories of people who contributed to the project, in unexpected ways. It's a time to be interviewed on others' sites, in videos, and in any other way that you can use all collaborative networks available to you. When you help others in advance or offer to reciprocate and do the same for these supporters when they need online word of mouth for their projects and initiatives, you expand your networks exponentially. Here's the time when your memberships and contributions to writers groups and publishing-related support groups works to your advantage.

If you have followed the steps in this book, you have already created a community support system that fosters and sustains a cooperative effort.

Advantages of a Virtual Book Launch "Tour"

The major benefit of having your book hot off the press is the opportunity to get people excited about the (long-awaited) publication of your book without you paying for travel costs.

More benefits include:

Web content that stays up for all time. Show the excitement surrounding your book launch, as it stays on the web permanently.

Enhanced visibility to your readership. Your name and book title recognition is increased by familiarity. Remember, it generally takes multiple exposures for a consumer to make the purchase.

Increased Amazon rankings. A blitz of appearances raises your Google search rankings and Amazon rankings as sales of your book increase with launch tour appearances.

Enhanced visibility to publishers, agents, and scouts. Establishing ties to your readership community attracts more opportunities. The editorial department at Mulholland Books, an imprint of Little, Brown, wants "authors who are engaged in the community, who reach out to their readers; authors who challenge the publisher on how to reach out further." Steve Elliot, publisher at Elsevier, also seeks "authors with a voice in the community, someone who strives to be a thought leader, a visible speaker in the industry who stays active on networks."

Strategy for Virtual Book Launch

There is every reason to appear as much as possible in person and online in the month spanning before and after the publication of your book.

Create local and virtual news. The strategy we advise is both to reach out, at least locally, with in-store book signings and a book launch party, and online through a virtual "tour."

Repurpose photos and video. Authors can live stream their book launch party for those who were not able to attend and/or include and repurpose videos and photos of the party as part of the virtual "tour."

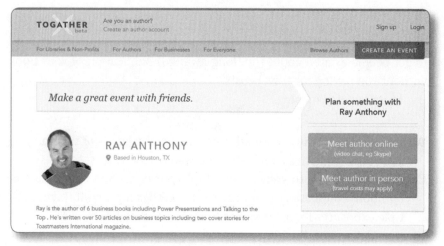

Author client Ray Anthony, listed in author roundup on togather.com. Coauthor with
Barbara Boyd of *Killer Presentations with your iPad*.

Maximize the celebration announcement with links, tying in as
many elements as possible between live appearances and online appearances at the publication of your book.

Create audience interactions with an event hashtag. Creating and
using your own event hashtag such as #authorplatformparty everywhere
you announce will give people a way to search and talk about the event
easily and create buzz about it through social media.

Steps to Creating Your Virtual Book Launch Tour

As with all elements of your author platform, find the book tour models
that appeal to you before you start planning your own. We've included
the main elements in this chapter along with models, but you can search
for and find many more. A simple virtual book tour includes the following elements, which can be expanded upon and customized. Authors
regularly schedule their own online "appearances" themselves rather than
paying a book publicist. Good publicists are also available to do the work
for a fee. Here are the steps:

1. **Make a target list of the sites and networks where you want to appear as a guest,** especially sites where you may already be active and have a presence. For guest blogging, one option is to join a community of guest bloggers at guestblogit.com or myblogguest.com. About .com also has a guest blogging forum. A quick route to possible online appearances is to ask those in your network if you can do guest posts for them; reach out to your groups, colleagues, clients, and industry friends.

2. **Contact your target sites.** Tell the site owners that you have a book about to be published and a firm publication date, and ask for a guest appearance. Tell the owners that you love their site and why, that you have a lot to offer their audience, and that you want to make it a stop on your virtual tour. Offer to give them an interview or write a post that meets their specifications, even a review of someone else's book or an editorial piece.

3. **Set up posts of interviews and/or articles.** See Chapter 7 for ideas on places to apply for interviews, and consult Chapter 10 on how to make interview videos to post on your site—and sites like YouTube—with your physical book in your hand.

4. **Research audiences for each stop.** Plan and coordinate the content you'll use for each type of audience.

5. **Create your schedule.** As you receive responses to your guest post inquires, you'll start to book dates for appearances. Maintain an internal calendar and keep a public version of it updated in the media room of your author website.

6. **Post and promote the dates and online places of your virtual book tour.** List your tour stops on all parts of your author platform and also blog about your book and tour. During the launch of your book, add a splash page to your website—where your book and a Buy button are front and center.

7. **Write out your interview or agreed-upon posts for guest blogs,** then send in your copy for approval from your hosts. You can ask your hosts if they would, for example, announce that they are happy to introduce you and your hot-off-the-press book for an expert question-and-answer session over a specified amount of time.

8. **Be sure to include live links to additional articles** that you've written; if your readers follow your links to additional locations where you have written, your rankings increase.

9. **Double-check your byline.** Make sure your byline includes your name, book title, a photo of the cover of your book, and a Buy button.

10. **If a host wants to interview you, suggest questions.** Give hosts some suggested questions, the words you'd like used to introduce you, and especially for video, make sure a copy of your book is in hand as you are introduced. Keep the focus on your ultimate goal of selling copies of your book.

11. **Orchestrate book giveaways and contests.** People love freebies, so consider some giveaways as part of your virtual book tour. Sites like Goodreads and LibraryThing host book giveaways (see Chapter 13). You might also want to give away copies of your book via your author website. To win a free copy, readers would just need to give you their name, postal address (for physical copies), and email address with the winner(s) named at the end of the virtual book tour. Collect your entries in a spreadsheet and use Random.org to select your winner. You would be responsible for delivery and shipping costs, unless your publisher is willing to participate in the promotion.

Literary Podcasts

Literary podcasts are mostly used for fiction and poetry, but scout some out to see if they may also be candidates for your virtual book tour. Consider the following podcasts, all of which you can subscribe to through iTunes or RSS feeds.

- *NY Times Book Review* Podcast. The *New York Times Book Review* editor discusses literature with authors, publishers, editors, and critics in this weekly literary podcast.
- *NPR: Books* is a weekly podcast featuring readings and interviews with contemporary authors. Podcasts explore fiction and nonfiction alike.
- *Selected Shorts* is an award-winning podcast that features famous actors (from the stage and screen) reading short stories by famous authors.
- *New Yorker.* This monthly podcast features a reading and conversation with Deborah Treisman, the fiction editor for *The New Yorker.*
- *EscapePod* is devoted to science fiction. The podcast presents a new short fiction story each week from today's best science fiction authors.

Virtual Tour Stops

The sky is the limit for appearing online, and authors tailor tours to their personalities, capabilities, and time constraints. Focus on the events and video capabilities of your social networks to coordinate an "event" at each of your online locations.

Facebook Events. From your Author Page, click the **Event** button to set up your date, time, and location. Schedule a live Facebook chat session, or a more formal Q&A on your Author Page. For the latter, announce that you'll answer questions submitted to your page at a given time. Consider an ad campaign to promote the event. Perhaps you can offer a giveaway of your book to either a random questioner or just your favorite question.

LinkedIn group. Use your book title to create a discussion group. Attract new people and get them talking about you and your topic. If enough users engage in your group, you could become a LinkedIn Influencer. Read more about LinkedIn groups in Chapter 6.

Google+ Events and Hangouts. Google+ Events can be live and in person or strictly online. Always put whatever you're doing on Events. Host a Hangout on Air to talk about your book and take questions from your readers. This feature allows up to 10 people to video chat at one time and for up to 200 people to watch the Hangout live (the Hangout is always recorded and posted to YouTube, so millions can watch it later). This group video chat is a perfect tool to use for your virtual book launch upon publication. See Chapter 4 for more about Google+.

Virtual Book Signings

You can hold a virtual book signing using Skype or teleconferencing tools like iSight and iChatAV. This technology allows authors to talk directly with book buyers and give them a signature that they can print out and paste into their books. Margaret Atwood, best-selling author of *The Handmaid's Tale*, conducted a virtual book signing in 2004 for her book *Oryx and Crake* with the LongPen. This is a robotic arm that works as a remote signing device, replicating the hand movements of the author. Neil Gaiman and Michael Chabon have also done virtual signings using the LongPen. For more information on how this technology works, visit blog.longnow.org/02007/11/20/longpen-makes-short-work-of-distance.

Twitter chat. Create a hashtag and ask your Twitter followers to use it during an hour-long Twitter chat. Your chat can be a Q&A about your book, during which you can take questions from followers for an hour at a designated time. For example, tweet six questions, at ten-minute intervals, to create a chat. Remind participants to include the hashtag in their answers so that you can easily track the responses (using a Twitter platform like HootSuite or TweetDeck) and answer as many questions as possible during the chat.

Reddit. This user-generated Internet link site has a popular feature called AMA (Ask Me Anything). Everyone from Arnold Schwarzenegger to President Obama has used this forum to answer questions from users. Use this forum to promote your book, your current project, or your authority. People can ask questions about your platform or other random questions, and it generates user interest.

Pinterest. If your book lends itself to a more visual presentation, create a Pinterest board full of images related to your topic. Create an infographic of interesting and fun facts you generated while researching your book.

Instagram. This Facebook photo-editing site now allows very short (3 to 15 seconds) video clips. Use these to tease details from your book, or other spots on the tour.

Audio Tours: Taped readings, audio interviews, and podcasts at these sites:

- Writers Out Loud
- BlogTalkRadio
- Lively Words

Mini Books

To create buzz while you are still waiting for your book to come off the press, you can create an electronic mini-version of your book. Publishers still create these mini books leading up to publication by printing one single formatted chapter, staple folded inside its real cover. You can create an online version of this type of mini-version of your book to send it out in advance of your virtual book tour.

Blog Tours. A blog tour means you'll be posting on one blog after another. The quantity of guest blogging depends on your schedule, but some virtual book tours go so far as to include twenty blogs over a four-week period.

Blog reviews. Your book launch is the ideal time to announce your book publication to top book-review bloggers in your subject area, sending them requests for reviews plus an advance copy of your book. To find reliable blog review sites, look at the Goodreads website under Book Blogger Awards.

Bloggers Who Interview Authors

Here's a list of top book bloggers who interview authors:

- Eri Nelson's Wonderful Reads of the Month (dearharts.com/UnorthodoxBlog)
- Teddy Gross on Jewish-themed books (teddygross.blogspot.com/p/book-reviews-interviews.html)
- Sylvia Browder (sylviabrowder.com/category/women-authors)
- Paper Dragon Ink (paperdragonink.com)
- Kris Wampler (kriswampler.wordpress.com)
- Morgen Bailey (morgenbailey.wordpress.com/blog-interviews)
- Kate Brauning writes excellent book reviews (katebrauning.wordpress.com)
- MUTT (muttonline.com)
- Indies Unlimited (indiesunlimited.com)

—List courtesy of Delin Colon

Regardless of how many elements you choose to include in your book launch, the blitz of your author appearances surrounding the "news" of publication of your book gives you a huge advantage in creating a spotlight and stage for your book to become highlighted, bought and read, and reviewed.

Successful authors make multiple appearances closely in advance of the publication of their books and often give away advance copies marked "not for sale," like Barbara Kingsolver did with *Fight Behavior* to seed the market, giving her fans a chance to read first and tell their friends. We love watching the many authors who speak on panels at Book Expo America in advance of their new titles. Mary Roach, a best-selling pop-science author with ingeniously startling titles like *Gulp, Bonk,* and *Packing for Mars,* is an author who is clearly having fun, reaching out to widen the audience for her books right before they hit the market. Each time before her latest book is published, she speaks—mostly about embarrassing biological facts we can all relate to—at science centers and book conferences. We love her fun book trailers, especially the broccoli on the roller coaster for *Gulp,* and watching her enjoyment while appearing on television on *The Colbert Report.*

We are hoping time will be an ally, not a thief, so that you can use every one of the 14 steps in this book to announce your book to your newly created and ever-expanding audience. Our most successful author clients have found that the initial work that goes into creating an author platform pays off and, once established, works on its own, resulting in increased sales, a ready audience for future books, and opportunities to create additional related products and services.

May you enjoy creating your author platform and may you reap the benefits and rewards for many years to come!

Checklist, Step 14: Launch

- ➤ Plan your launch to include a live book party and a virtual launch.
- ➤ Send invitations two months in advance to give media time to schedule coverage.
- ➤ Plan your virtual tour a couple of months before your book is published.
- ➤ Create schedules for the launch party and virtual book tour to coincide with your publication date.
- ➤ Post every aspect of your launch to your social networks and sites.
- ➤ Query for guest blog spots and interviews, and create multiple virtual appearances.
- ➤ Try to get reviews on prominent book blog sites.
- ➤ Promote your book tour on all of your online locations.
- ➤ On all guest blog posts, include your byline and a Buy button for your book for easy purchase.
- ➤ Enjoy and celebrate every step of the way during your launch!

Further Reading

Author and Book Websites

Plumley, George. *WordPress 24-Hour Trainer*. Indianapolis, IN: John Wiley & Sons, 2011.

Plumley, George. *Website Design and Development: 100 Questions to Ask Before Building a Website*. Indianapolis, IN: John Wiley & Sons, 2010.

Smith, Bud E. and Michael McCallister. *WordPress In Depth, 2nd Edition*. Que Publishing, 2012.

Blog

Butow, Eric and Rebecca Bollwitt. *Blogging to Drive Business: Create and Maintain Valuable Customer Connections, 2nd Edition*. Indianapolis, IN: Que Publishing, 2013.

Social Networks

Butow, Eric and Kathleen Taylor. *How to Succeed in Business Using LinkedIn: Making Connections and Capturing Opportunities on the World's #1 Business Networking Site*. AMACOM, 2009.

Elad, Joel. *LinkedIn For Dummies*. Hoboken, NJ: Wiley Publishing, 2011.

Feiler, Jesse. *How to Do Everything: Facebook Applications*. McGraw-Hill, 2008.

Harvell, Ben. *Teach Yourself VISUALLY Facebook (Teach Yourself VISUALLY (Tech))*. Indianapolis, IN: John Wiley & Sons, 2012.

O'Reilly, Tim and Sarah Milstein. *The Twitter Book.* Sebastopol, CA: O'Reilly Media, Inc., 2012.

Stay, Jesse. *Google+ For Dummies.* Hoboken, NJ: John Wiley & Sons, 2011.

Stay, Jesse. *Google+ Marketing For Dummies.* Hoboken, NJ: John Wiley & Sons, 2012.

Taylor, Dave. *The Complete Idiot's Guide to Growing Your Business with Google.* Alpha Books, 2005.

Personal Appearances

Gallo, Carmine. *The Presentation Secrets of Steve Jobs: How to Be Insanely Great in Front of Any Audience.* McGraw-Hill, 2009.

Ray, Anthony and LeVitus, Bob. *Killer Presentations with Your iPad: How to Engage Your Audience and Win More Business with the World's Greatest Gadget.* McGraw-Hill Education, 2013.

Ray, Anthony. *Talking to the Top: Executive's Guide to Career-Making Presentations.* Prentice Hall Trade, 1995.

Articles

Ruberg, Michelle, ed. *Writer's Digest Handbook of Magazine Article Writing.* Cincinnati, OH: Writer's Digest Books, 2005.

Audio, Video

Carucci, John. *Digital SLR Video and Filmmaking For Dummies.* Hoboken, NJ: John Wiley & Sons, 2013.

Morris, Tee, Evo Terra, and Ryan C. Williams. *Expert Podcasting Practices For Dummies.* Hoboken, NJ: John Wiley & Sons, 2007.

Morris, Tee, Chuck Tomasi, Evo Terra, and Kreg Steppe. *Podcasting For Dummies.* Hoboken, NJ: John Wiley & Sons, 2008.

Sahlin, Doug and Chris Botello. *YouTube For Dummies.* Hoboken, NJ: John Wiley & Sons, 2007.

Tear-Out Sheets:
Author Platform Publicity Plan

Step 1: Your Author Website: Home Central

➤ Know your audience needs and your own value and plan your author site accordingly.
➤ Choose an existing author site model to customize for your needs.
➤ Map out your landing page site strategy.
➤ List your site pages and create a tab for each.
➤ Write content for each page.
➤ Determine your website design.
➤ Publish your website—go live.
➤ Track and measure the users of your website.

Step 2: Blog

➤ Create and link your blog to your home base website.
➤ Choose a model and customize your blog accordingly.
➤ Post original-content blogs consistently at least once a week.
➤ Add reposts of others' blogs or articles with a comment to add blog frequency.
➤ Write from the perspective of what your audience needs.
➤ Promote your blog.
➤ Learn more about your audience preferences on your blog with Google Analytics.

Step 3: Twitter

➤ Sign up for Twitter.
➤ Use your consistent author brand name and photo.
➤ Construct your audience-centric author profile.

➤ Emulate model tweets of others.

➤ Connect your Twitter account with your blog.

➤ Create and automate your Twitter posts.

➤ Respond to your Twitter comments.

➤ Follow others to create a broad network.

Step 4: Google

➤ Create a Google+ Account.

➤ Include your friends, associates, and clients. Find people to follow and repost others' works.

➤ Try to post once a day; automate posts to save time. You can duplicate Facebook and Twitter posts.

➤ Post when you have a new blog entry and/or announcement.

➤ Use Google Alerts and What's Hot to find articles to post.

➤ Join Google Authorship.

Step 5: Facebook

➤ Create a personal profile.

➤ Keep your author photo and name consistent across your author platform.

➤ Write your profile bio for public eyes.

➤ For your personal profile, keep as friends only family and those close to you.

➤ Create and customize a book Page consistent with your book website.

➤ Post updates and events to your book Page without advertising.

➤ Respond to comments on your book Page.

➤ Encourage Likes on your book Page.

➤ Join Facebook groups with common interests.

Step 6: LinkedIn

➤ Join LinkedIn.

➤ Optimize your author brand profile with photo, name, and keywords consistent with all parts of your author platform.

➤ Upload your address book contacts into LinkedIn.

➤ Grow your contacts list and post updates.

➤ Join groups and post your news.
➤ Seek joint book-marketing opportunities.

Step 7: Personal Appearances

➤ Organize your subject matter into teachable lists.
➤ Plan your mix of live and online personal appearances in advance of your publication date.
➤ Create and deliver a short course or series of courses.
➤ Give live talks.
➤ Attend industry conferences.
➤ List your personal appearances in your media kit on your websites and all parts of your author platform.

Step 8: Article Bank, Repurposing Content

➤ Create an article bank of 500-word original articles.
➤ Include your byline description with your name, photo, and book titles listed.
➤ Create articles that repurpose portions of and outtakes from your book.
➤ Publish articles on your blog and sites and get permission to publish these on blogs and sites of people in your network.
➤ Submit original articles to large and small publications and article directories.
➤ Repurpose original material into spin-offs for publications addressing various audiences.
➤ Work to get quoted in others' articles and on others' websites.
➤ Blitz the web with as many articles as possible with your byline, which should mention your name and book title, especially near the time of your book launch.

Step 9: Audio

➤ Practice recording yourself with a headset.
➤ Post the best audio clip on your author website.
➤ Pitch local and national radio shows for interviews.
➤ Find podcasters in your niche for interviews.
➤ Create your own podcast.

Step 10: Video

➤ Practice and videotape a short author interview about your book.

➤ Videotape all talks and instruction.

➤ Tag videos carefully with keywords for searchability. Include your book title and URLs.

➤ Create a short book trailer video.

➤ Upload your book trailer to YouTube, Vimeo, and other video sharing sites.

➤ Create a YouTube channel and upload all your author/book videos and grow over time to include related videos of others for cross-promotion.

➤ Connect YouTube and Vimeo to all your book and author websites, social networks, and author platform locations.

Step 11: Book Website

➤ Create a book website in addition to your author website built during Step 1.

➤ Use your book title as your URL.

➤ Showcase a large photo of your book cover on the landing page.

➤ List your book's back-cover copy in short, succinct points on the landing page.

➤ Place a Buy Now button next to the book, linked to Amazon.

➤ Create pages beyond your landing page.

➤ Include a link back to your author site.

Step 12: Amazon's Author Toolbox

➤ Join Amazon's Author Central.

➤ Create your Author Central page and keep it updated.

➤ Upload photos and videos to your Author Central page.

➤ Cross-link to all your online locations.

➤ Solicit as many book reviews as possible from colleagues and Top Reviewers.

➤ Join and participate regularly in Amazon Customer Communities.

➤ Create Listmania lists to link your book to similar titles.

Step 13: Reviews

➤ Ramp up your outreach to potential reviewers the minute you deliver your final manuscript to your publisher.

➤ Three months prior to publication, send out galley proofs to reviewers.

➤ Send out free copies to potential reviewers as soon as your book is published.

➤ Review others' books positively and let the authors know you did.

➤ Join or use all of your group memberships as support systems for reviews.

➤ Ask audience and colleagues to post positive comments specifying things about your book that helped them.

➤ Join review sites. Find and query book review blogs.

➤ Connect all information together on your author website.

Step 14: Launch: Book Parties and Virtual Tours

➤ Plan your launch to include a live book party and a virtual tour.

➤ Send invitations two months in advance to give media time to schedule coverage.

➤ Plan your virtual tour a couple of months before your book is published.

➤ Create schedules for the launch party and virtual book tour to coincide with your publication date.

➤ Post every aspect of your launch to your social networks and sites.

➤ Query for guest blog spots and interviews, and create multiple virtual appearances.

➤ Try to get reviews on prominent book blog sites.

➤ Promote your book tour on all of your online locations.

➤ On all guest blog posts, include your byline and a Buy button for your book for easy purchase.

➤ Enjoy and celebrate every step of the way during your launch!

About the Authors

Carole Jelen, founder of Jelen Publishing and vice president of Waterside Productions, has been representing authors as a top-producing agent for over two decades. She specializes in areas of tech, business, and self-help. Jelen has worked as editor at major publishing houses and holds a master's degree in English/Linguistics from the University of California, Los Angeles. She holds a California teaching credential, instructs author platform seminars, and works as a publishing consultant, aiding authors and companies in the publishing process.

Michael McCallister has been helping ordinary people understand and master computer software and the World Wide Web for the past two decades. He is the author of *openSUSE Linux Unleashed* and coauthor (with Bud Smith) of *WordPress in Depth*. McCallister was named one of the Mindtouch Most Influential in Technical Communication and Content Strategy for two years running. He is a past president of his local Society for Technical Communication chapter and works as the Senior Document Architect at PKWARE. He's active on many social networks, usually as WorkingWriter.

Index

Don't Be Anonymous

Join Carole Jelen, with Mike McCallister, and special guests

Platform for Authors Webinars

Sign up at jelenpub.com

- Learn author platform essentials now that new rules have changed publisher, author, and audience perspectives.

- What are these new requirements for visibility and how do you use them to widen your audience?

- This series of webinars gives answers to your biggest questions, offering strategies and hands-on techniques to create your complete author platform.

Part of Authors Opt-In Program.